ACTION AND ITS
EXPLANATION

ACTION AND ITS EXPLANATION

David-Hillel Ruben

CLARENDON PRESS · OXFORD

OXFORD

UNIVERSITY PRESS

Great Clarendon Street, Oxford OX2 6DP

Oxford University Press is a department of the University of Oxford.
It furthers the University's objective of excellence in research, scholarship,
and education by publishing worldwide in

Oxford New York

Auckland Bangkok Buenos Aires Cape Town Chennai
Dar es Salaam Delhi Hong Kong Istanbul Karachi Kolkata
Kuala Lumpur Madrid Melbourne Mexico City Mumbai Nairobi
São Paulo Shanghai Taipei Tokyo Toronto

Oxford is a registered trade mark of Oxford University Press
in the UK and in certain other countries

Published in the United States
by Oxford University Press Inc., New York

British Library Cataloguing in Publication Data
Data available

Library of Congress Cataloging in Publication Data
Data available
ISBN 0-19-8235887

1 3 5 7 9 10 8 6 4 2

Typeset by SNP Best-set Typesetter Ltd., Hong Kong
Printed in Great Britain
on acid-free paper by
Biddles Ltd.,
Guildford & King's Lynn

בָּרוּךְ אוֹמֵר וְעוֹשֶׂה

Blessed is He Who Speaks and Acts.

PREFACE

Some of the material in this book has appeared previously, although in almost all cases I have introduced important and substantial changes to that material. An early version of much of Chapter 1 appeared as 'A Puzzle about Posthumous Predication' in the *Philosophical Review*, 97, 1988, © Cornell University, and reprinted by permission of the publisher. Most of the remainder of Chapter 1 first appeared as 'Act Individuation: The Cambridge Theory' in *Analysis*, 59, 1999.

Some of Chapter 4 and a small part of Chapter 5 had an earlier existence in 'Doing without Happenings: Three Theories of Act Individuation', in Ghita Holmstrom-Hintikka and Raimo Tuomela, eds., *Contemporary Action Theory*, i, Kluwer Academic Publishers, 1997. Other versions of the same or different parts of Chapters 4 and 5 are to be found in 'The Active and the Passive', *Aristotelian Society, Supplementary Vol. 71*, 1997, in 'Actions and Their Parts', *Proceedings of the 20th World Congress of Philosophy*, ii, Boston, 1999, and in 'Mental Overpopulation and the Problem of Action', *Discipline Filosofiche*, 1993, no. 2 (Italian version), and *Journal of Philosophical Research*, 20, 1995 (English version).

The main part of Chapter 6 first saw light as 'A Counterfactual Theory of Causal Explanation', *Nous*, 28, 1994, © Blackwell Publishers Inc., and reprinted by permission of the publisher. After some initial uncertainty, I have omitted the final section of that article, 'The Disappearance of Causal Pre-emption', for Chapter 6. I still regard causal pre-emption as an important challenge to my account of causal explanation, but, because of the specific character of my account, making that challenge requires a terminology that moves even further away from the prevalent orthodoxy about causation, so that an event would cause another only in virtue of some specific property it possesses. That did not seem to me an issue that it was appropriate to take on in a book about action and its explanation.

My reliance on symbols has been kept to a minimum and in most cases is conventional and easily understood. For example, I use upper-case letters to refer to types; lower-case letters, to tokens. I only depart from this when quoting other authors who may use different conventions. Expressions such as 'doing A' or 'intending to A' should be understood as 'doing some action token of type A' or 'intending to do some action token of type A'. However, I should note my use of the special bracket, { . . .}, which I use indifferently both to represent wholes by listing their parts and to represent ordered pairs, triplets, and so on. Although not strictly correct, that use did not seem to me to be a likely cause of any misunderstanding.

I do not think that use of grammatical gender in personal pronouns or possessive adjectives reveals anything of any importance, and so I use 'his', 'he', and so on, to indicate persons of any, or no, gender in the sexual sense. I hope that the reader sensitive to these issues will bear that in mind.

Many people have saved me from faults and errors galore. Michael Zimmerman and Randolph Clarke deserve special thanks. Peter Momtchiloff, of Oxford University Press, has been especially wise and patient. Ever supportive, he has excused many missed deadlines. He also read through the entire manuscript and made helpful suggestions for its improvement.

Is it even necessary to say that the remaining errors are my responsibility alone, since I was not coerced or compelled to make them against my will? It has always seemed to me something bordering on a moral platitude to accept sole responsibility for one's own, freely made, mistakes.

David-Hillel Ruben

London

Contents

Contents

Introduction

I don't suppose that any, or many, contemporary philosophers believe that one can 'prove' or 'demonstrate' a substantial philosophical view or theory beyond any reasonable doubt. Nor do I imagine that many philosophers hold that one can 'disprove' or 'refute' an alternative view with any degree of finality, given the ways in which philosophical theories can absorb and adapt to the criticisms made of them. I certainly have no such illusions. What I try to do in this book is to articulate a view of action and its explanation that most closely fits the way I conceive them, and to dismiss some alternatives to my view on grounds that I consider strong, or plausible.

What one can demand of a theory is that it be internally consistent and not have too many consequences that are agreed by all sides to be wildly implausible and unintuitive. Not that a philosophical theory can have no unintuitive consequences whatever; it should simply try and keep them to a minimum. Of course, it is not always clear and beyond dispute what is implausible and unintuitive. One person's reductio of a position can be another's happily embraced consequence of that view. And what philosopher has not had the experience of considering a view that at first seems to fall in one of the two camps and which, after a little reflection, then seems to fall into the other? So, in some places in what follows, I stick with a view because it 'saves the appearances', as Aristotle would have said. In other places, I part company from the appearances. I think every action theorist must make choices like this; I can only hope that I have chosen wisely.

I believe that the theory of action and its explanation herein presented meets the demands of consistency and plausibility at least as well as any alternative account. The theory will not be to everyone's tastes. It is certainly out of keeping with perhaps the best-known and most widely accepted theories of action current. As I explain the term in Chapter 1, I am prolific, not austere, in my metaphysics and ontology, both about action specifically and about other matters more generally. I have never liked desert landscapes, always preferring luxuriant hothouses in the midst of well-tended gardens (jungles being far too dangerous). I don't aspire to convince the austere theorist but do hope to win his respect, by presenting a perfectly coherent and credible alternative.

A philosopher should have heroes, without ever becoming their, or anyone's, disciple. I, at any rate, have some heroes—different ones for different topics. My action heroes are Aristotle and Marx, because I view both as defenders of the thought that at least some basic actions are physical actions. I think that there are mental actions, but I do not trace the source of all agency back to them. My conception of the physical world is one that makes room for agency within it, and not just as a consequence of mental agency. It is not easy to find quotes from these heroes that have them saying just what I have said; it is more an appreciation of the general tendency of their thought. Certainly, to assign a view about basic agency to Marx, for example, would be highly anachronistic, as he was not even aware of that concept. But I think that a fair reading of *The Nichomachean Ethics*, and of the *Theses on Feuerbach*, two of the great classical contributions to action theory, presents us with attractive pictures of basic physical agency. In my view, genuine agency can, at least sometimes, start at the agent's physical surface, by his moving of parts of his body. Being a prolific theorist, though, I just don't think that agency stops at an agent's physical surface. Physical action can extend both 'outwards' and 'inwards' from that bodily surface.

What is in this book? In Chapter 1, I address the question of the identity conditions for actions: what must be true for action a_1 = action a_2? I contrast austere and prolific theories of action individuation. Austere theories tend to find multiplicity in descriptions but uniqueness in the action to which multiple descriptions may refer. Prolific theories find multiplicity in the actions themselves.

Through the introduction of something I call 'the puzzle of posthumous predication', I make use of Peter Geach's idea of Cambridge changes, in contrast to real ones. Using the parallel idea of a Cambridge action, I state and defend a variant of prolific theory, which I dub 'the Cambridge theory of action individuation'. Although not necessarily the most prolific theory on the conceptual map, the Cambridge theory tends to find multiplicity in the actions, but at the price of also finding many, even most, of those multiple actions to be merely Cambridge actions. This discussion provides me with the metaphysical framework within which, in the remainder of the book, to discuss theories of action and its explanation.

In Chapter 2, I introduce some further distinctions and terminology for

the ensuing discussion of action. I note the distinction between action and
activity. I introduce the idea of events intrinsic to actions and consider
which, if any, causal antecedents or consequences of one of my actions are
themselves events intrinsic to actions of mine. I distinguish three kinds of
chains that are action-involving: action-causal chains, action chains, and
teleological chains. I discuss the concept of a basic action. Finally, I argue
that there are both physical and mental actions (I do not mean to beg the
question of whether every mental action is identical to some physical action
or event), and also argue against the proposal that every basic action is a
mental action. As I indicated above, I believe that there are at least some
basic physical actions.

In Chapter 3, I introduce the idea of a particular sort of philosophical
naturalism, folk naturalism, and I explain what this doctrine says about
action. I describe its commitment to a reconstructive analysis of action in
folk terms, but ones thought to be acceptable to the naturalist. I describe
three theories of action, pointing out a crucial assumption that all three
share, and concentrate on one of the theories, the one favoured by folk
naturalism, the causal theory of action. I state some of its main ideas, and in
particular focus on the requirement of rationalization that is part of the
causal theory's requirements for action.

In Chapter 4, I take head-on the causal theory of action. I spend some
time clarifying the idea of belief and I argue that there is no genuine sense of
'belief' in which there are sufficient beliefs to meet the requirements of the
causal theory of action. I describe some possible responses by the causal theorist and reject them. Finally, I discuss the category of mental action and
claim that the causal theorist cannot provide a convincing reconstructive
analysis for an important subset of them.

In Chapter 5, I introduce two versions of another theory of action, the
agent-causal theory. One version is involved in a reification that I find
gratuitous; the other, I reject on other grounds. In my view, all three of the
theories, the causal theory and both versions of the agent-causal theory,
share an assumption that I identify and reject, and I describe my own view
of action by considering the implications of that rejection. Many have told
me that my rejection of this common assumption is under-motivated and
wildly implausible. I can only add that, the more I have considered my rejection, the more it has appealed to me. I try to both motivate and make credible that rejection as best I can.

In Chapter 6, I turn to the question of the explanation of action. I do not
argue that all action explanation must be causal, and I am agnostic on that

point in this book. I am neutral on the question of whether every action has a cause. But I believe that at least some do. I begin by making some remarks about explanation generally and action explanation in particular, which guide my subsequent discussion of causal action explanation.

Certainly, at the very least, sometimes action explanations are causal and I set out what I believe is involved in the idea of causal explanation, as it would apply both to actions (folk psychology) and to ordinary macro-events of the common-sense world (folk physics). On the understanding of causal explanation that I elaborate, there is no explicit commitment to the existence of laws or law-like generalizations. This is, I think, good news for those who think that at least some action explanations are causal explanations. Whether there is an implicit commitment to the existence of generalizations in my analysis, one not immediately apparent, depends on what analysis might be offered in turn of the idea of a counterfactual.

Finally, in the Appendix on the Epistemology of Action, I discuss briefly the idea that we could have certain or indubitable knowledge, as agents, about our own basic physical actions, either those we are doing or about those we are not doing. I can find no sense in which such a thesis can survive various interesting counter-examples. Perhaps not altogether unsurprisingly, I think there is no certain knowledge about our own basic physical actions.

The Cambridge Theory
of Action

Token action a = token action b iff . . . Well, iff what? An agent, X, bends his finger, pulls the trigger, shoots the gun, kills the Queen, and thereby reduces the world's population by one. X did each action on the list by doing its predecessor (if it has one). How many things did the person do?

The alternative theories that attempt to answer this question are well known. The most austere theory says that X did only one thing, and that what the list above provides are five different descriptions of one token action. All actions are, on austere theory, movings of the body, variously described.

The most prolific theory says that, in the list above, X performed five different actions. Each action description on the list is a description of an action different from the action any other description on the list describes. A prolific theorist finds the plurality in the action, not in the description.

What considerations might incline us towards one or the other of the competing theories of action individuation? Some of my colleagues have told me that it could not matter. Accept either theory, they say, just making sure that one's usage is consistent throughout.

But that cannot be right. There are other considerations that we take to be truth-making: in science, for example, simplicity. In philosophy, there is another sort of consideration: choose that theory which is minimally counter-intuitive, which has the least unacceptable consequences for our ordinary ways of thinking about things. Such a consideration has no probative force in science, but at least since Aristotle, who desired to 'save the appearances', it has often been thought to have such force in philosophy.

A problem with this method is that both theories are thought to have counter-intuitive consequences in roughly equal measure. For one writer, Kent Bach, the consequences of both theories of individuation are so bad as to lead him to believe that it is wrong to think of actions as entities of any sort, requiring any criteria of individuation at all: 'But if actions are [not entities but] instances of a relation, we are not obliged to produce a theory of individuation of actions'.[1]

Both the austere and prolific theories are thought to have numerous counter-intuitive consequences, but I wish to focus only on those having to do with the times (and, to less of an extent, the locations) of action. My arguments are intended to support a version of prolific theory, although it has some similarities to austere theory as well. I shall argue that my variant of prolific theory has fewer unacceptable counter-examples than any alternative theory, at least in so far as the spatial and temporal location of actions is concerned.

I shoot the Queen in London at t. Imagine that the Queen dies in Balmoral six months after I shoot her, at $t+$ six months; poor dear, she lingers that length of time in her country estate before expiring. The time argument against the austere theory is this: if my killing of the Queen = my bending of my finger, and since I bent my finger at t, then I must have also killed her at t, fully six months before she died. But how can I have killed her before she died? It is not credible, so the argument goes, to accept the consequence that I kill the Queen long before she dies.

The argument against placing the time of the killing only at t is consistent with the view that the time of the killing is more extensive but includes t. For example, the argument is consistent with the view, held by some, that the killing started at t and extended over the whole period t–t'. But this view does not escape the paradoxes that beset the simpler austere view that the killing happened only at t, when the finger bending did. On the new suggestion, we would have at least to accept that some temporal part of the killing occurred before the Queen died (and not just that something that led to the killing occurred before she died, which is surely true), and having to accept that seems little improvement on having to accept that the whole killing occurred before she died. How could any part of the actual killing occur before her death?

---

[1] Kent Bach, 'Actions are not Events', *Mind*, 89, 1980: 114–20. Quote from p. 119. Why, it might be asked, do we *not* have to provide criteria of identity and individuation for instances of a relation? What is an instance? Can't we count instances, and wonder if one instance is numerically the same as another?

The location argument against the austere theory is similar in form. Location arguments are not generally as convincing as time arguments, because (I think) we have reasonably secure intuitions about the temporality of events, but less secure intuitions about their spatiality. Still, let me try running location arguments as far as they will take us, in adjudicating between the theories.

I bent my finger in London. If my killing of the Queen = my bending of my finger, and since I bent my finger in London, then I must have also killed her in London. But how can I have killed her in London? When she left London for Balmoral, she was very much alive. True, she was wounded in London, but that was some hundreds of miles away from where she died. If she did not die in London, I could not have killed her in London, even though I did something in London that led to her death elsewhere, in Balmoral. If she died in Balmoral, surely that must be where I killed her, on the grounds that I can hardly kill someone in a place other than in the place where they die.

Note that the location argument against the austere theory does not have to presuppose that the killing did take place in some place at all, as I did presuppose in the paragraph immediately above. The location argument against the austere theory merely assumes that, unlike the shooting, which was in London, the killing was not in London, either because it occurred elsewhere or because it had no location at all, and that is argument enough against the identification.

So much for arguments against the austere theory. The prolific theory is thought to have problems of its own. The time argument against the prolific theory is this: if my killing of the Queen ≠ my bending of my finger, then the finger bending occurs at t, but the killing occurs only when she died, namely at $t + 6$ months. Of course, it does not follow from the non-identity of the two actions that they must occur at different times (we shall see later that Alvin Goldman does not think that they do), but this is the way in which prolific theory has standardly been understood, and it is this version of prolific theory that I shall discuss in what follows. I will return to the Goldman possibility, non-identity but same temporal locations, later in this chapter.

Now, there are a number of different ways in which to state the difficulty that the prolific theory faces from the following no-further-effort argument (as Bennett calls it): on the prolific theory, my action of killing the Queen is not finished or completed at t, or more strongly, has not even begun by t, even though there is, it seems, literally nothing further for me to do after t. After t, there is *nothing further that I do*, relevant to the killing at any rate, so how could it be that I kill her only after *t*, or even only finish killing her after *t*?

This way of putting the difficulty for the prolific theory is not compelling. The alleged difficulty seems to be that, on prolific theory, my action would occupy temporal points at which I am no longer moving any part of my body. Put like that, the argument seems question begging. One cannot infer from the fact that I am not moving parts of my body to the fact that I am not acting at all, unless one is already assuming the truth of the austere theory's thesis that 'we never do more than move our bodies: the rest is up to nature'.[2]

What proponents of the time argument against the prolific theory almost invariably say is not just that, if prolific theory were true, the action may occur when the agent is no longer moving some part of his body, but that the agent's action may commence or continue even after the agent dies. This *seems* a more telling objection that could not be met in the same easy way as above. Suppose that I bend my finger at *t*, the Queen dies at *t*+six months, and I die at *t*+three months, no doubt from finger strain induced by all that finger bending.

I will have killed her *after* I have died (and of course *a fortiori* after I have moved (finished moving) my body). Thus Bennett: the prolific theory entails 'that the action has to run its course after the agent's death. When put thus plainly, it is incredible.'[3] And Bach, against the prolific theory: on the prolific theory, 'the camper killed the coyote a day after he fired the gun. He himself could have been killed before then.'[4]

So there are two different time arguments against the prolific theory: if the prolific theory were true, then (*a*) some actions could occur at times when the agent is no longer moving a part of his body; (*b*) some actions could occur at times when the agent no longer exists. (*b*), of course, entails (*a*), but not conversely. The first argument is not compelling on its own, since it seems to beg the question against prolific theory, but may gain whatever plausibility it does have in light of the second sort of argument.

What is the location argument against the prolific theorist? Presumably, if my killing≠my finger bending, and *if* my killing of her is to have any location at all, then my killing should be placed wherever the Queen died rather than where I bent my finger, namely in Balmoral. But I may never

[2] Donald Davidson, 'Agency', in his *Essays on Actions and Events*, Oxford and New York: Clarendon Press, 1980: 59.
[3] Jonathan Bennett, *Events and their Names*, Oxford: Oxford University Press, 1988: 196–7.
[4] Bach, 'Actions are not Events', 117.

have been north of the border, and how, it might be asked, could I have acted at a location where I may never have been? Locating the killing in Balmoral seems no less counter-intuitive than locating it in London, since I may never have been to Balmoral.

Both austere and prolific theories have, or seem to have, location and time difficulties. I think the temporal and spatial arguments against austere theory hit their mark. Let me rebut the spatial and temporal arguments against prolific theory. In so far as I can do this, I will have, to that extent, justified my adoption of some version of prolific theory.

Presumably, the temporal argument against prolific theory assumes this:

(1) If agent X acts, does something, at time t, then X must exist at t.

The spatial argument against the prolific theory seems to assume this:

(2) If an agent X acts, does something, in place p, then X must be in p when he acts.

The idea, then, is that since I might have died at t+three months, it cannot be the case that I killed the Queen at t+six months, because I would not have existed then and hence could do nothing at that time. Further, since the Queen died in Balmoral and I may never have been north of the border, it cannot be the case that I killed her in Balmoral (even were I to have been alive then).

Since an action is a type of event or change, in one sense of that term (for more on this, and an important qualification to this claim, see Chapter 5), (1) and (2) are instances of a more general thesis about change:

(3) If an object o changes in place p at time t, then o must exist in p at t.

And this general thesis about change is itself an instance of an even more general thesis about property possession, since change might be thought of as an object's having and then not having a property (although we shall see, in a moment, that this is too liberal a criterion for real change):

(4) If, at time t, and in place p, o has a property P, then x exists at t in p.

Of course, if 'o' is a name or a definite description and if 'at t and in p, o has property P' is true, then o's existence is a necessary condition of that statement's truth, in a timeless sense. But (4) goes beyond that and insists that o must exist at t and in p, in order for that statement to be true.

(3) and (4) are, in my view, certainly false. There are many counter-examples to them, as I try and show below. Showing that (3) and (4) are false is not, of course, to show that (1) and (2) are, but it does undermine any support that the latter might have been thought to provide the former.

A Puzzle about Posthumous Predication

Many kinds of things begin to exist and cease to exist at specific times. If the reader is tempted by the view that at death persons lose their bodies but do not cease to exist, he can easily substitute an example of some physical object or artefact like a stone or a desk for my example of a person. In what follows, I extend the meaning of 'posthumous' to cover certain things that arise or continue after the ceasing-to-be of an object, whether or not a person. Some, although not all, of the difficulties I discuss under the heading 'posthumous' have their analogue in difficulties which can be called 'antenatal' and which concern certain things that happen before the coming-to-be of an object. I similarly extend the meaning of this latter term to cover objects that are not persons.

Two closely related topics need distinguishing: posthumous reference and posthumous predication (although some sentences do both). The following sentence is a pure case of posthumous reference, no posthumous predication being involved:

(5) Napoleon was emperor of France in 1808.

In (5), reference is made to a person who no longer exists, and so the reference is posthumous. The property predicated of him is one he had only when or while he existed, so the property is not predicated posthumously. Of course, if (5) is asserted now, the *act* of predicating the property of Napoleon is posthumous to him, but the time of the predicating act is not, in general, the same as the time at which the predicated property is or was possessed.

The point is that the property so predicated is not one that he had posthumously. On the other hand, (6) both posthumously predicates and posthumously refers:

(6) Napoleon is now being eulogized.

(6), like (5), refers to someone who no longer exists, so (6) is an example of posthumous reference. (6), unlike (5), ascribes to Napoleon a property he has now, being eulogized, long after his demise. For this reason (6), unlike (5), is also an example of posthumous predication.

(6) uses tense; it fixes Napoleon's eulogy in what Hugh Mellor, following McTaggart, calls 'the A series'.[5] The puzzle will still arise if we

---

[5] Hugh Mellor, *Real Time*, Cambridge: Cambridge University Press, 1981: 13–28. For a discussion of the debate between tensers and detensers, see Jeremy Butterfield, 'Prior's Conception of Time', *Proceedings of the Aristotelian Society*, 84, 1983–4: 193–209.

translate assertions like (6) into their dated and detensed counterparts in the B series:

(6′) Napoleon is tenselessly being eulogized in 2003.

So the puzzle arises for both tensers and detensers. (6′), like (6), appears to predicate the property, being eulogized in 2003, of Napoleon, although he died in 1821, and that seems puzzling. How could Napoleon, even in a timeless sense, have *that* property, since he died in 1821? As we shall see in discussing Harry Silverstein's views later, tensers and detensers may deal with that puzzle differently. In what follows, I often move back and forth freely between tensed and dated posthumous predications.

Some sentences can posthumously predicate without posthumously referring at all. For example:

(7) There is one and only one person who was a French general and who was an emperor of France in 1808 and he is being eulogized in 2003.

(7) predicates three properties of Napoleon, one of which he possesses at a time after his death, and therefore involves posthumous predication. Since (7) does not involve any reference at all, at least on one standard view of the matter, *a fortiori* it cannot involve any posthumous reference.

I regard posthumous reference as wholly unproblematic.[6] In this regard there is a disanalogy between posthumous and antenatal matters, since antenatal reference is puzzling in a way in which posthumous reference is not.

In what follows, I am interested only in posthumous predication. If I mainly consider sentences that involve both posthumous reference and posthumous predication, it is only for the sake of convenience, since sentences like (7) are generally more cumbersome than sentences like (6).

The thought that generates the puzzle of posthumous predication seems to me to be deep and initially convincing, even though finally wrong. It is the thought conveyed in (3) and (4). Properties are instantiated, exemplified, displayed at specific times, or at any rate this is true for those sorts of objects, unlike numbers and propositions for instance, which begin to exist and cease to exist. But if a property is true of some object at t, then surely

---

[6] Ardon Lyon argues that this distinction is too facile. Consider the property, 'is being referred to'. This is a property that can be predicated posthumously of an object. If there is a puzzle about the posthumous predication of this property, then there must be a puzzle, according to Lyon, about posthumous reference. If Lyon is right, then this paper resolves both puzzles.

There are predication and reference problems for objects which never exist, if there be such, similar to those for objects which no longer exist, but I do not discuss them here.

the object of which the property is true at t must itself exist at t, just in order to display or exemplify that property at that time.

As Lawrence Lombard has put it: 'nothing has a property when it doesn't exist . . .'; '. . . if an object . . . changes . . . between t and t' . . . [that object] must exist between t and t''.[7] On his view, no properties can be had or acquired by things at times or places at which the thing in question is not there to have or acquire the property. That is precisely what (4) above asserts.

But if (4) is true, and since Napoleon is now dead, Napoleon cannot now have the property of being eulogized. Or, to express the same issue for the detensers: if (4) is true, and since he died in 1821, Napoleon cannot have the property of being eulogized in 2003.

Indeed, since Napoleon does not now exist, (4) claims, by contraposition, that it is not the case that any property is true now of him. (It can of course be the case that it is timelessly true that he has certain properties.)

In general, (4) says that if x does not exist at t, then, for all properties P, it is not the case that x has the property P at t. It follows too that x cannot change at t, if (4) and hence (3) are true. Note that the assertion, 'It is not the case that, at t, x has the property P', ascribes no property to x, not even a negative one, if such there be. So if (4) is true, posthumous predication seems impossible.

If we accept (4), what shall we say about an assertion like 'Napoleon now fails to have any properties'? Doesn't this assertion ascribe a property to Napoleon that he now has, namely the property of failing to have any properties? I think that we need to distinguish between a weak and a strong sense of 'failing'. In the weak sense of 'failing' in which it is true that Napoleon now fails to have any properties, 'Napoleon now fails to have any properties' is equivalent to 'It is not the case that Napoleon now has any properties.' In the weak sense, 'Napoleon now fails to have any properties' does not ascribe a property to Napoleon, since 'It is not the case that Napoleon now has any properties' ascribes no property to him.

There is a stronger sense of 'failing', in which to fail to have some property is itself to have a property, namely the property of failing to have the specific property in question. For example, to say that Napoleon failed to become emperor of Russia is to ascribe a genuine property to Napoleon. In this strong sense, to fail is to try unsuccessfully. In this strong sense, it is false that Napoleon now fails to have any properties, since it is false that

    [7] Lawrence Lombard, *Events: A Metaphysical Study*, London: Routledge & Kegan Paul, 1986: 82 and 84.

Napoleon is now unsuccessfully trying to have properties. Thus, in neither of the two senses of 'failing' is it true that Napoleon now has the *property* of failing to have any properties.

Finally, a word of caution. The posthumous predication puzzle should not be conflated with an entirely benign and non-puzzling implication of the plausible, if not uncontroversial, view that a proposition, if true, is time-lessly true, and hence that 'true' itself needs no temporal qualification, not even 'at all times'. If it is true that x is P at t, then it is true timelessly that x is P at t. That x itself only exists at t and the temporal interval 'surrounding' t is irrelevant to the timeless truth of 'x is P at t'.

The posthumous predication puzzle arises because there are cases in which it seems that 'x is P at t' can be true, even timelessly true, even though *at t x* no longer exists. Also, in considering cases of posthumous predica-tion, I restrict myself to cases, which are unproblematically cases of predi-cation of properties. I do not, therefore, consider so-called counterfactual predications, or assertions of non-existence. I think it is plausible to regard 'Napoleon is now dead' as roughly equivalent to 'Napoleon does not exist now and Napoleon existed at some time before now', where this latter involves no genuine predication at all. (It will not matter to my discussion of the puzzle if existence does turn out to be a property, since the property of existence is surely one property that no one can have posthumously.)

I assume that we do wish to make sense of posthumous predications like (6) (or (6′)). What possibilities are open to us? I can think of four:

(a) (6) predicates the property, being eulogized, of Napoleon at a time after his death, and hence (4), at least in its unrestricted form, is false.

(b) (6) does not predicate, of Napoleon, any property at all, so there is no property that (6) ascribes to Napoleon posthumously.

(c) (6) asserts, of Napoleon or of some temporal segment of Napoleon, that he timelessly has the property of being eulogized, or of being eulogized in 2003; properties ascribed timelessly cannot be had posthumously.

(d) (6) really predicates, of Napoleon, the future tensed property of going to be eulogized; and since this is a property he had while alive, there is no posthumous predication involved.

My own solution to the puzzle is (a). I think that there are sufficiently strong objections to (b) and (d) to rule them out as solutions. I examine a version of (c) advanced in the literature, and try to improve on it. (c) may, I take it, be attractive to detensers.

I compare the improved version of (c) and (a) and offer some reasons why one ought to opt for solution (a). I think that the decision between improved (c) and (a) raises some very important issues, and I attempt nothing more than a few remarks about that choice.

I begin with (b), which I take to be the view of Lawrence Lombard.[8] Since, as Lombard says, 'nothing has a property when it doesn't exist', and since some sentences like (6) are true, it must follow that such sentences do not predicate properties to no-longer-existent objects. Lombard does not draw out the implication of his claim in this way, but if this is not an implication of his view, then I cannot understand what his view is meant to be, since there is no indication that either (c) or (d) attracts him as a solution.

Perhaps this is not entirely implausible when one considers a sentence like 'Napoleon is now being eulogized'. That sentence is surely equivalent to 'Someone is now eulogizing Napoleon', and one might take the view of that latter sentence that it is non-relational, on the grounds that 'Napoleon' occurs in an opaque context, and hence that the sentence ascribes no property to no-longer-existent Napoleon at all, but only ascribes a non-relational property to the indefinite but existent someone doing the eulogizing. I would not myself subscribe to any non-relational analysis of (6), but still one might see a certain plausibility to this suggestion, in so far as allegedly posthumous predications involve epistemic and intensional properties.

But such plausibility as (b) might have disappears when we consider other examples of posthumous predication, such as:

(8) Since Smith has just now been born, Smith is now the latest remote descendant of Adam and Eve.

Indeed, it is easy to construct an indefinitely large number of examples, which, like (8), involve lengthy causal chains. Each long past cause gains a new remote effect, whenever that effect occurs. Given that fact, one can always then construct a corresponding posthumous predication involving no epistemological or intensional property: 'c has remote effect e at t'. c's remote effect, e, occurs at t, long after c has occurred.

(8) seems clearly to predicate a property of Adam and Eve. The property is a relational property, true now of them and Smith, in spite of the fact that they no longer exist.[9] Such a property could not have been truly predicated

---

[8] Lombard, *Events*, 82 and 84.

[9] I am not sure if my terminology is standard; let me make it explicit in any event. Being the latest remote descendant of, or being taller than, are relations (I use the term 'relational property' synonymously with the term 'relation'); they are at least dyadic. A non-relational property, like being tall, is monadic.

of them while they existed, since when they existed, they had no remote descendants at all. (Say that a descendant of x is remote iff the descendant is born at least one thousand years after x. So even Methuselah had no remote descendants while still alive.)

I claim that (8) predicates a relational property of Smith and Adam and Eve. Couldn't the proponent of (b) just deny that this is so? Why not say that (8) ascribes a non-relational property to Smith, namely, being-the-latest-remote-descendant-of-Adam-and-Eve (the hyphenation is meant to indicate that there is no quantifying inside the whole expression), and that this is a property, which Smith has while he is alive?

Consider:

(9) Whoever is Smith's remote ancestor was human.

From (8) and (9) it follows that Adam and Eve were human, but no analysis of (8) which does not make that ancient pair one of the relata of the relational property, being the latest remote descendant of, will be able to preserve this inference. Second, there is a test for relationality that I have elsewhere defended.[10] If P is a non-relational property, then it is logically possible for there to be a world in which there is but one object, x, and x is P (note: the test is not that there be a world in which there is only one object which is P). On this test, (8) ascribes a relational property, not a non-relational property, for there could be no world in which only Smith ever

What about being taller than Joe or being the latest remote descendant of Adam and Eve? Some have called these 'relational properties'. There are two ways in which to construe them. If one understands them as if there were hyphens inserted between the words, these properties become unbreakable, i.e., there is no quantifying into them, then these are, in my terminology, non-relational properties, because they are irreducibly monadic.

On the other hand, suppose they are construed without the hyphens, so that they are breakable, i.e., one can quantify in. In that case, the whole expression is to be understood as expressing an incomplete sentence, specifying that a relational property, or a relation, holds between two items, with only one but not the other of the relata specified. I think that the second way is the best way to construe most sentences like this, and argue the point elsewhere, and also in my *The Metaphysics of the Social World*, London: Routledge & Kegan Paul, 1985.

[10] See my *Metaphysics of the Social World*, 1985: 26–9. David Lewis, in 'Extrinsic Properties', *Philosophical Studies*, 44, 1983: 197–200, argues that this could not be a definition of relationality, since if it were, then a clearly relational property such as being lonely would come out as non-relational.

But nothing I am aware of suggests that this cannot be construed as a sufficient condition for relationality. If we know of some property P that there cannot be a world in which there is but one object x, and x is P, we can infer that P is relational. What we learn from Lewis's remarks about loneliness, and other negative relational properties, is that we cannot conclude from the fact that there can be a world in which there is but one object x and x is P, that the property in question is non-relational.

existed and yet it was true that he was someone's remote descendant. I conclude that (8) does ascribe a relational property to Smith and to the pair, Adam and Eve, and that therefore (b) could not serve as a general solution to the puzzle of posthumous predication.

If we disregard his tendency to conflate posthumous reference and posthumous predication, we can attribute (c) to Harry Silverstein.[11] Following Quine, Silverstein reads all predication as timeless predication. He holds that the posthumous predication puzzle can only arise on an adverbial reading of 'at t', on which the expression indicates when the property is had. On the other hand, Silverstein thinks, the puzzle will disappear on the Quineian reading, since properties had timelessly cannot be had posthumously. The Quineian reading will allow a reconstruction or analysis of (alleged) posthumous predication on which the puzzle cannot arise. The Quineian thesis of timeless predication needs to be distinguished sharply from the thesis of eternal truths. I reject timeless predication in what follows, but I do not necessarily dispute the view that truths are eternally true.

If predication is timeless, 'in 2003' can hardly be construed adverbially, as modifying the verb. So this reconstruction of predication as timeless predication must find an alternative method of recapturing the information given by what was naïvely thought to be the adverbial modification, that is, at what time the property is possessed. Suppose the tensed 'Napoleon is now being eulogized' becomes the dated and detensed 'Napoleon is being eulogized in 2003'. We still need to make sense of the puzzle that Napoleon, who died in 1821, is being timelessly eulogized in 2003, a date long after his death. How shall we understand the 'in 2003' if not as an adverbial modification of the property possession?

One way in which Quineian reconstructions might attempt to recapture the requisite temporal information is by selecting an appropriate time slice of an object, of which a property can be timelessly predicated. Dates can be construed as identifying appropriate time slices of objects. Thus, 'Napoleon was emperor of France at t' might become 'Napoleon-at-t is timelessly emperor of France'.

But another method has to be found for posthumous predications, since objects of which properties are posthumously predicated are the very ones that lack an appropriate time slice by which the temporal information can

---

[11] Harry S. Silverstein, 'The Evil of Death', *The Journal of Philosophy*, 77, 1980: 401–24. For a development and refinement of the Quineian view see H. M. Lacey, 'Quine on the Logic and Ontology of Time', *Australasian Journal of Philosophy*, 49, 1971: 47–67.

be recaptured. Napoleon has no 2003 time slice. In cases of posthumous predication (and no doubt in other cases of predication for different reasons), Silverstein allows the predication to be of the whole object, and not just of a time slice of the object, and finds an alternative way to recapture the temporal information contained in 'at t'.

How will this work for (6) and (8)? Silverstein paraphrases (6) into timeless predication discourse, but it will be simpler if we construct a similar paraphrase of (6′), the detensed version, letting the date of the eulogy extend from t_3 to t_4, Napoleon's life span extend from t_1 to t_2, and reading all the verbs in the paraphrase tenselessly, which is indicated by the subscript 'a' (for 'atemporal') that occurs under the verbs:

(10) Napoleon is being eulogized$_a$, and if Napoleon's temporal dimensions extend$_a$ from t_1 to t_2, and if the eulogy's temporal dimensions extend$_a$ from t_3 to t_4 in 2003, then t_2 is$_a$ earlier than t_3.

Presumably Silverstein's thought is to recapture the temporal information in the timeless predication by introducing a second object, in this case, an event, the eulogy, which timelessly has the temporal dimensions required in what was naïvely thought to be the posthumous predication. In (10), no property is predicated of anything at a time, and hence not posthumously either.

The main difficulty with this idea is that not all sentences that posthumously predicate make use of verbs like 'is being eulogized' that lend themselves to the construction of events or states of affairs that can serve as relata and timelessly have the appropriate temporal extensions. Indeed, 'Adam and Eve now have yet another remote descendant' uses no such convenient verb, so Silverstein's particular proposal could not serve as a general solution to the puzzle.

However, it is fairly easy to see how a Quineian view might accommodate this point. I take it to be true that all posthumous predications are at least implicitly relational. I intend this claim about the relationality of posthumous predications in a sense stronger than that in which time itself is counted as a relatum. I shall try to explain later why this should be so, but let us here merely note its plausibility by the consideration of some examples.

If Napoleon is being eulogized, then there is some unnamed eulogizer of Napoleon. If Adam and Eve acquire another remote descendant, then there is someone such that he is the additional remote descendant of them. So if we are looking for an appropriate time slice of an object by which to recapture the temporal information in a Quineian analysis, we have more than one object available, namely the other relatum, at least in the posthumous cases.

On this alternative, we are back to time slices of objects after all. If Napoleon is now being eulogized, there is the possibility of a now time slice, or a 2003 time slice, of the unnamed eulogizer, rather than just a temporally extended eulogy. If Adam and Eve now gain an additional remote descendant, there is the possibility of a now or 2003 time slice of that descendant.

Even in cases in which the posthumous predication is explicitly relational, there may be further implicit relata that have appropriate time slices. For example, in the explicitly relational 'Hume is more famous than Reid in 2003', there is no 2003 time slice of either Hume or Reid. But further analysis of this posthumous predication will show that the relation in question is not really only dyadic. If it is true that Hume is more famous than is Reid in 2003, there must be more people in 2003 who think highly of Hume than who think equally highly of Reid. And there will, then, be the possibility of 2003 time slices of those unspecified persons.

However, the following posthumous predication finally shows, I think, that it will not always be possible to recapture the temporal information in a Quineian analysis either by time slices of objects or by events with the right temporal extensions:

(11) Napoleon has by now, 2003, been eulogized at least three times.

Let's assume that the third eulogy of Napoleon occurred in 1890. Imagine that Napoleon has not been eulogized throughout the whole of 2003. (11) posthumously predicates the property, being at least three times eulogized, of Napoleon. It is a property that he gained in 1890, and which he continues to have ever after, and, in particular, has in 2003. But there is neither a 2003 Napoleon time slice nor a 2003 eulogizer time slice nor a 2003 eulogy. At least in these sorts of posthumous predications, the time itself must count as an additional relatum.

Some will welcome times as relata on other grounds, namely that persons and not their time slices eulogize; that a person and no time slice of a person is a descendant. This response is controversial.[12] For those inclined to make it, what I said a Quineian would take as an n-adic relation can be construed as $n+1$-adic, time itself counting as the additional relatum. (6) can be construed as being about a triadic relation, ____eulogizing____at____, holding

---

[12] See e.g. Lacey, 'Quine on the Logic and Ontology of Time', esp. 65–6; David Wiggins, *Sameness and Substance*, Oxford: Blackwell, 1980, esp. 193–7; Peter Geach, 'Some Problems about Time', *Proceedings of the British Academy*, 1965.

timelessly of the ordered triplet, {some eulogizer, Napoleon, and 2003}, rather than only a dyadic relation holding timelessly of some time slice of a eulogizer and Napoleon; (8) as being about a triadic relation, ____being the latest remote descendant of____at____, holding timelessly of the ordered triplet, {Smith, Adam and Eve, and 2003}, rather than a dyadic relation holding timelessly of a time slice of Smith, and Adam and Eve. In this way, temporal information about property possession can be preserved by letting time itself serve as an additional relatum. If so, all property ascriptions can be timeless, and properties ascribed timelessly cannot be had posthumously.

Whether this revised version of (c) is adequate raises some very complex questions, but let me simply state briefly why I am inclined to look for an alternative solution to the puzzle of posthumous predication.

Consider a simple (and not necessarily posthumous) predication of the form, 'x is P at t'.[13] Our ordinary way of thinking about property possession, and property change, is that the 'at t' does play an adverbial role: 'at t' qualifies the 'is P', and tells us when, at what time, that possessing occurs. The Quinean–Silverstein view invites us to see things quite differently. On that view, the 'at t' is not to be read adverbially. The whole property is 'is P at', and the 't' simply stands for a relatum of that relation, a relation borne timelessly by its relata.

We have a choice, then, between two quite distinct sets of metaphysical commitments. The first includes a commitment to times, time slices of objects, and timeless property possession; the second, a commitment to temporally extended objects and properties possessed at times. I believe that the second set of commitments reflects our pre-philosophical or natural way of thinking about the world, and especially about change. In that sense, it represents our natural metaphysics. I do not say that we never have reason to abandon our natural metaphysics for a more artificial one; indeed, I do precisely that elsewhere in the book, where it seems to me the weight of the argument is on the side of such abandonment. We abandon natural metaphysics when certain philosophical difficulties or problems are irresolvable unless we do so.[14]

[13] See e.g. Michael Shorter, 'Subjective and Objective Time', in The Proceeding of Aristotelian Society, suppl. vol. 60, 1986, esp. 226–7.

[14] I claim that thinking about property possession as being dated accords with our ordinary way of thinking. Does our ordinary way of thinking, however, also have it that whatever has a property at t must exist at t, namely, at the time that it has that property? If so, am I giving to ordinary ways of thinking with one hand, only to take back with the other? No, for I would deny, pace (1) and (2), that our ordinary way of thinking does make that second commitment. At any

One such reason for switching from the natural to the Quineian account might be that there is no other way of dealing with the puzzle of posthumous predication. But if there are other ways of dealing with the puzzle that permit us to retain our natural metaphysics, then to that extent we have one less reason for abandoning it in favour of the unnatural one.[15]

I intend to try and sketch just such an alternative solution to the puzzle. I claim, then, that whatever other reasons there may be in favour of adopting the alternative metaphysics, the resolution of the puzzle of posthumous predication is not among them. I do not say that there is any technical difficulty in resolving the puzzle on the unnatural metaphysics (although I do think that its reconstruction of our idea of change comes dangerously close to being no idea of change at all), but only that it is unnecessary to adopt it in achieving the resolution of the puzzle we are discussing.

Although I know of no one who has suggested (d), it is an obvious enough suggestion. I have been thinking of properties like the property of being red, the same property that something might have at a past, present, or future time. But might there really be three different tensed properties: going to be red, being presently red, having been red?[16]

I earlier said that 'Napoleon was emperor of France' was capable of an alternative reading. For example, if tensed properties are allowed, we could say that the property of going to be an emperor is a property Napoleon had when, for example, he was a little boy. Or we could say that the property of having been an emperor is a property Napoleon had only when on St Helena.

Using this idea of tensed properties, we might try a reductive strategy for all alleged instances of posthumous predication. Reconsider 'Napoleon is

---

rate, I see no evidence for thinking that it is so committed. In my view, the slogan, 'No properties can be had or acquired by things at times or places at which the thing in question is not there to have or acquire the property' is a piece of metaphysics, which I reject, not a pronouncement of ordinary thought.

[15] See Mark Johnston, 'Is there a Problem about Persistence', *Mind*, suppl. vol. 61, 1987: 107–35, for a treatment of the 'at t' in 'x is P at t', as an adverbial modification rather than along the lines of 'x-at-t is P'.

Colin McGinn draws a distinction between two views about necessity and other modal notions, in his *Logical Properties*, Oxford: Oxford University Press, 2000: 74–83, that also has some similarities to the view I am advocating. For McGinn, modals like necessity do not modify the property, to yield a new, modal property, but are modes, ways in which a property is had or possessed. He puts it this way: it is not that Socrates is necessarily-rational, but that he is-necessarily rational.

[16] Tensed properties are briefly discussed in John Watkins, *Science and Scepticism*, Princeton: Princeton University Press, 1984: 233–5.

being eulogized'. If we permit the tensed property, going to be eulogized, why not say that this is a property he had while alive, and that this is all that the alleged posthumous predication comes to? In every alleged case of posthumous predication, so (d) claims, such predication of a property to a no-longer-existent object can be rephrased as a future tense predication of a property to an existent object.

This, we might hope, could yield a general solution to the posthumous predication puzzle. The idea behind (d) would instruct us to admit only those tensed properties which are true of existent objects.[17] Of course, on this view, a statement like 'Napoleon is being eulogized' can sometimes be true; it is just that it would be analysed as equivalent to a statement like 'Napoleon, while alive, was going to be eulogized'. Similarly, (5) becomes: 'Adam and Eve had the property, going to have Smith as a remote descendant', and this is a property they had while alive.

What is wrong with (d)? Perhaps many things are, but one is this: it would cure the posthumous predication puzzle only by introducing a new puzzle about antenatal predication. Suppose that Adam and Eve did have, while they were alive, the future tensed property of going to have Smith as a remote descendant. But this property is, as I have argued, a relational property. The future-tensed property must also be true of Smith. And that future tensed relational property can't be true of Adam and Eve at one time and of Smith at another. So it must be a property that was true of Smith when Adam and Eve were alive.

And that means that a property was true of Smith a very long time before he was born. But how could Smith have a property before he was born? That contradicts (4) in the same way as does the posthumous predication. Smith was not in Eden 5,763 years ago, any more than Adam and Eve were wherever and whenever Smith was born.

The Puzzle Resolved: Cambridge Change

The alternative way in which I wish to handle the puzzle, (a), and retain our natural metaphysics, involves challenging (3) and (4), which seemed to be the same principles that also generated the difficulties we faced in accepting a prolific theory of act individuation. On prolific theory, I have to kill the Queen in some p and at some t in and at which I no longer exist. (a) makes

---

[17] Mark Twain once commented on the premature reports of his death. Might he have been eulogized, while alive, in those premature reports? Well, perhaps it could not really have been a eulogy, when he was alive, just an encomium.

a similar claim about Napoleon's eulogy and Adam and Eve's gaining a new remote descendant: Napoleon can be eulogized and Adam and Eve can gain a new remote descendant where and when they no longer exist. I believe that my discussion of the Napoleon and Adam-and-Eve cases and the schoolchild-admiring-Socrates case, which I introduce below, offers a different way of dealing with actions such as my killing of the Queen.

I start by making a working distinction between states and events. Examples of states are: being red, being taller than, being the remote ancestor of, being brittle, believing, admiring, and desiring. Examples of events or changes are: kicking, killing, acquiring, starting to admire, eulogizing, becoming red, starting to want, and beginning to believe. In what follows, I focus only on events or changes, not on states of affairs, although a complete solution to the puzzle of posthumous predication would have to be extended to cover cases of the latter as well.[18] Notice that events can be either relational or non-relational. We can speak of non-relational changes or events, like becoming red or growing fat, and relational changes or events, like kicking, admiring, and killing.

Are relational changes reducible to pairs of non-relational ones? Lawrence Lombard thinks they are.[19] I remain unconvinced. I won't cite as evidence various Cambridge events, like acquiring a new remote descendant, since he disputes that there are such things. What about a kicking? Consider first the change involved in Smith's kicking Jones. Intuitively, the change, at least in Smith, is real.[20] Lombard must argue that the change in Smith, if real, is non-relational, despite appearances to the contrary. He does so in the following way. If we describe Smith's kicking as a kicking of Jones, there is an appearance of relationality. But, according to Lombard, this appearance arises only from the description we have chosen for Smith's kicking, and not from the change itself.

There is, according to Lombard, another possible world in which exactly the same token change occurs in Smith, the very same kicking, even though in that world there is no Jones for the kicking to be a kicking of. (It can't just be a numerically different kicking with qualitatively identical intrinsic properties.) So, says Lombard, if Smith kicks Jones in the actual world, the change in Smith is non-relational and hence real.

---

[18] I provide that extension in my 'A Puzzle about Posthumous Predication', *Philosophical Review*, 97, 1988: 211–36.

[19] Lombard, *Events*, 102–4.

[20] One often needs background information to locate which of two relata really changes. In the example given, it is possible that Jones as well as Smith undergoes a real change. See Paul Helm, 'Detecting Change', *Ratio*, 19, 1977: 34–8, for a discussion of this.

It would be desirable to have a criterion for distinguishing real from Cambridge change that did not rely on controversial judgements about the identity of changes across possible worlds. In any case, there are counter-examples to Lombard's rejoinder. Consider the change involved when Smith comes to be acquainted with Jones. Intuitively, this change involves at least a real change in Smith. But such a change is essentially relational, although real, on any plausible account of relationality that I can think of. There is no possible world in which Smith undergoes the same token change, and yet Jones does not change by coming to be known by Smith. So, I doubt that there are no irreducible relational changes.

Peter Geach has introduced into the literature a distinction between real change and Cambridge change.[21] On the classical account of change, an object o changes at t iff o acquires a property at t that it did not have before t. The inadequacy of that classical account (as I intimated earlier) can be seen in the examples above, and in many others like them, since Socrates gains a property that he did not have before when a new schoolchild comes to admire him, and yet he does not, in the most intuitive sense, really change at all. A real change is a change as ordinarily and intuitively understood. The change in a schoolchild if he comes to admire someone he did not admire before, the change in a woman when she gives birth to a sixth child, the change in an object when its colour changes, are all real changes.

Cambridge changes are Cambridge qua changes: the change in Socrates every time a fresh schoolchild comes to admire him, the change in the number six each time it becomes or ceases to be the number of someone's children,[22] the change in Adam and Eve each time they acquire a new descendant.

Notice that to predicate even a Cambridge change of an object is to predicate of the object a perfectly good property. To say of some person that he has acquired a new cousin upon the birth of a child to his aunt or uncle, is to ascribe a perfectly genuine property to that person, but it is *not* to ascribe to him a perfectly genuine change.

The sorts of Cambridge event examples that I have been or will be using really break down into at least two different types.[23] The first type includes

---

[21] Peter Geach, *Logic Matters*, Oxford: Blackwell, 1981: 318–23; and *God and the Soul*, London: Routledge & Kegan Paul, 1969: 66–7, 70–3, 98–9.

[22] For Cambridge changes in numbers see Michael Dummett, *Frege: Philosophy of Language*, London: Duckworth, 1973, ch. 14, 'Abstract Objects'.

[23] The reader interested in my somewhat fuller account of Cambridge change should see my 'A Puzzle about Posthumous Predication'.

cases like admiring and being admired by, becoming taller than and becoming shorter than, and eulogizing and being eulogized by. In the case in which Chirac eulogizes Napoleon and Napoleon is eulogized by Chirac, there is but a single token event or change. Let's say that, for example, the schoolchild's coming to admire Socrates and Socrates' coming to be admired by the schoolchild, or Chirac's eulogizing Napoleon and Napoleon being eulogized by Chirac, provide an 'active–passive' pair of event descriptions, which refer to a single token event, when the descriptions are related by simple grammatical transformation between active and passive voice, but extended to capture straightforward semantic relations like that between 'taller' and 'shorter', for example (even though the contrasting terms, 'active' and 'passive', do not quite work for examples like the latter).

In this sense, 'Cambridge' or 'real' do not denote two kinds of events or states, but rather refer to two different senses in which the multiple subjects of a single relational event may change. Is the event itself Cambridge or real (in the sense in which 'real' gets its meaning in contrast to 'Cambridge')? This is an ill-formed question as it stands. Concerning a single event with two (or more) subjects of change, one subject may change really and the other may change only in a Cambridge fashion. Strictly speaking, the event itself is neither real nor Cambridge.

Still, we can apply the Cambridge–real distinction even to these changes, in a somewhat derivative way. We tend to think of the change as categorized by what happens to the positionally first grammatical subject of the change. So we can say, if we wish, that Socrates coming to be admired by a fresh schoolchild is Cambridge, meaning thereby that the change in Socrates is Cambridge. On the other hand, if we describe the *same* token change as the fresh schoolchild coming to admire Socrates, we could call it a real change, meaning thereby that the change in the schoolchild is real. I will use the terms 'Cambridge' and 'real' in this derivative sense, as well as in the nonderivative sense that I explain below, but it is crucial to remember what these terms mean in the case of active–passive pairs.

What about the other type of example? In the cases above, as we have seen, there is but one token event under discussion, described in two different, an active and a passive, ways. But other real–Cambridge event pairs, unlike the eulogizing and admiring cases, do not follow this active–passive model, and seem, indeed in my view are, different: Socrates' death and Xanthippe's becoming a widow; the birth of my daughter in 1972 and Adam and Eve's acquisition of an *n*th remote descendant.

Assuming that, in these cases, the partner changes are *not* numerically identical, the real–Cambridge distinction applies to the two changes or events themselves, and not just to the numerically same change or event as it differentially involves the two subjects. Socrates' death and the birth of my eldest daughter are real changes; Xanthippe's widowing and Adam and Eve's descendant-gain are different from (not identical to) the former but are only Cambridge events. In these cases, although the Cambridge change is always relational, the real change need not be. Socrates' death is not a relational change; the widowing of Xanthippe and Adam and Eve's acquisition of an nth remote descendant are both relational.

I return again to this question at the very end of the chapter, in a discussion of some views of Lawrence Lombard, where I shall give further reasons for refusing to identify some (but not all) Cambridge changes with any real change. But let me offer some reasons now, as well.

Of course, questions of event identity are controversial, but, following Kim, I think that the events in the Xanthippe's widowhood–Socrates' death pair, and others like it, are not identical.[24] Kim says that Socrates' death happened in an Athens prison; Xanthippe's widowing, if it happened anywhere, happened wherever she was. It seems true, he would say, that she did not become a widow in the prison. I don't put any weight on this consideration, and I do not agree with Kim on this point. As will be seen, I read the dating and locating of the Cambridge change from the dating and locating of its partner real change, so I do think Xanthippe became a widow in an Athenian prison (if anywhere) and when Socrates died.

But there is another, more compelling reason against the identification. Goldman says[25] that if two events have different subjects, or temporal locations, or exemplify different properties, they can't be identical. Without agreeing with him on the temporal locations he assigns to the events (more on this later), and without committing myself on the question of property exemplification, the two event descriptions in the pairs immediately above have different subjects, unlike the two event descriptions in the active–passive pairs, and this alone seems to me to rule out the identity of the events they describe.

No event that happens only to Socrates (his death) could be identical to an event that happens to Xanthippe and Socrates (her becoming his widow), and no event that happens to my daughter (her birth) but not to Adam and Eve could be identical to an event that befalls both her and them

---

[24] J. Kim, 'Noncausal Connections', *Nous*, 8, 1974: 41–52.

[25] Alvin Goldman, *A Theory of Human Action*, Princeton: Princeton University Press, 1970: 10.

(their gaining her as their latest remote descendant), no matter how intimately or even logically related the events might be. When I reuse this argument in Chapter 2, for the case of actions and their intrinsic events, I shall have something more to say about the meaning of 'happening to' or 'befalling'.

Finally, there are important asymmetries: Xanthippe became a widow by Socrates' death, and not conversely; Adam and Eve gained a new remote descendant by my daughter's birth, and not conversely. No doubt, more can be said by way of reply; for example, the asymmetries might be attributed to descriptions of events rather than to the events themselves. But I hope I have said enough to motivate, without 'proving', the non-identity thesis concerning some Cambridge events and the partner events on which they depend. I will return to this issue below, and again in Chapter 2.

Geach, as far as I am aware, never offered an account of this difference between real and Cambridge changes. I think that the basic idea is that somehow there is an asymmetry in terms of their dependence on one another between what changes really and what changes in a Cambridge fashion. In some sense, the latter depends on the former in a way in which the former does not depend on the latter. Like other writers, I exclude cases of pure change of spatial position. Such cases, for example, a's becoming 500 metres from b, offer special problems for analysis, quite unlike examples of other changes, and I deliberately exclude them from consideration here.[26]

I take the relational versus non-relational change distinction as given. If 'Rab' ascribes any change, it ascribes a relational change. For these purposes, I do not count a change as relational simply because time itself might be construed as a relatum. That is, 'Napoleon turned red in 1801' is not relational just because '1801' might be taken as a relatum of the relation 'turning red in'. I take it that some changes are not relational, and since all change happens at a time, the consequence of taking such changes as relational, on the grounds that time itself was a relatum, would be to erase the distinction between relational and non-relational change altogether.

If we help ourselves to the independent distinction between relational and non-relational change, we can then explicate the real versus Cambridge change distinction in terms of the asymmetric dependencies that we need. The idea is that a real change in an object has a basis in some non-relational change in that object, whereas a Cambridge change in an object

---

[26] Terence Paul Smith, in his 'On the Applicability of a Criterion of Change', *Ratio*, 25, 1973: 325–33, excludes them, and Lombard, *Events*, attempts to introduce a special proviso in his criterion of change to avoid their difficulties.

has no such basis in any non-relational changes in that object. (Let's call such changes which the real changes in an object presuppose its 'basic' non-relational changes. In the sense in which I am using 'basis', a real change that is non-relational may have its basis in itself.)

Thus characterized, some real changes in an object may be essentially relational. However, if they are, then they must have a basis in some non-relational change in that very object. If the fresh schoolchild comes to admire Socrates, and so Socrates comes to be admired by the fresh school-child, there must be some non-relational changes in the schoolchild but there might not be any in Socrates. The change in the schoolchild is real, but the change in Socrates is Cambridge. In that sense, the real change is 'in' the schoolchild, and not 'in' Socrates.

The account below applies to the Cambridge–real distinction both as two kinds of events and as two features of the same events. Any wording suggesting only the one can be rephrased to cover the other case as well.

(12) An object, x, in going from having to lacking the property P, at t, undergoes a *real* change iff

(i) x, in going from having to lacking P at t, changes, and

(ii) there is no possible world in which x goes from having to lacking the property P at t and x undergoes no non-relational change at all at t.

x's change is Cambridge, then, iff x changes and there is some possible world in which x changes from having to lacking P at t and x undergoes no non-relational change at all at t. Changes, relational and non-relational, are real when rooted in the object's simultaneous non-relational changes; otherwise, they are Cambridge (again, a non-relational change may be rooted in itself). (12) helps us answer an earlier question: why can't there be non-relational Cambridge changes? If x Cambridge changes at t, then x might not undergo any non-relational change at t. Since every change is either relational or non-relational, Cambridge change must then be relational.

How does any of this help us with the posthumous predication puzzle? It seems clear from the examples that we have been using that only the Cambridge changes (in both senses) are posthumously predicable, never real changes. If Napoleon gets eulogized, Adam and Eve gain a new remote descendant, Hume becomes more famous than Reid, all in 2003, all such changes are Cambridge because posthumous. If all posthumous changes are Cambridge changes, then we have a further reason to believe that all post-humous changes are relational. I have already argued that all Cambridge changes are relational, so it will now follow that, if all posthumous changes are Cambridge, all posthumous changes are relational too (and not just in the trivial sense in which a time itself may be taken as a relatum).

So the puzzle of posthumous predication can be resolved by biting the bullet and rejecting (4) outright. Things, objects, can have properties, and can change, in places and at times at which they do not exist. Note again that there is no legitimate real versus Cambridge distinction for properties themselves. We can accept only a modified version of (3), which I believe will still account for the intuitions about change that we have, intuitions which may have wrongly led us to think that unmodified (3) was correct:

(3′) If an object o *really* changes in place p at time t, then o must exist in p at t.

Napoleon can now have the property of being eulogized, Adam and Eve can have the property of acquiring a new remote descendant, and so on, since the sentences that express the two foregoing thoughts ascribe only Cambridge changes to them. Things can undergo Cambridge changes when they do not exist. But real change at t requires the existence at t of the thing really changing, and it was this insight, correctly captured by (3′), which may have misled us into misplaced acceptance of (3). Since this solution, perhaps appropriately called 'the Cambridge solution', accepts that one can sometimes truly posthumously predicate, it is a version of (a).

As an aside, the fact that all predications of posthumous change are predications of Cambridge change will, I think, help sort out what is involved in the long-running dispute concerning whether one can harm the dead. If one regards x's being harmed by y as always involving a real change in x, the relatum which is harmed, and if people cease to exist at death, then it will follow that one cannot harm the dead. On the other hand, if x's being harmed by y is or can be a Cambridge change in x, then there is no reason in principle why one cannot sometimes do things which do harm the dead.

I believe that the Cambridge solution is preferable to the solution offered by (c), however formulated or reformulated. The Cambridge solution, unlike (c), is able to preserve the thought that properties are possessed at times, in its most natural interpretation. That, as I have tried to make clear, seems to me to be an important point in its favour.

Cambridge Actions: Their Times and Places

What we have shown thus far is that there can be cases of change in a Cambridge changer, or can be Cambridge changes, at times and in places, in or at which the Cambridge changer does not exist. Adam and Eve

Cambridge changed in 1972, by obtaining another remote descendant, and if anywhere, in Glasgow, where and when my eldest daughter was born. Xanthippe became a widow in an Athenian prison, in spite of herself never having been a prisoner or even having visited one, where and when Socrates died. The correct placing and dating of the Cambridge event is taken from the placing and dating of the partner real event, or the partner real changer. In cases in which there is a pair of non-identical events, a Cambridge event and a real one, as in the two cases above and not as in the case of Chirac eulogizing Napoleon, there is a third event to be considered, which we might call the 'grounding' or 'initiating' event. Adam and Eve procreated, which involved them undergoing some real changes, 5,763 years ago, just outside the Garden of Eden (they were quick off the mark), and that act of procreating is on a causal line that leads all the way to my eldest daughter's birth in 1972. The relational change, the new remote-descendant-gaining that they undergo now, is a Cambridge event, dated and placed where they no longer exist, but when and where my eldest daughter was born.

So too for Socrates and his good missus (*pace* Kim). He drank some hemlock at t in p, one room of an Athenian prison, and that, for the purpose of this example, was the initiating event. At t', he died in p', a different room of that Athenian prison, as a causal consequence of that drinking. Place p' and time t' are where, if anywhere, and when, Xanthippe became a widow. The dating and locating (if such there be) of partner Cambridge relational changes are tied to the date and location of the partner real change, not to any temporal or spatial features of the Cambridge changer.

The Cambridge event is certainly not dated and placed by the grounding or initiating event. That is, no one would date or place Adam and Eve's remote-descendant-gain by the dating and placing of their 'grounding' act of procreation so long ago, rather than by my eldest daughter's birth. So too, no one would, or should, date or place Xanthippe's widowing by using the date and place of Socrates' hemlock drinking earlier in that other room, in p at t, rather than by using his death at t' in room p'.

Let's return the discussion specifically to actions, and focus the discussion only on pairs of distinct 'partner' Cambridge–real events, one of which is an action. The same account as I gave above for events, I think, holds for actions. Indeed, it would be surprising if there could be Cambridge changes or Cambridge events, but no Cambridge actions. I name my version of the prolific theory 'the Cambridge theory' of act individuation. If we distinguish between real and Cambridge specifically for acts, what Bennett found 'incredible' is true: agents can act, Cambridge act, after they cease to exist.

It is true that actions, 'positive' actions at any rate, are changes (but qualified by what I will say in Chapter 5). But what about acts that involve no
change, 'negative actions', as they are sometimes called? Lying perfectly still
upon awakening is something I do, as is standing perfectly still while on
military parade. They evince inactivity, rather than activity, but they seem
to be actions none the less. Forbearances and omissions are negative actions
too. But if we can offer a plausible account for the central cases of positive
actions that involve change, we can then offer a derivative account for forbearances, omissions, and inactions, which do not involve change, based on
the former account.

Reconsider in this light my action, my killing of the Queen. There is my
earlier bending of my finger (compare the initiating or grounding events:
Adam and Eve's procreating; Socrates' drinking hemlock). There is also a
subsequent pair of non-identical 'partner' changes: the Queen's death and
my killing of the Queen. In Chapter 2, I have more to say about why these
partners are not identical, and what the relationship between them is.

The Queen's death, a real event, is a causal consequence of my finger
bending (compare: birth of my daughter and the death of Socrates, as causal
consequences of A and E's act of procreation and Socrates' hemlock drinking, respectively). And there is the Cambridge change, an action in this case,
namely, my killing of the Queen (compare: A and E's gaining another remote
descendant and Xanthippe's becoming a widow). In the cases above, both
partners were non-actional events (Socrates' death and Xanthippe's widowing; my eldest daughter's birth and A and E's gain); of these new partners,
only one is a non-actional event and the other is an action.

So, there are three 'elements' to consider: (a) the initiating or grounding
act, my finger bending, is a real act of mine, dated (let's say) at t; (b) the
action, my killing of the Queen, is relational; it relates me to the Queen. The
act presupposes a change in me and a change in the Queen (the Queen's
being killed by me). Of course, this is a single change, but is both in me and
in her. My killing of her = her being killed by me, but I refer to my killing of
her as a Cambridge act, in the derivative sense of that term. Finally, (c) there
is the Queen's death at t'.

What really happens at t'? It is the Queen who really changes at t' (by
dying). But when did I kill her? At t', when she dies, or at t, when I bent my
finger? I merely Cambridge change by killing her. If I am dead when the
Queen dies, that the change, my killing of the Queen, can be only
Cambridge is clear. But even if I am alive, my body may have stopped moving by then (at least my bending of my finger will be six months in the past).

My killing of the Queen, (*b*) above, takes its temporal and spatial locations from the Queen's death, (*c*), just as Adam and Eve's gaining another remote descendant took its date from its 'partner' real event, my eldest daughter's birth and not their own much earlier act of procreation (and similarly for the Socrates–Xanthippe case). So, as in the Adam and Eve case, my killing of the Queen is to be dated when its partner real change occurs, that is, at t', when the Queen dies, and (if it has a location at all) at the place where its partner real change occurs, Balmoral. My killing of the Queen no more has the place and date of my finger bending, (*a*), than do Xanthippe's widowing and A and E's gaining an nth remote descendant get placed and dated by Socrates' hemlock drinking and A and E's act of procreation, respectively.

On my view, my killing of the Queen ≠ my bending of my finger, since my bending of my finger occurs six months earlier, in London. My killing of the Queen is a Cambridge action, placed and dated by her death. Although my action, my killing of the Queen, is not identical to my bending of my finger, yet it is only a Cambridge action, because it attributes only a Cambridge change to me.

We have no difficulty, in the case of non-actional events, in saying that the change in one of the relata is merely a Cambridge change for that relatum. So the remarks I made about Adam and Eve gaining a new remote descendant seem right. Why might we be more reluctant to say in the case of actions, like my killing of the Queen, that the Cambridge change, the killing, is in the actor, the real change, the dying, in the patient?

Perhaps this is because we tend, albeit wrongly, to associate the idea of effort with our idea of action. How can Cambridge action be any sort of action, since, as Bennett pointed out, the agent expends no effort additional to the effort expended in the bona-fide act, say in his pulling of the trigger? To that extent, the observation is simply correct: there is action without additional effort: 'the rest is up to nature'. When I Cambridge act, what my action is no longer depends on my effort, but on, for example, whether the Queen dies. I act, yet without exercising any more effort beyond what I did when I bent my finger.

What about my shooting of the gun? Since all the arguments about the dating and locating of the Queen's death apply *mutatis mutandis* to the gun's going off, the real change is in the gun, the Cambridge change in me. So my shooting of the gun occurs at the time that the gun undergoes a change, and since this time is not identical to the time at which my finger bent, the bending of my finger ≠ my shooting of the gun. My shooting of the gun, like my killing of the Queen, is one of my Cambridge actions. The dating of my shooting of the gun is taken from where and when the gun goes off. Most, but not all, of my physical actions are Cambridge actions.

Although my own view is close to that of Alvin Goldman,[27] it differs from it in at least one significant respect. Goldman says that the actions that form a series like the ones we have been discussing are related by causal generation (there are other sorts of generational relations in Goldman's account, but let us look only at this first kind). Causal generation, he says, is not the same relation as that of causation, and that, I think, is true. Indeed, no two actions that are related by causal generation can also be related by causation. In the chain of actions we have been using as the stock example, no action is caused by its predecessor, although one does each action *by* doing its predecessor, if it has one. (So 'by' is not to be construed causally; I discuss this more fully in the next chapter.) Actions, even Cambridge ones, have causes and effects, but the series or chain of related actions we are using does not provide an account of the causes and effects of actions, whatever the latter might be.

The reason Goldman gives for this, though, seems to me wrong. A cause and an effect must be differently dated, the former earlier than the latter. But, he claims, if two actions, a and a', are related by causal generation, they are 'always done at the same time'.[28] 'Although the light does not go on until a few seconds later, it would still be incorrect to say that he flipped the switch "and then" turned on the light.'

I disagree. Suppose a time switch that creates a longer delay than normal between an agent's flipping and the light's going on. He flipped the switch at t. The light went on at t', some time later. When did he turn on the light? Not, I think, at t, for the reasons already given: a person can't have turned on the light before the light went on. It may indeed, at first, sound unnatural ('incorrect') to say that he flipped the switch and *then* turned on the light, but so too does it sound unnatural ('incorrect') to say that he turned on the light before the light went on.

The longer the time delay, the less unnatural it sounds in any case. He flips the switch at t, and the valley floods hours later. He did not flood the valley at t, when he flipped the switch. Of course, he did something at t that led to the flooding. And he certainly flooded the valley by flipping the switch, but he flooded it after t, after he flipped the switch.

When it does sound unnatural, I think one can explain the unnaturalness

---

[27] Goldman, *Theory of Human Action*, and esp. ch. 2.   [28] ibid. 21–2.

of saying, in such a case, that a person A-ed and *then* B-ed, while accepting its literal truth, in terms of remarks I made above: 'I act yet without exercising any more effort beyond what I did when I bent my finger'. There are, of course, genuine cases of a series of related actions in which extra effort is required: a person walks to Balmoral, shoots the Queen, climbs into his waiting get-away car, and then drives away. In the latter case, there are, on everyone's view, four actions: the walking, the shooting, the climbing, and the driving. The four actions might be part of an agent's overall action plan. Each is both later in time than its predecessor(s), and requires additional effort on the agent's part. In cases like this, later-in-time and more-effort-required go together.

In the different case of the flipping of the switch and the turning on of the light, it is literally true that the second action is dated later than the first. But the later-time-thus-more-effort nexus is broken. In cases like the flipping and the turning on, saying 'later' may sound wrong, since so saying carries the pragmatic or informal implication that more effort is required by the agent to turn on the lights, in addition to what he expended in flipping the switch, and this is, of course, not so. This informal or conversational (as it is sometimes called) implication is no part of the semantics of 'he A-ed, and then he B-ed', but saying 'he flipped on the switch and then he turned on the lights' can lead to a conflation of that case with cases like the walking-shooting-climbing-driving case.

So (to employ terms I explain later), unlike Goldman's, my prolific theory dates and places the non-basic action at the time and place of its associated event, not at the time and place of the basic action. I, like Goldman, am a prolific theorist, but unlike Goldman, I do not think the distinct actions that stand in this relation of causal (or other types of) generation must occur at the same time, even though some might.

As long as there is a finite time interval (or locational difference), however small, between the bending of my finger and the event associated with an action I do by the bending of my finger (like the shooting of the gun or the killing of the Queen), the same argument will apply. What about my reducing the world's population by one? As far as I can see, I reduced the world's population by one exactly when I killed the Queen and at the same place, if anywhere. If events e_1 and e_2, or actions a_1 and a_2, occur at different times or different places or occur to (or are done by) different subjects, then they cannot be numerically identical. But I have not committed myself to, and wish to remain neutral about, the Goldman–Kim view that if e_1 and e_2 exemplify different properties, then $e_1 \neq e_2$. My own intuitions tell me that my reduction of the world's population by one = my killing of the Queen, but nothing in my view, concentrating as it does on times, places, and subjects, would force me to take a stand on this one way or another.

So my account is also neutral on the question of the identity of actions, done at the same time and in the same place, by the same agent, like the bending of my finger and my giving of the signal (by so doing), or my saying 'I promise' and my promising (by so doing), or my bending of my finger (when it is as a matter of fact the left index finger that I bend) and my bending of my left index finger. Where there is a series of action descriptions that run from the very general to the very specific, the descriptions in the series may refer to one and the same action, as far as my own theory goes (but see my discussion of hierarchies of properties in Chapter 6). My prolific theory is something of a hybrid. So a Cambridge theory may be a prolific theory, but it need not be a most prolific theory.

Finally, what of (what seems to be) my basic action, my bending of my finger? Could this action involve a real change to only one relatum, a mere Cambridge change to another, as in the case of my killing of the Queen, and so on? I do not think that cases of basic action could be construed in this way. The change in my (attached) finger is real. What change, Cambridge or otherwise, in me, as opposed to the change in my attached finger, could be the change in question? Presumably, the bending of my finger just is the relevant change in me! I am not distinct from my attached finger; the change in my finger just is a change in me. There is no real change and Cambridge change, or even two real changes. There is only one change in this case, a real one: my bending of my finger.

The theory here proposed might be called the Cambridge theory, since when he acts in cases like his killing of the Queen or his shooting of the gun, the change in the actor is Cambridge. Like the austere theory, it limits real (i.e. non-Cambridge) actions to movements of one's body. Like prolific theory, it holds that actions like an agent's shooting of the Queen are nonidentical to basic actions like his bending of his finger. But many (though not all) of the distinct non-basic actions that it licenses are not real actions, only Cambridge ones, because the actors in such cases only Cambridge change. The challenge to the prolific theorist by the austere theorist was to account for the fact that, on prolific theory, I may be credited with acting at a place where I am not, and either after I die, or anyway after I stop moving my body. The prolific reply is that these are my Cambridge actions, since they presuppose only Cambridge changes in the actor.

In the chapters that follow, the terminology I use, in which I discuss various issues and problems, assumes prolific rather than austere theory. It is an assumption to which I regard myself as entitled, given the results of this chapter. However, much of what I have to say could transpose into the terminology of austere theory, without its central point being lost. For example, in what follows, I often talk of basic and non-basic actions. Most of this could be restated with similar effect as a distinction between basic and non-basic action descriptions.

Jonathan Bennett's Theory Compared

Jonathan Bennett attempts to draw the sting from the time argument against the austere theorist.[29] I find his position somewhat under-described in his *Events and their Names* (I am thinking particularly of his distinction between consummated and unconsummated events), but I assume that the view posed somewhat cryptically there is the same as the more extended view he developed in his much earlier 'Shooting, Killing and Dying'.[30]

Using my examples, Bennett's view is as follows: my shooting of the Queen is identical to my killing of her. My shooting occurs at the earlier time, t, and in London. What, if anything, happens at $t+6$, in Balmoral? Of course, the Queen dies then. But also, says Bennett, the shooting acquires a new characteristic at $t+6$ (and maybe in Balmoral): namely the characteristic of being a Queen-killing, or, as he says in the book, a consummated Queen-killing. Bennett's view holds that the shooting (namely, the killing, since they are identical on his view) at $t+6$ acquires the delayed characteristic of being a killing or acquires the property of being a consummated Queen-killing.

On Bennett's view, the shooting acquires that new characteristic long after it has ceased to exist, since the shooting occurs at t and that event does

---

[29] Bennett, *Events and their Names*. That is his solution on p. 197. He seems to have a distinct solution on p. 198. See also his 'Shooting, Killing and Dying', *Canadian Journal of Philosophy*, 2, Mar. 1973: 315–23.

[30] In the book, Bennett says (putting his point in terms of my example) that my killing of the Queen occurred at t, when I bent my finger and so shot the gun, even though she did not die until six months later. On the other hand, my killing of her was *consummated* six months later, when she died, even though I killed her at t. 'An action is a consummated felling [of something] at time T just in case it is a felling of something that falls before T.' But, the action can be an unconsummated felling even before the tree falls. So although an action is *consummated* only after its intrinsic event (as I shall call it later) occurs, and is consummated forever thereafter, the action, my killing of the Queen, albeit unconsummated, itself can occur before it is consummated (i.e. before she dies).

This is, I take it, the same solution as in the article, but I find it less clear.

not exist any longer at later times. (His view is not that the event extends from t to $t+6$.) Bennett certainly thinks that his view is austere, since it needs only one event, as long as that event is able to acquire new properties after it goes out of existence.

I have no problem with events acquiring characteristics after they cease to exist, since my own Cambridge solution requires something similar for objects. But we now seem to have a second event, on Bennett's story: an acquisition or a consummation. We have the shooting's acquisition of the delayed property of being a killing. (Or: the consummation of the shooting as a killing.) How do we date these events?

Call an event that occurs to another event a 'meta-event'. Objects or entities can be the subjects of events, and there is no reason why events cannot be the subjects of events as well. An acquisition (or a consummation) is itself an event, indeed, a meta-event, and in this case a Cambridge meta-event, since it is an event that befalls a no-longer-extant event. Moreover, I assume that meta-events can have a time, perhaps a place, and it appears that this meta-event, the shooting of the Queen becoming a killing of the Queen, occurs at $t+6$ (it is Bennett's view that this is so), and at Balmoral, if anywhere.

So the ontology behind Bennett's proposal seems, as far as I can tell, more complex than mine, if anything, and introduces a second event after all, which is also a Cambridge event, and whose time (and location) is the same as the Cambridge event my account requires. I can't see any advantage to Bennett's proposal, when compared to mine. Bennett's view requires Cambridge meta-events, namely acquisitions and consummations; mine, only ordinary Cambridge events.

Austere theorists often argue in a similar vein, and although their views are not so obviously involved in the rather baroque ontology that Bennett makes explicit, I believe that their views have similar consequences. For example, here is what Lawrence Lombard says:[31] 'p' unless 'q' does not entail 'p' until 'q'. So, he would say that whereas it may be true that I can't kill the Queen *unless* she dies, it does not follow that I don't kill her *until* she dies.

Consider an analogy with objects. Suppose I saw Bill Clinton when he was a little boy in Arkansas, at t. And suppose I, with great prescience, said: 'The 42nd president of the United States is playing on the swings at t'. If he is indeed playing on the swings at t, what I have said may be misleading but

---

[31] Lawrence Lombard, 'The Cambridge Solution to the Time of a Killing', *Philosophia*, 30, forthcoming: 1–14. See also his discussion in *Events*, 92–104.

it is true none the less. Clearly, scope needs sorting out. He was not yet the president when I saw him, but he was later to become the president. But the assertion is true, literally true, because the little boy on the swings = the 42nd president of the United States.

One might rewrite the statement to bring this out: 'The man who was later to become the 42nd president was playing on the swings at t'. But it does not need to be rewritten, to produce a truth. Although the statement is not true *unless* he becomes president, it does not need to wait *until* he becomes president, in order to be true. It is true even before he actually becomes president.

How would this observation help us with the dating and placing of events? I don't think that it will. On the austere theory, my killing of the Queen = my bending of my finger, and since the bending occurs at t, before she dies, so does my killing. So, on the austere theory, this is true: 'My killing of the Queen occurred at t', even though the bending had not yet become a killing at t, just as 'The 42nd president of the United States is playing on the swings at t' is true, even though Clinton had not yet become president at the time he was spotted by me in the playground.

But just as we can ask: *when* did little boy Clinton become president (answer: in 1992, many years after he was on that swing), so too we can ask *when* the bending became a killing. It was not always a killing, on any plausible view. It had to become one. The bending was not a killing at t, any more than Clinton was president when he was on the swing.

Clinton's election was, of course, an event. That event is dated a long time after the swings-sighting, in 1992. At t, the bending was not yet a killing. So too, the bending's becoming a killing must be an event; that event must be dated when the Queen died, at $t+6$, and not when the bending occurred. With events, we will quickly be back to the same issue that we pinpointed with Bennett's theory. There seems to be no gain in insisting that the bending = the killing, and so I deny the identity. (Lest I be misunderstood, I hasten to add that we of course do not have the same problem with Clinton = 42nd president of the United States.)

Again, no one should take it that I am disputing that identities, if true, are always or eternally true. If 'The 42nd president of the United States = the little boy on the swings in Arkansas' is true, then it is timelessly true. But that cannot stop us from asking the question about change: when did the little boy become the president? And his election was an event, occurring in 1992, long after the playground sighting.

Any plausible austere theory will have to tell us when the one event acquired a new feature (when some new description becomes true of that event), and, on the austere theory, that is bound to involve us in an ontology of acquisitions by long-extinct events of new properties posthumously. I think that the prolific theory has a better answer.

Lombard's Objection

Lawrence Lombard has objected to the position I have taken in this chapter.[32] He says that, for example, Socrates' death = Xanthippe's widowing given the marital circumstances, and that, by denying this, my account unnecessarily reifies Cambridge events. I have also argued that my bending of my finger ≠ my killing of the Queen, since they are differently dated and possibly differently placed. The latter I have termed an example of a Cambridge action (in the derivative sense).

Lombard holds that we do not need to include Cambridge events or actions as separate items in our ontology, on the grounds that what we wish to say does not need quantification over them. Assuming Davidsonian theory for the moment, we hold that there are butterings, or runnings, because the logical form of sentences like 'John buttered his toast quickly' and 'John ran at full speed' requires quantification over butterings and runnings, namely, over events. Lombard says: '. . . it seems clear that, because of the dependent character of Cambridge change, there is no comparable argument for the claim that there are Cambridge events and actions as parts of a best explanation of the semantic facts'. It does not seem clear to me.

Lombard holds that if the analysis of 'Socrates died' is '$(\exists e)$ (e is a dying & e's subject is Socrates), then:

(13) Xanthippe became a widow iff $(\exists e)$ $(\exists x)$ (e is a dying & e's subject is x & Xanthippe was married to x at the time of e).

So Lombard says: 'Precisely because things change Cambridge-ly only because they are related in some way to things which alter, we can always express the idea that a thing changed Cambridge-ly in terms of the underlying alteration and the relation between the subject of that alteration and the thing that changed Cambridge-ly'. Analyses like (13), if correct, would make Cambridge events redundant. Of course, my account of Cambridge change accepts that a necessary condition of a change being a Cambridge change is that it bears an appropriate relation to something that really

---

[32] Lombard, 'The Cambridge Solution to the Time of a Killing', *Philosophia*, 30, forthcoming: 1–14. See also his discussion in *Events*, 92–104.

changes, but I do not accept the reduction that Lombard appears to infer from this dependence.

(13) gives the logical form of 'Xanthippe became a widow' if and only if we can express all that we need to say using the form (13) offers. An alternative to (13), which I have been assuming above, is:

(14) Xanthippe became a widow iff ($\exists e$) (*e* is a widowing and *e*'s subject is Xantippe).

(Since (14) is relational, it has a second, unspecified subject as well, but I ignore that complication here.) Which should we prefer, (13) or (14), and why? Let me cite two considerations.

(A) Hecuba's widowing was more tragic than Xanthippe's was. It was certainly an occasion for greater public mourning. Moreover, Hecuba's, but not Xanthippe's, was immortalized by Virgil. So Hecuba's widowing was both more tragic than Xanthippe's and was immortalized by Virgil. How would we convey this information, using Lombard's preferred form?

Socrates died and Priam died, and Xanthippe was married to Socrates when he died and Hecuba was married to Priam when he died. So it follows that they were both widows. This might deal with simple assertions of the existence of widowings, perhaps assertions of the existence of Cambridge events in general. But sometimes we wish to say things about Cambridge events, to talk about them rather than just to assert their existence.

For example, how will we express any further thought about the comparative tragicness of the two widowings, without 'reifying' widowings? Or how will we express the truth that Hecuba's widowing was immortalized by Virgil, without speaking of widowings? The difficulty for Lombard's position will surface in dealing with assertions that ascribe features or characteristics to Cambridge events. Note that Hecuba's widowing could be more tragic than Xanthippe's, without it necessarily being the case that Priam's death was more tragic than Socrates'. Further, it could surely be the case that Virgil immortalized Hecuba's widowing (in such a long, moving passage!) without it also being true that he immortalized Priam's death (only a brief mention, in a rather prosaic passage). There will be many truths about the widowings that are not translatable into truths about husbands' deaths and which appear to be uncapturable in forms such as (13).

A fortiori, if the view cannot capture assertions that appear to predicate features of widowings, it cannot capture entailment relations between such assertions: 'Hecuba's widowing was immortalized by Virgil' follows from

'Hecuba's widowing was immortalized by Virgil and was more tragic than Xanthippe's'. That too will require quantification over widowings. Lombard merely asserts that '. . . all of the adverbial modifiers that might have been attributed to the alleged [Cambridge] change can be parsed out as attributions of features to the things that [really] changed . . . and to the [real] changes involved'.[33] But this seems to me a mere hope. Lombard does not consider examples and, in light of the ones I adduced above, I see no way that it can always be done.

(B) Lombard requires, as in (13), that someone who understands what a Cambridge event is, the widowing for example, can actually produce a determinate proposition only about real events (and persons), into which the proposition seemingly about a Cambridge event can be translated. I think that requirement is far too strong.

We can bring out why it is too strong by asking this question: in the case in which two Cambridge events of the same type occur, must they occur in virtue of two non-Cambridge events of the same type? Xanthippe and Hecuba both became widows; the same type of Cambridge event happened to both of them, a widowing. And, in this case, they are both widowed in virtue of the same type of non-Cambridge event, namely, a death of a husband.

But this pattern is not always so. Sometimes the same type of Cambridge event befalls two subjects, in virtue of different types of non-Cambridge events. For example, consider a social example, like becoming a father. A person can become a father in virtue of a birth of his child to a woman, or in virtue of an adoption. (Suppose, for the sake of simplicity, that it is always and only the wife who effects the legal process of adoption, so that the change is always only Cambridge for the father.)

One might imagine that this need not disturb Lombard's view: might he not just adopt a disjunctive analysis of what a Cambridge event like becoming a father is: to become a father is either to have one's child born to a woman or to have one's wife adopt a child. The translation of 'X became a father' would simply be in terms that permit either adoptions or births, both a type of real event.

A problem with this solution is that, in such social cases (and one might consider in this regard other social cases, like coming to hold an honorary title, or becoming a mayor), there is no definite end to the ways or methods by which one might become a father; the list is open-ended.[34] Different

---

[33] Lombard, *Events*, 103.   [34] See my *Metaphysics of the Social World*, 119–21.

societies might have, surely do have, still other routes by which one can become a father. So the translation of 'X became a father' would in principle be open-ended and uncompleteable in terms of the enabling real changes on which the fatherhood can depend. So, Lombard's view notwithstanding, I do not think that there always are determinate, specifiable propositions, mentioning only real events, that translate propositions which otherwise might be construed as about Cambridge events.

By way of reply, in private correspondence, Lombard suggested to me that 'I do not think it is necessary to spell out in advance what real events must occur in order for someone to change Cambridge-ly . . . After all, ["becomes a father"] does not mean ". . . by means of this or that social/legal practice", but rather, ". . . by means of whatever social/legal practices [are] in force".' But '. . . by means of whatever social/legal practices are in force', does not get the idea that Lombard needs quite right. Lots of legal and social practices are in force, which have nothing to do with fatherhood. Lombard means or should mean: 'whatever social/legal practices are in force that allow one to become a father'.

The reference to 'becoming a father' seems quite indispensable in the purported analysans after all, if we are looking for a determinate proposition to serve as the translation we need. So we seem to be caught on the horns of a dilemma: either the list of underlying real changes, on which a Cambridge change can depend, will, at least in some cases, be quite indeterminate, yielding no determinate proposition, or one can produce a determinate proposition, but only by introducing a circularity in the alleged analysis, incorporating a reference back to a Cambridge event, in order to close the indeterminacy.

Contrary to what Lombard would have us believe, the dependence of Cambridge events on non-Cambridge ones does not guarantee the non-circular translation of talk of the former into talk of the latter.

2

Some Preliminaries

Action and Activity: A Distinction

Aristotle says in the opening lines of the *Nichomachean Ethics*: 'Every art and every inquiry, and similarly every action and pursuit, is thought to aim at some good; and for this reason, the good has rightly been declared to be that at which all things aim'. Aristotle's examples are: the good at which medical art aims is health; the art of shipbuilding, a vessel; the art of strategy, victory; and the art of economics, wealth.

What is the distinction Aristotle seems to be recognizing between an action and a pursuit or activity? A pursuit or activity, like shipbuilding, is typically composed of more than one action, usually a large number of actions. There is no harm in calling a pursuit an action as well, since the whole made up of actions might also be an action, just as a whole composed of things physical is also physical. But I shall tend to use 'pursuit' or 'stretch of activity' or simply 'activity' for the composite items that have multiple actions as their parts.

Moreover, the distinction between actions and pursuits is only relative to the occasion and context. For one person, bending his finger may be an action that is a part of a larger activity or pursuit, for example, as a part of building a ship. Under unusual circumstances, perhaps a disability of some kind, another person may set himself a goal, to bend his finger, and when he does so, his bending of his finger may be both the action and the activity, the activity having in this case but a single part. An activity with a single action as its part is the limiting case, in which the activity is token identical to the action.

The distinction is neglected in contemporary action theory.[1] Judith Jarvis

---

[1] An exception is G. H. von Wright, who draws a similar, but not the same, distinction between acts and activities in his *Norm and Action*, London: Routledge & Kegan Paul, 1963: 41–2.

Thomson, for example, speaks of her cleaning the house as 'an act of mine'.[2] As a matter of ordinary language (not in itself of much importance), it sounds wrong to refer to house-cleaning as 'an action'. Aristotle's distinction seems right. I would have said that house-cleaning was a pursuit or activity, not identical with any single bodily movement, somewhat akin to shipbuilding, managing a household, or treating a patient, each made up of many actions as its parts.

As presented here, the point I am making is merely terminological. But, one fairly obvious point follows. Unless activities and actions are distinguished, it would be patently false to say that every token action (like house-cleaning, for example, were it an action) is identical to some token bodily movement.

Of course, there is no single bodily movement with which every house-cleaning is identical, since house-cleaning can be, as it were, multiply realized. Sometimes house-cleaning involves vacuuming, but sometimes not, and sometimes it involves polishing, but sometimes not, and both vacuuming and polishing require different bodily movements on different occasions.

But the point I am making is different from that above. It is that there is no single bodily movement with which any token house-cleaning is identical. Consider merely a single, token house-cleaning. Even with our focus so narrowed, there is no one bodily movement with which that token house-cleaning is identical. That token house-cleaning will be made up, or composed of, many successive bodily movements. Perhaps first a vacuuming, then a polishing, then a floor mopping. (In truth, each of these latter is itself made up of a succession of bodily movements as well.)

At best, what might be true is that there is an ordered series of such token bodily movements with which the token house-cleaning can be identified. We shall have to see, later, when I turn to the examples of skilled activity, whether or not anything of greater philosophical importance than this simple point hangs on the distinction.

In the above discussion, and elsewhere, I rely on readers' intuitions as to what counts as a single, simple, non-complex action, or one simple, non-complex bodily movement. Throughout the book, I use an action, like my bending of my finger, and a bodily movement, like my finger's bending, as stock examples of these. I discuss this more fully later in the chapter, where I say something about the distinction between a simple action and its many parts, which are not themselves further actions.

[2] Judith Jarvis Thomson, *Acts and Other Events*, Ithaca, NY: Cornell University Press, 1977: 51.

Actions and their Intrinsic Events

Suppose an agent *a*-ed, where his *a*-ing is a token physical action. On one view of the matter (but be forewarned: not one that I will ultimately accept in its full generality), in the case of physical action at least, 'Someone *a*-ed' logically entails 'there was a token event *e*', where the converse entailment does not hold. So, for example, if someone kills the Queen, or he shoots the gun, then '*e*' stands for the event, the Queen's death, or the gun's firing. I will sometimes refer to the token action as an a_e-ing, rather than just as an *a*-ing, and to the event as e_a, rather than just as *e*, to mark the fact that *e* is *a*'s intrinsic event, as I shall call it.

Different writers use different terms for this event, 'e_a'. von Wright calls it 'an event-result'. Davis calls it 'a doing-related event'. Bishop says that it is the event that is 'intrinsic' to the action.[3] Others have called it 'the associated event'. In similar vein, Hornsby and Hamlyn distinguish between the transitive and intransitive sense of verbs like 'to move'. Hornsby holds that there is an inference from 'aV_tb' ('*a* moved his finger') to 'bV_i' ('his finger moved').[4] David Hamlyn says that '. . . it is undeniable that, when we make a bodily movement [i.e. when we act], a bodily movement in the intransitive sense [an event] occurs; when we move an arm certain arm movements take place'.[5] The intransitive sense of the verb describes the intrinsic or associated event.

I shall follow Bishop's terminology (indeed, I already mentioned events intrinsic to an action in Chapter 1). Actions (or some of them, at least) can be paired with intrinsic events. On the view I am using pro tem, if such an action occurs, it is conceptually or metaphysically necessary that the intrinsic event does. Is it also sufficient? On some theories, some actions at least are identical with their intrinsic events; on this sort of theory, and for those cases, it follows that the intrinsic event is both necessary and sufficient for those actions. On other theories, the intrinsic event may only be necessary for the action, but never sufficient for it.

The question of the necessity/sufficiency of a token intrinsic event for the action token to which it is intrinsic, and their alleged identity, can be con-

[3] von Wright, *Norm and Action*, 39–40; Lawrence Davis, *Theory of Action*, Englewood Cliffs, NJ: Prentice-Hall, 1979: 5; John Bishop, *Natural Agency*, Cambridge: Cambridge University Press, 1989: 105.

[4] Jennifer Hornsby, *Actions*, London: Routledge & Kegan Paul, 1980: 2. Think of an action as what makes a sentence with the form 'aV_tb' true ('Simon moved his hand'), and an event as what makes a sentence with the form 'bV_i' true ('Simon's hand moved'). '*a*' names a person, '*b*' a bodily part, '*V*' stands for a verb, and the subscripts '*i*' and '*t*' for intransitive and transitive occurrences of the verb respectively.

[5] David Hamlyn, *In and out of the Black Box: On the Philosophy of Cognition*, Oxford: Blackwell, 1990: 130.

fusing. For example, consider these remarks by Hugh McCann: '[Intrinsic events] are events that are necessary for those actions . . . But . . . they are never sufficient for those actions.'[6] If intrinsic events are not sufficient for their actions, they can't be identical.

The views of action I shall be considering (and *rejecting*) in subsequent chapters hold that, even in the case of basic action, the basic action and its intrinsic event are identical, so *a fortiori* the intrinsic event is sufficient for the action. If McCann had a swift, sound argument for the insufficiency of all intrinsic events for their actions, basic and non-basic, we would have a short way indeed with the views on which basic actions are identical to their intrinsic events, and much of my subsequent discussion will have proved unnecessary.

What are McCann's reasons for holding this view of the matter? 'An event appropriate to serve as [the event intrinsic to] action A might occur without A occurring at all . . . An upward motion of my arm does not guarantee that I have raised it.' But McCann's reason is a bad one, even though I agree with his conclusion. McCann's reason might show that the event type, a death (or an arm rising), is not sufficient for the action type, a killing (or a raising of an arm), but it goes no way in showing that the token death (or arm rising) was not sufficient in the circumstances for this particular killing (or arm raising).

However, I do agree with McCann's conclusion: an event intrinsic to an action is not sufficient for the action to which it is intrinsic. Take the case of my token killing of the Queen and her token death, the former of which is, as we shall see, a case of a non-basic action. My argument for the non-sufficiency of the token death for the token killing is not that the death could have occurred without that action's occurring, for the reason I gave above. I shall argue the case for non-identity directly, and not via non-sufficiency. The non-sufficiency follows from the non-identity (plus some additional assumptions). Nor is my argument that they occur at different times and places, since, on the basis of my position in Chapter 1, I regard them as occurring at the same time and, if in any place, at the same place.

Rather, one of my arguments for the non-identity of an action with its intrinsic event (at least in cases of what I shall call non-basic action) is the same as one that I gave in Chapter 1, for the non-identity of pairs consisting of a Cambridge action or non-actional Cambridge event and a real event. Not surprisingly is this so, since I think that many actions are Cambridge actions, and their intrinsic events are the real events with which they are paired.

---

[6] Hugh McCann, 'Volitions and Basic Action', repr. in his *The Works of Agency*, Ithaca, NY: Cornell University Press, 1988: 75–93. Discussion of this point on pp. 76–7.

First, the action and its intrinsic event may have different subjects. The Queen's death happens only to her; my killing of her concerns or involves her and me. I accept, of course, that the Queen's death was in fact the death of her caused by me. So why did her death happen to, or concern, only her? If it was caused by me, does not her death involve her and me?

Anything can be given some relational description. But we shall need to distinguish between what is essential to an event or action and what is only contingent. What is at stake here is what an event or action essentially concerns or involves, and so who is or are its subject(s) in that sense. This same qualification applies to cases like Socrates' death and Xanthippe's widowing, that we dealt with in Chapter 1. Xanthippe's becoming Socrates' widow was relational and happened to Socrates and her; Socrates' death is non-relational and befalls only him. Of course, Socrates' death was in fact the death that caused Xanthippe's widowing, but that relational description of this death attributes something non-essential to it.

My second argument for their non-identity focuses on properties that one but not the other has. My killing of the Queen is punishable; her death is not. Her death is tragic, but not dastardly; my killing of her is dastardly but not tragic. The killing and the death can have different causes. One cause of her death, along with my shooting of her, was her loss of blood. But her blood loss was no part of the cause of my killing her. If a and b have different properties (including of course different causal properties), $a \neq b$, so my killing of the Queen $\neq$ the Queen's death.

It is not always possible to name the event intrinsic to an action just by being able to describe the action to which it is intrinsic. The terminology, 'he a_e-ed' and 'the event e_a that is intrinsic to his a_e-ing', might wrongly suggest that the two descriptions are merely trivial grammatical transformations of one another, as in 'he moved$_T$ his arm' and 'his arm moved$_I$'.

But matters are not always so trivial. The intrinsic event associated with 'he ran' is something like, the moving of his legs rapidly in such-and-such a fashion. Still, if someone grasps the idea of an action of type A, he must have some rough access to the nature of the event intrinsic to actions of that kind, on the assumption of course that his action has an intrinsic event. Perhaps some actions lack events intrinsic to them, so I shall argue later, but if they have them at all, an agent should be able to say something about what they are like, on the basis of a priori knowledge alone.

I would extend the above claim to cases of non-identical pairs of real and Cambridge events generally. As I asserted at the end of Chapter 1, in order to understand that Xanthippe became a widow, one certainly does not need to know who her husband was. But it is to have some understanding that her becoming a widow depends on the death of her husband, whoever that might be. But what of cases of Cambridge events like becoming a father, since, as I argued at the end of Chapter 1, one can become a father in virtue of any one of a disjunction of real events (birth, adoption, and so on)? In order to grasp what it is to become a father, one surely need not know the entire disjunction; indeed, it was part of my argument in Chapter 1 that such a disjunction is by nature open-ended and uncompleteable. So I would say that in order to grasp what becoming a father means generally, one needs only to have a grasp of some of the disjuncts in the disjunction of real events that is paired with it.

To return to the case of action: to understand running is to know that legs moving rapidly in a specific fashion is intrinsic to running. The agent may be hard-pressed to refine further the description of the intrinsic event, but he must have access to at least such an unrefined conception. So, if an action has an event intrinsic to it, not only is the latter necessary for the former, but also there is an a priori connection of sorts between them. Understanding what the event intrinsic to an action is, if there is one, is part and parcel of the agent's understanding the action in which he is engaging.

The above claim is conditional: if an agent grasps the type of action in which he is engaging, then he must grasp the type of event intrinsic to his action, if there is one. But must an agent always grasp the type of action in which he is engaging? In my view, agents might be truly said to engage in all sorts of actions, the concept of which they do not grasp either in general or as applying to their particular case. For example, I can see no difficulty with the idea of a group of anthropologists telling us that one group in a native society is exploiting another, even though neither group, neither the exploiters nor the exploited, has even the most tenuous access to the concept of exploitation. Let's refer to such examples as acting in an 'ungrasped' way.

An ungrasped action may be, in principle, graspable; being grasped or not grasped is a matter-of-fact affair, not a matter of what the agent's abilities and powers could lead him to grasp in principle.[7] However, when

---

[7] Do or can agents perform an action, the concept of which is in principle ungraspable by them? We should first have to decide how seriously to construe 'in principle'. Second, answering that question requires deciding whether all languages translate into one another, whether there are semantic universals, and so on. After all, if all languages inter-translate, the native language should have enough resource so that, in principle, the natives could come to learn what exploitation is.

an agent acts in a way which he does not grasp, does the possibility of his so doing depend in some way on his acting in some other way which he does grasp? To put it succinctly, does the ungrasped depend on the grasped? To anticipate, even if their non-basic actions might be ungrasped, must agents at least grasp what their basic actions are, when they are acting? Even though the concept of exploitation is quite alien to them, don't they at least grasp that one group is taking goods from the other, and it is by doing that that the anthropologists regard them as exploiting one another? I discuss this question further in the Appendix on the Epistemology of Action.

Notice that the event intrinsic to an action is not the same as the action's consequences. There are at least two ways in which to draw this distinction: in terms of necessity and contingency; in terms of the a priori and the a posteriori. (I already began to employ both contrasts at different places above.) Event-consequences of an action are contingently related to that action, or it can only be known a posteriori what they are (e.g. the effects of my raising of my arm might be that a plate is overturned, the soup is spilled, my trousers soiled, and the dry cleaner enriched); on the other hand, an event intrinsic to an action is not contingent but necessary (but, on my and some other theories, insufficient) for that action, or it can be known a priori what they are (e.g. the event intrinsic to my spilling of the soup is that the soup is spilled).

It is not a contingent consequence of my spilling the soup, or only knowable a posteriori, that the soup is spilled. Rather, as I explained above, it is a necessary condition for my spilling the soup, or knowable a priori, that the soup is spilled. Even if the action and intrinsic event descriptions are not simple verbal transformations of one another, their connection is still necessary or knowable a priori. When a person acts, his action has certain contingent causal consequences in the world. But the intrinsic event is not a contingent consequence of the action, since it is meant to conceptually follow that a token of the intrinsic-event type occurs when the action does.

Just events, or mere events, as I shall call them, are events that are not intrinsic to any action (like the exploding of a supernova or the eruption of Vesuvius or the cascading of water over Niagara Falls). These three seem clear cases of mere events, intrinsic to no one's action. But, as we shall see, the line between mere events and events intrinsic to actions is problematic.

Consider actions like my bending of my finger and all its effects. It is true that sometimes actions can have other actions (both the agent's and those of others) as causes and effects. For example, my doing something might cause you to do something. I will henceforth avoid these two-or-more persons cases, since the inclusion of the actions of a second person will throw our intuitions awry, at least for the purposes of this chapter.

But even if we restrict our discussion to the actions of a single agent, actions can still have other actions as causes and effects. If I bend my finger at t, and thereby break it, I may go to the doctor at t', and one of the causes of my going to the doctor is my breaking of my finger.

Does my bending of my finger, in addition to my breaking of my finger, also cause my going to the doctor? It seems utterly natural to also say that a cause of my going to the doctor was my bending of my finger. If so, isn't my going to the doctor overdetermined, caused as it is by both the bending and the breaking? Note that what we cannot say is that my bending causes my breaking that in turn causes my going, so that the former is a mediate cause of my going and the latter a (more) immediate cause of my going. My bending does not cause my breaking, because I break *by* bending. (As we shall see shortly, I don't give 'by' a causal meaning.)

Would not the identification of my bending with my breaking help solve this overdetermination difficulty? Indeed it would help, but I have rejected, in Chapter 1, that identification on other grounds. And there is an alternative way of dealing with this alleged overdetermination. Let there be three token actions of an agent, a, a^*, and b, such that he does a^* by doing a, and such that both a and a^* cause b, as in the example above. (There might be other actions of mine which I do by doing a, but that do not cause b.) In this case, we can say that a caused b only at-a-remove. a^* might cause b at-no-remove, but even if a^* causes b only at-a-remove as well, there will be some other action of the agent, a^{**}, and only one such action, such that he does a^{**} by doing a^* and a, and such that a^{**} is the cause of b at-no-remove. There is no overdetermination; any effect (like my going to the doctor) can have many at-a-remove causes. As long as the effect has only one cause at-no-remove, it is not overdetermined.

Causation-at-a-remove is not the same as indirect or mediated causation. The account I give of causation-at-a-remove does not apply when all the items stand in the relation of cause and effect to one another. In causation-at-a-remove and causation-at-no-remove, the several actions, a and a^*, that stand in those relations to another action, b, do not stand in the relation of cause and effect to one another (since a^* is done by doing a, and 'by' does not have a causal meaning). There is no overdetermination of b by both a and a^*, *not* because a and a^* occur at different times as they would in a case of mediate and immediate causation (although they typically do occur at different times), but because of the different positions of a and a^* in the non-causal 'by'-chain leading to b.

So, an agent's actions can have other of his own actions as causes and effects. But, in what follows, I avoid these cases as well. I consider only 'simpler' cases in which an agent's action has no other action of his, or of another agent, as either cause or effect. So I exclude cases like the one in which my breaking my finger causes me to go to the doctor.

I want now to introduce three different kinds of chains: (A) action-causal chains, (B) action chains, and (C) teleological chains. I am mainly interested in (B), but I require (A) in order to explain (B). That is, I need the idea of an action-causal chain, in order to introduce the idea of an action chain. Unlike many other action theorists, I am going to say little about (C).

(A) In line with the above restriction, the actions on which I focus have non-actional events and not other actions as their causes and effects. Consider, say, my bending of my finger, and all the causal consequences (and causes, if it has any, and to which I advert later) of that bending: the trigger's being pulled, the gun's being fired, the Queen's being shot, the Queen's death, the reduction of the world's population by one. Each of these causal consequences is an event, not an action, and the relation between my bending of my finger and each of them is causal (either immediate or mediate causation). Call this an 'action-causal chain'.

An action-causal chain, as I am using the term, isn't just any old chain of events, but rather a chain with exactly one action on it (by stipulation), and with all the events which are its causes (if any, but I shan't keep repeating this qualification) and effects on it, and all of whose links are causal links. As is clear in my example, many of the events on the action-causal chain will be intrinsic to other of the agent's actions. But it is the events intrinsic to those actions which are on the action-causal chain, not the actions themselves. What the action, say my bending of my finger, causes is the event (e.g. the Queen's death), rather than the action to which the event is intrinsic (e.g. my killing of the Queen).

If my finger bending causes the Queen's death, it cannot also cause my Queen-killing. If c is the mediate or indirect cause of e, there must be an intervening causal mechanism that goes from c to e. Because the death and the killing are non-contingently related (the former is necessary for the latter), there can be no causal mechanism that goes from the death to the killing, or vice versa, and hence none that goes all the way from my finger bending, via the Queen's death, to my killing of her, or from my finger bending to the

Queen's death via my killing of her.[8] Nor, given their non-contingent relation, can the death and the killing be joint independent effects of a single cause, the finger bending. So my finger bending must cause only one of her death and my killing of her; it causes the former and not the latter.

Actions also cause events that are mere events as well as events intrinsic to actions. Imagine that something I do causes the mere event of soil erosion somewhere. Soil erosion is a mere event, intrinsic to no action. I can cause the soil erosion, but neither I, nor anyone else, can erode the soil (that's what the rain 'does'). So, both sorts of effects may occur on an action-causal chain: events that are intrinsic to actions and mere events that are not.

(B) Consider an action chain, constructed from an action-causal chain like the one above. The action chain and the action-causal chain share an action (e.g. the action, my bending of my finger, is on both). But action chains have only actions on them, and no non-actional events. Consider all the actions whose intrinsic events are among the events on the action-causal chain. These are the actions on the action chain.

It was in fact an action chain that we discussed in Chapter 1: my bending of my finger, my pulling of the trigger, my shooting of the gun, my killing of the Queen, my reducing the world's population by one. Each action on the action chain is done *by* doing its predecessor, if it has one.

The by-relation, as I have repeatedly said, that relates these actions, is not a causal relation. As I reported in Chapter 1, Goldman calls the relation, 'causal generation'.[9] Goldman characterizes additional relations between actions on action chains, in addition to the relation of causal generation: conventional, simple, and augmentation generation. I shall not extend the discussion here to capture these other cases.

Notice also that not all of the actions on the action chain are intentional actions. My bending of my finger may have some effect that I did not intend. Perhaps my assassination starts a war. The start of the war will therefore occur as an event on the action-causal chain. But it may also be true that I started the war; that is, it might be that one can move from the effect, the start of the war, to its being an event intrinsic to my action, my starting of the war. If so, the action, my starting of the war, is on the action chain with my bending of my finger, but unlike the bending, it is not one of my intentional actions.

---

[8]   This argument is borrowed from J. Kim, 'Noncausal Connections', *Nous*, 8, 1974: 49. The argument also shows, more generally, that the real events that partner with Cambridge events cannot be causes of the latter.

[9]   Alvin Goldman, *A Theory of Human Action*, Princeton: Princeton University Press, 1970.

Overdetermination looms yet again. (Overdetermination is an ever-present danger of any prolific theory, and one that must be avoided.) An action-causal chain includes an action, say my bending of my finger, and all of its effects. One of its effects is the event, the gun's discharge, which in term causes the event, the Queen's death.

Now consider my shooting of the gun, to which the gun's discharge is intrinsic. Might the effect of my shooting of the gun also be the Queen's death? And herein lays the worry of overdetermination. The discharge and my shooting can't be identical (as I have argued), since one concerns or involves only the gun and the other is something I do and hence involves both the gun and me. The gun's discharge caused the Queen's death, but it would now seem that my shooting of the gun caused it too.[10] The action and its intrinsic event must occur at the same time. So is the Queen's death overdetermimed by two causes, both of which happen at the same time?

The shooting of the gun and the gun's discharge might not be identical, but they are not logically distinct either, since the latter is necessary for the former. The two items are not independent, in the way in which two genuinely overdetermining causes would be. If the gun's discharge caused the Queen's death, then it is perfectly acceptable to say that my shooting of the gun caused her death as well, on the grounds that something necessary for my shooting, namely, the gun's discharge, caused it.[11] These are not two independent and therefore overdetermining causes. Rather, the shooting gets this particular causal power by mere courtesy, from whatever causal powers the gun's discharge has. I said, in an argument above for the non-identity of actions and their intrinsic events, that one cause of the Queen's death, along with my shooting of her, was her loss of blood. The claim that the shooting was one of the causes of her death should be understood in light of the distinction drawn here (this will not affect the soundness of that earlier argument).

I think that my shooting of the gun could have an action-causal chain of its own, not by mere courtesy and not thanks only to the causal power of its intrinsic event. Suppose my children were distressed at the turn of events involving me and the Queen. It wasn't the Queen's death that bothered them, for they are anti-royalists. Nor was it the pulling of the trigger, which

---

[10] Nor is it like the case in which a simultaneous storm and lightning both bring about some damage, since the precise part of the damage that the storm brings about is different from the precise other part of the damage that the lightning brings about. If the shooting and the discharge both bring about the Queen's death, it would be precisely the same whole death to which they both lead.   [11] Randolph Clarke suggested this idea to me.

they might not even have thought about. It wasn't even the gun's discharge that annoyed them, for it wasn't that loud. It was rather that they, committed to the moral probity of their father, were appalled that their father could do such a deed as shoot a gun; it is my shooting of the gun which upset them, and nothing else.

(C) Finally, there are teleological chains. Teleological chains are subparts of action chains. They include only the foreseen and intended actions from the larger action chains with both intended and unintended actions on them. Unintended and unforeseen actions, and foreseen but unintended actions have no place on teleological chains.

Teleological chains provide the plan that an agent will use: my goal was to assassinate the Queen, so I had to shoot her, which I could do by pulling the trigger, and so on. The actions on a teleological chain are such that the agent plans to do each action by doing its predecessor, if it has one. 'By' is not ambiguous in the ideas of an action chain and a teleological chain. 'By' has the same sense, but the idea of a teleological chain includes the idea of planning as an additional ingredient.

The Extent of Action Chains

I now concentrate on some of the properties of action chains. How far forwards and backwards do action chains extend? How shall we answer this question: for every consequence, e, that I bring about, or play some part in bringing about, is there some action I do, perhaps one of my Cambridge actions, such that e is intrinsic to it?

Joel Feinberg speaks of the accordion effects of action.[12] Feinberg says that we can describe a person's action(s) either narrowly or broadly (hence, the accordion), because 'we can, if we wish, puff out an action to include an effect . . . Instead of saying that Smith did A . . . and thereby caused X in Y, we might say something of the form, "Smith X-ed Y" . . .'.

As Donald Davidson pointed out, Feinberg's terminology vacillates somewhat between austere and prolific theory. 'Puffing out an action to include an effect' suggests both (*a*) that bending one's finger and killing the queen are identical (because it is a single action that gets puffed out or contracted) and (*b*) that they are distinct (because bending one's finger does not 'include' the effect of the Queen's dying). I will couple Feinberg's accordion with my own prolific understanding of action.

[12] Joel Feinberg, 'Action and Responsibility', repr. in A. White, ed., *The Philosophy of Action*, Oxford: Oxford University Press, 1968: 95–119. Quote below from pp. 106–7.

Following Joel Feinberg's terminology, let's call this putative principle the unrestricted accordion effect:

> The unrestricted accordion effect (UAE): if e is a consequence of some action of X, then X a_e-ed, where e is the event intrinsic to the a_e-ing.

If the (UAE) were true, then the agent will act in an indefinitely large number of ways which are unintended, or in ways in which he does not even know that he is acting, or in ways such that he does not even grasp the type of action he is said to be doing. But these are consequences that I have already accepted for other reasons, and so I don't take these considerations to be arguments against the (UAE).

Some writers seem to think that the (UAE) is true. For example, consider these remarks by Lawrence Lombard: '. . . if x did do something which caused y's death, and if neither x nor anyone else did something, after x did what he did, which causally contributed to y's death, then x killed y'.[13] So, disregarding cases of what Lombard calls 'multiple agency', in which someone, X himself or another person, has to do something more, in order to bring about e, if X caused e, then it is true that X a_e-ed.

I think that the (UAE) is false (even after disallowing cases of multiple agency). Consider, for example, distant consequences of my current action, such that my action is part but only part of the cause of that consequence, there being many other independent causal conditions for the latter, in addition to my action, although—let us suppose—none brought about by other agents.

For example, suppose that a thousand years from now, my writing of a letter will be one of many causal factors responsible for the burning of a forest. Chaos Theory will provide many somewhat dramatic examples of this. Whatever else had to happen on the causal chain between my letter writing and the fire, suppose that nothing I or anyone else did played any role. Let all intermediate causal links on the chain be natural ones.

It does not follow that I burned the forest (by my writing of the letter), or even that I helped to burn the forest, or played even a small part in burning the forest. What is true is that I did something that causally contributed to the forest's burning. It is not true that I helped burn it or that I played even a small part in burning it, unless one hears that last claim, 'I helped burn it' or 'I played a small part in burning it' only as meaning the former, 'I causally contributed to its burning'.

---

[13] Lawrence Lombard, 'Actions, Results, and the Time of Killing', *Philosophia*, 8, 1978–9: 341–54.

It is a principle of many legal systems that (UAE) is false. A clear example, it seems to me, is the principle in English law that defines the Actus Reus of Unlawful Homicide: 'When a man of sound memory and of the age of discretion unlawfully killeth any reasonable creature in *rerum natura* under the King's peace, so as the party wounded or hurt, dies of that wound or hurt, within a year and a day after the same'. The principle here enunciated says that a person is not guilty of homicide if the person he injures dies after a year and a day. The law's interest is in legal responsibility ('*actus reus*'), not in the analysis of action, but I take this to mean that, if the death occurs as an effect of what I do after 366 days (in a non-leap year), it is untrue that I have killed the man. If this is right, Lombard is wrong even about the particular example of killing that he offers.

Might one argue that the example from the English legal system does not prove that I have not killed someone? All that the example from the English legal system proves, on this reply, is that, although I killed the person, I am not responsible for the killing. But why would I not be responsible for my killing, if it were a killing? I intended the death and indeed foresaw the death, and may have even intended and foreseen that it would occur only after 366 days had elapsed. No, I am not responsible, it seems, because I did not kill the person in question at all, although he did indeed die as a consequence of what I did do.

Jewish Law offers even more dramatic examples of the same sort of restrictions on the accordion effect. It is forbidden to activate the thermostat of a heating system on the Sabbath. It is not forbidden to open a door on the Sabbath, even though a possible, perhaps even likely, consequence of opening the door is to lower the temperature of a room and hence lead to 'a thermostat activating a heating system'.[14] The person does open the door, and does cause the change in room temperature, and so his opening the door is a mediate cause of the thermostat activating, but it is not true that he activates the thermostat. Or, it is forbidden to turn on a light on the Sabbath. But it is not forbidden to activate a time switch, only minutes before the Sabbath commences, that will lead to the light turning on a few minutes later, just after the commencement of the Sabbath. So whatever happens when the light switches on, it is not true that I have turned it on, or anyway so Jewish law says.

Again, we might try the same reply as we tried above. Have I really not turned on the light on the Sabbath? Perhaps I did so, but only

[14] Rabbi Eli Pick, *Guide to Sabbath Observance*, Southfield, Mich.: Targum Press Ltd., 1998: 132, app. II, 127–33, provides a good overview discussion of such principles of action.

unintentionally? Perhaps the result was foreseen but unintended. This is not the way, apparently, that Jewish Law would describe the case. For Jewish Law, no one has, even unintentionally, activated the heating system or turned on the light. First, I have intended for just those very events to occur, so it is hard to see how, were these actions of mine, they could be unintentional. Second, the Jewish legal system says that if someone engages, however unintentionally, in a forbidden activity, he is obliged to cease as soon as he becomes aware of what he is doing and indeed to make various forms of atonement for it. In the case at hand, even when I realize that my opening the door or throwing the time switch has the consequence of the heating system being activated or the light going on, I am not obliged to stop opening the door or throwing the time switch from then on, because I am *not* activating the thermostat or turning on the light, even unintentionally. Nor am I obliged to atone in ways that are required for the unintentional violation of the Sabbath.

When I spill the soup on myself, not only is the soup spilled, but lots of micro-events occur—soup molecules change place, the mean kinetic energy (MKE) of the molecules of my trousers rises, and so on. In order to grasp the action of spilling soup, one does not need to understand anything about soup molecules or MKE. Are these micro-events intrinsic to some actions of mine or are they only mere events? Did I raise the MKE of the molecules of my trousers, did I alter the positions of the soup molecules, both by my spilling of the soup? In general, suppose I raise the temperature of some item, i. Do I also increase the mean kinetic energy of i's constituent molecules, or do the latter just increase, as a consequence? Is the increase of the MKE a mere event or an event intrinsic to an action of mine?

Partly, the answer to these questions depends on one's views about event identity. Suppose one were to think in a rather austere fashion that the event, the temperature of i rising = the event, the MKE of i's constituent molecules increasing. If there is an action, my raising the temperature of i, is there not also an action, my increasing the MKE of i's constituent molecules, and since their intrinsic events are identical, would not the actions be identical too? On the assumption of the identity of their intrinsic events, it would be natural to suppose that these were one and the same action. On this austere view, intrinsicness (like basicness and intentionality) would become description-relative. So an event might be intrinsic to an action of raising the temperature under its description, 'the temperature rising', but not under its description, 'the mean kinetic energy of the constituent molecules increasing'.

On my more prolific view, on the contrary, intrinsicness is not description-relative. In terms of dealing with the above case, I do not hold with the alleged event identity. To make good that claim, I need not argue about the identity or non-identity of the two properties, temperature and mean kinetic energy. I invoke only the same consideration I have already used in Chapter 1 and above. I believe that the two events have different subjects, since macro-object $i \neq$ the set/aggregate, a, of i's constituent molecules. Needless to say, I believe that there is a close relationship between i and a, but that that relation is not one of identity.[15] I won't argue that here.

But even if we adopt the prolific view, there remains the difficulty of where to draw the line between intrinsic and mere events. The line between events intrinsic to my actions and mere events is vague. My own intuitions are not clear as to whether I raised the MKE of the molecules of my trousers, or whether their temperature simply rose as a consequence of my spilling the soup on them.

There are many cases in which there seems to be no right answer to the question, 'Did I do (or participate in doing) that?' Imagine a Heath Robinson (or Rube Goldberg) device, such that I flick a switch, that engages a lever, that lights a candle, whose dripping wax accumulates on a scale, that triggers a gear, that . . . , and that finally lights a bulb some time later (an hour? a day? a year?). Clearly, I did something (flicked the switch) that led causally to the light going on. But did I turn on the light, or play a part in turning on the light, in this kind of case?

There are, then, lots of cases which show that unrestricted (UAE) is false, and lots of cases about which it is simply unclear whether the accordion effect is or is not true of them. As a consequence of my eating my lunch, my stomach digests the food I swallow. Is digesting my food one of my actions, or is it a mere event that occurs in my body? I think it is unclear whether it is the case that I digest or only that digestion occurs.

I do not think we have any very clear principles of how far in the future the consequence needs to be or how small a causal contribution my action must make to the consequence, to block the inference to there being such an action of mine with that consequence intrinsic to it. The causal consequences of what I do become increasingly remote and distant, and my action has an increasingly diluted effect on those consequences, due to other, independent causal influences on that same outcome. To that extent, it becomes increasingly less plausible to claim that I have acted, with that

---

[15] See Mark Johnston, 'Constitution is not Identity', *Mind*, 101, 1992: 89–105.

remote outcome as my action's intrinsic event. So, from the fact that a consequence of what I did was that e occurred (so I brought it about, at least in part, that e occurred), it does not follow that I a_e-ed or even that I played a part, however small, in a_e-ing.

Do Action Chains Extend 'Backwards'?

If we imagine ourselves standing 'where' we act, let's look now backwards on an action-causal chain, in the other direction, rather than forwards. Return to Feinberg's accordion. I wrote earlier as if action-causal chains temporally commence with an action on them, but of course this is not really true. Even before the action-causal chain reaches the agent's bending of his finger, certain temporally prior causes, or causal conditions, must occur—a person's muscles must contract, his neurones must fire in a specific way, and so on. These are certainly causally necessary conditions for his bending of his finger; let's assume that they are also among its causes.

Could at least some of these causally earlier events also be events intrinsic to some of my actions, and hence those actions have a place on the corresponding action chain? Does the action chain 'shadow' some temporally earlier segment of the action-causal chain as well as some later segment? Can at least some of these causally earlier events, like my muscles contracting or my neurones firing, be events intrinsic to some of my actions, just as some causally later events can be events intrinsic to my actions? Do they also yield actions that have a location on the action chain that includes my finger bending?

Much of the earlier literature in the philosophy of action seemed convinced that these are causal conditions of a person's actions, but not themselves events intrinsic to something he does.[16] When I bend my finger, my muscles have, of course, contracted. The orthodox view was that an agent's muscles contract when he bends his finger, but there is nothing he does which has muscular contraction as its intrinsic event.

From the fact that a person bends his finger and that a cause, or causal condition, of his so doing is that his muscles contract, I agree that it certainly does not follow that he therefore contracts his muscles. However, I can see no compelling reason to deny that he does this action, that he has contracted his muscles, when he bends his finger. Nor can I see any reason to deny that he has fired his own neurones, whether intentionally or not, when he bends his finger. When we moved forward from bendings, we

---

[16] See e.g. A. I. Melden, *Free Action*, London: Routledge & Kegan Paul, 1961.

encountered unintentional actions; so too we will confront them when we move temporally backward. Aristotle knew nothing about the firing of neurones in his brain, yet, when he bent his finger, I think he also fired the neurones in his brain. He did so, but not intentionally. I think action chains that commence with some action a include actions whose intrinsic events are (perhaps unknown to the agent) causal conditions for a.

The spatial metaphors of 'backwards' and 'forwards' should not mislead us. If one takes an action such as my bending of my finger as a fixed point, the action-causal chain for that action does stretch temporally backwards and forwards from that action, since the action has temporally prior causes and temporally subsequent effects. 'Earlier' and 'later' are temporal ideas for action-causal chains.

But not so for an action chain. Since the action chain is constructed using the 'by'-relation, if an action like my bending of my finger is taken as the fixed point, two action chains proceed only 'forwards' from that action: (1) I kill the Queen by shooting the gun by pulling the trigger by bending my finger; (2) I fire my neurones by contracting my muscles by bending my finger (even though the neurones firing is causally necessary for and precedes the contracting and the bending). The bending of my finger 'anchors' both action chains. Both chains commence with the bending. The 'forwards' in 'action chains proceed only forwards' has no temporal meaning, only a diagrammatic one. For action chains, 'earlier' and 'later' do not have temporal meanings. An action a's being earlier than b on an action chain could only mean that a person does b by doing a. Temporally, a might precede b, or b might precede a, or a and b might co-occur.

Accordion effects of action can be supplemented by accordion causes of action, and the 'puffing out' of an action can be made to include its causes as well as its effects. We might then consider whether a principle analogous to the (UAE) is true:

> The unrestricted accordion cause (UAC): if e is a cause of some action of X, then X a_e-ed, where e is the event intrinsic to the a_e-ing.

The (UAC) is of course not true, just as (UAE) was not true. The accordion cause has clearer limits than does the accordion effect. The accordion effect certainly goes external to the body of the agent, so that ways in which I act can be described essentially in terms of some external effect; the accordion cause does not go external in this way. No non-basic action of mine can be described essentially in terms of its external causes. I turned on the lights, although the effect of my bodily movement, the light going on, is external to my body. But I doubt that I did anything, described essentially in terms of causal conditions of my action, when those causal conditions are external to my body. (Of course, it would be easy to get true action descriptions in terms of external causes, if the descriptions can be inessential to the actions.)

Basic Actions

In thinking about the topic of basic action, it is easy to conflate a number of distinctions.[17] Writers, I think, often intend a causal or a metaphysical distinction and yet explicitly speak in terms of a teleological one, or vice versa. An example of this confusion, to my mind, is to be found in much writing on basicness, for example, by Hugh McCann and Arthur Danto. McCann says he is defining 'B is causally more basic than A', and argues for the view that there must be causally basic actions. Danto says that if a is an action, either a is basic or a is the effect of a chain of causes which commences with a basic action, so Danto too constructs a concept of causally basic.

What is their argument for there being any basic action whatever? McCann's argument is typical: unless there were basic actions, 'one would have to bring about an infinite series of further changes in order to bring about any changes or set of changes at all. Humans cannot do this.'[18] Arthur Danto's classic paper, 'Basic Actions', also argues that unless there were basic actions, there would be a regress and hence that 'the agent could perform no action at all'.[19]

Some regresses are vicious and some not. I do not have a theory that I can articulate, that distinguishes between vicious and virtuous regresses, but some examples will, I hope, suffice for my discussion of this issue.

Zeno's Racetrack argument, for example, describes a regress:

If a runner is to reach the end of the track, he must first complete an infinite number of different journeys: getting to the midpoint, then to the point midway between the midpoint and the end, then to the point midway between this one and the end, and so on. However, since it is logically impossible for someone to complete an infinite series of journeys, the runner cannot reach the end of the track.

[17] Austere theory speaks in terms of basic and non-basic descriptions of action; prolific theory in terms of basic and non-basic actions. I, of course, employ the latter terminology.
[18] McCann, 'Volitions and Basic Action', 78–9.
[19] Arthur Danto, 'Basic Actions', repr. in Alan White, ed., *The Philosophy of Action*, Oxford: Oxford University Press, 1968: 43–58. His argument, from which the quote is taken, appears on p. 51.

All motion is therefore impossible.[20]

Whatever the solution is to this alleged paradox, the paradox cannot be posing a vicious regress. There *are* an infinite number of journeys between the starting and end points, if 'journey' is given the meaning it has in the statement of the paradox, and no successful solution to the paradox can deny that. Yet, since motion is possible and the runner can reach the end of the track, he does manage to complete all of them.

Other regresses are vicious. One that is usually accepted as vicious is the regress of justification, described by Karl Popper as one lemma of 'Fries trilemma'.[21] Suppose that, in order for any belief *b* of a person to be justified, he must justify every belief that he requires in justifying *b*, that only a belief can justify another belief, and that no belief can justify itself. This will lead to an infinite regress of justification, apparently vicious, since it requires the person to have actually gone through an infinite number of justifications, and to hold an infinite number of beliefs, and this is impossible.

Is the regress of actions like the vicious regress of justification or the non-vicious regress of journeys? In my view, McCann's and Danto's arguments only support the view that there must be some basic action on every teleological chain, since if there were a regress of actions on a teleological chain, it would be vicious and planned action would become impossible. Every plan must start somewhere, with something the agent does. An agent could not execute any plan at all if he actually had to plan an infinite number of actions in order to complete the plan. He could not even get started, much less finish. So I think that only the regress of actions on a teleological chain is like the vicious regress of justification.

But their arguments do not show that a regress on an action chain, if there were one, would be a vicious regress. So the arguments do not demonstrate (*a*) that there must be a basic action on every action chain, or (*b*) that there must be some causally basic action, in any plausible sense of 'causal' that I can think of. The arguments tell us nothing about the causal structure of an action-causal chain, or anything about action chains. McCann and Danto only address the requirements of planning and strategies to gain desired ends, and hence their arguments only relate to teleological chains.

What I want to do in the rest of this section is to distinguish three notions of basic action, and then ask whether there are any basic actions of each kind (I have already agreed that there are basic actions on teleological chains, for the reason McCann and Danto offer).

(D) The central concept of basicness, for my purposes, is basicness on an action chain. That is the central concept; it does not follow that there are any actions that are basic in this sense. It does not follow, but we still want to know whether there are any basic actions on action chains.

Recall all of the sorts of actions I allow on action chains, including ones I have never heard of, cannot grasp, neither foresee nor intend, and hence ones that will have no place in my plan. An action a on an action chain c is basic on c iff a is such that some other action on c is done *by* doing a, but a is not done *by* doing any other action on c. (This disallows an action being basic on any action chain with only itself on the chain.) I will henceforth refer to this as basicness, *sans* qualification.

If a were basic on an action chain, it would not follow that I intended to do it, since both intended and unintended actions occur on an action chain. But, whether it follows from the idea of basicness itself or not, are actions that are basic on an action chain, if any, ones that I intend(ed) to do?

An action that is basic on an action chain may be, as we have seen, no part of my plan. (Teleological chains are proper parts of action chains.) In planning my killing of the Queen, it may simply not be true that my bending of my finger was part of my plan. My plan may have 'started' with the shooting. I did bend my finger, but I did not consider the matter and settle on the bending. I just bent it, which is what I had to do if I was to succeed in shooting her.

It may also be true to say that I did not intend to bend my finger. I may have bent it intentionally, but without intending to do so. More on this later, but I mark this possibility at this point only as a concession that we might wish to make regarding basic actions on an action chain (although I do in fact think that it is true).

But even if we make that concession, I do not think that such basic actions on action chains can be ones that the agent intended *not* to do. It would seem strange to assert, even if I did not explicitly consider that action (so that it might not be on the corresponding teleological chain), that I moved my body contrary to my intentions, that I bent my finger, waved my hand, or whatever (when these are basic actions), intending not to do so. And this, at the very least, I think must be true: those actions, that are basic on an action chain, if there are any, cannot be ones that I do contrary to any intentions that I may have. I might not have intended to do them, but I can't have intended not to do them.

I shall henceforth mean by 'unintended', 'contrary to my intention'. My claim is only that I cannot do a basic action, having intended not to do it (and without altering that intention). This is weaker than the claim that I intend to do my basic actions. Non-basic actions, on the other hand, could certainly be unintended, both in the sense that I do them without intending to do so and in the sense that I intend not to do them. I may have intended to reduce inflation by some economic measures that I introduce, but I may actually increase inflation instead by those same measures. If I do, I not only do not intend to increase inflation, but I intended not to do so. Increasing inflation runs counter to my intentions.

But the case is different for basic action. Trying to imagine doing a basic action (unlike the inflation-increase example) that I intended *not* to do seems to collapse into a case of bodily movement rather than action. I meant to bend my index finger and I intended not to bend my thumb, but what happened was that my thumb bent. In such a case, I did not bend my thumb (a basic action) at all; my thumb just bent (for more on this example, see the Appendix).

That, I think, is what basic actions on action chains would be like, if there are any. But are there basic actions on action chains? I think the answer here is far from straightforward. Suppose on some occasion that there is no action I (seem to) do, such that I bend my finger by doing it. So perhaps my bending of my finger is basic on this action chain. My difficulty is not with the possibility of there being a trying, willing, or volition, such that one bends one's finger by so mentally acting, so that the mental act becomes, contrary to supposition, the basic action on the action chain (more on mental actions below and in Chapter 4). Rather, I think there is a problem with basic action on an action chain, even remaining within the realm of physical action.

That problem is this. When I bend my finger, I first bend it the first halfway, then I bend it the last halfway. Contrary to assumption, is the basic action really just my bending of my finger the first halfway, and so on? This returns us to the issue, first mentioned in the opening section of this chapter, of whether there are any absolutely simple, non-complex actions, or whether simplicity/complexity is always relative to some particular purpose for drawing that distinction.

It seems true that I bend my finger the whole way *by* bending it the first halfway, and then *by* bending it the second halfway. And if these, but not the whole bending of the finger, are basic actions on the action chain, will we not have set up a regress, since we can produce ever more minute spatial or temporal parts to the act? The truly basic actions on the action chain will be half-finger bendings, or quarter-finger bendings, or eighth-finger bendings, etc. There is indeed an infinite regress here, but there is no reason yet given for thinking that the regress is vicious. This regress just seems like the regress of journeys in Zeno's paradox. But, vicious or not, the regress will prevent us from identifying any action as the basic action on the action chain.

There are, I think, four ways that suggest themselves for dealing with this. First, we might deny that the fractional finger-bendings are actions at all. I do not believe that all the component parts of an action are themselves actions, and I discuss this further in Chapter 4. If the halfway finger bending is a mere event and not an action of mine, there is of course a swift way to deal with the issue. If they are not actions, they can't be actions more basic than the whole finger bending anyway. But this way out does not appeal to me. These fractional bendings seem to me to be actions and not mere events. They pass the tests for actionhood that I use elsewhere: done on purpose, things for which the agent can be held responsible, intentional, and so on.

A second way of dealing with the problem is simply to accept that there are no basic actions *sans* qualification; unlike teleological chains, action chains simply do not have basic actions on them. For every physically extended entity, there is a way to distinguish physically extended parts, ad infinitum. So too, one might hold, for actions on an action chain. My bending of my finger has action parts, and each of those has action parts, ad infinitum.

On this second way of dealing with the problem, these fractional part-bendings are not likely to be actions that a person intends to do (but they would not be contrary to his intentions either). They would be no part of one's action plan, and thus they would have no place on the teleological chain. But they would have a perfectly respectable place on an action chain. The teleological chain omits many actions that are on the corresponding action chain, and some of the omitted actions would include actions like the half and quarter, etc. bendings.

Even if my action *a*, has action parts *b* and *c*, and I do *a* by doing *b* and *c*, it does not follow that I *plan* or *intend* to do *a* by doing *b* and by doing *c*. In the normal case, I don't plan to bend my finger by bending it halfway and then by bending it the rest of the way, even though my bending it halfway and my bending it the rest of the way are actions of mine which are parts of my bending of my finger. I can describe a special story in which I am asked to bend my finger by first bending it halfway, and then the rest of the way, but that is not what normally happens.

The third way, which I favour, is to amend slightly the definition of basic- ness on an action chain, inserting the idea of 'disjoint', in the standard mereological sense: an action *a* on an action chain *c* is basic on *c* iff *a* is such that some other action on *c* is done *by* doing *a*, but *a* is not done *by* doing any other action on *c* which is disjoint from *a*. Two actions are disjoint if they have no part in common. Full finger-bendings share a part with frac- tional finger-bendings and hence the former are not disjoint from the latter. This third way allows that there are basic actions on an action chain, even though there is a non-vicious regress of parts of actions, themselves actions in their own right, but such that these latter actions have no place of their own on the action chain (and *a fortiori* no place of their own on the cor- responding teleological chain).

A fourth possibility would also do for my purposes, although I prefer the third option. The fourth possibility does not require the disjointness condi- tion, but does rest on some controversial judgements about the by-relation. It is true that I move my finger one inch by moving it half that distance and then by moving it the other half. But is it true that I move my finger by mov- ing it a millionth of an inch, then another millionth, and so on? One might say that the only way in which I can move it only a millionth of an inch is by moving it a much greater distance, thereby ensuring that it moves the mil- lionth of an inch. There is some smallest distance, *d*, which may vary from person to person, such that a person can move his finger distance *d* by doing nothing else, but such that moving his finger any distance smaller than *d* is something he can do only by moving it distance *d*. If there were some pre- cise *d*, for each person, it would give us a basic action for that person with- out a disjointness qualification. But I doubt whether there is such a precise distance for each person.

Whether we accept the third or fourth way of analysing the idea of an action being basic on an action chain, I shall accept that there are actions, like the bending of a finger, the waving of a hand, and so on, that are basic on action chains. I don't have a convincing argument for why there must be such; as far as I am aware, the only argument for basicness that works, works for teleological chains. But it does just seem true that on every action chain there is some action that is not done by doing any other action disjoint from it, or which is not done by doing any other action (as on the fourth option). Further, such basic actions are *not* actions that the agent intended not to do.

(E) Another sort of basicness concerns the place of the action within one's overall plan. This was the sense on which Danto and McCann seemed to rely. Such an action is basic on a teleological chain, itself a subpart of a longer action chain. This I call 'teleologically basic'. Only an agent's intended actions are a part of his plan, so an action that is basic on a teleological chain must be an intended action. An action *a* is teleologically basic on a teleological chain iff the agent plans or intends to do some actions by doing *a* but there is no other action on the chain such that he plans or intends to do *a* by doing it.

So, if an action that is basic on an action chain is one that the agent does not intend to do (recall that he may still do it intentionally), then that action will have no place at all on the corresponding teleological chain, and *a fortiori* it won't be basic on the teleological chain. There may be some action *a*, such that actions on his teleological plan are done by doing *a*, but that doing *a* is no part of his plan and so is not on his teleological chain at all. If token action *a* is simultaneously part of two action plans, as it could be, then *a* might be a node shared by two teleological action chains. One action can serve two or more purposes; I might both mop my brow on a hot day and give a signal by bending my fingers. In the right circumstances, an example such as this might provide two teleological chains with the same initial point.

Imagine that I am in a brain neurosurgeon's office, and he needs to examine the pattern of electrical firings in my brain. He tells me that if I do anything, say bend my finger, he will obtain the results he needs. He asks me to fire the neurones in my brain, and this I accomplish by bending my finger. So I have fired the neurones in my brain. In the above scenario, not only have I fired the neurones in my brain, but I have intended to do so. Indeed, it was part of my action plan to do so. My firing of my neurones was a teleologically non-basic action of mine, done by bending my finger. It was also a non-basic action on the action chain, of which the teleological chain is a fragment.

This is the way things are. They might have been different. It could have been the case that I had direct control over my neurones or over my muscles. Indeed, in other parts of my body, I am able to flex my muscles without moving another part of my body (my ears, for instance). Direct control abilities differ amongst people. There is no reason in principle why some of the teleologically non-basic actions that I do, whose intrinsic events lie 'leftwards' from a basic action on an action-causal chain could not have been teleologically basic for me and might not actually be teleologically basic for others.

(F) What about causal basicness, as distinct from teleological basicness and basicness on an action chain? We might say this: if *a* and *b* are two actions, an action *a* is causally basic relative to action *b* iff *a* or the event intrinsic to *a* causes either *b* or the event intrinsic to *b*. In this sense, action *a* can be causally basic relative to action *b* without *a* causing *b* (it may be their intrinsic events which stand in the causal relation).

My firing of my neurones and my contracting of my muscles are causally more basic (but neither teleologically more basic nor more basic on the action chain) than my bending of my finger, given this account of causal basicness. The event intrinsic to my firing of my neurones caused my finger bending. So causal basicness and teleological basicness yield different basic actions. My bending of my finger is, in the case imagined, teleologically basic (and basic on the corresponding action chain). But it is non-basic, in the causal sense, at least relative to the muscle contracting and the neurone firing.

An action can, then, be more causally basic than another. Are there any (absolutely) causally basic actions? As we move temporally leftwards on an action-causal chain for action *a*, for example, a person's bending of his finger, what would be the last event on the left, which is intrinsic to some other action of the agent? Would it be, for example, the firing of his neurones, intrinsic to his firing of his neurones? If we could identify which the last such event was, it would be, relative to some action chain *c*, constructed from the action and events on the corresponding action-causal chain, the causally most basic action on *c*, given the account of causal basicness that I have offered. Every event even further leftwards of it on the corresponding action-causal chain would be a mere event, intrinsic to no action. But, as I argued, it is unclear where actions stop and mere causal conditions of action occur, even remaining wholly internal to the agent, just as in the other direction, it was unclear where actions stop and mere later effects take over.

So, since the restrictions on the accordion cause are not firm and fixed, it is vague which action, whose intrinsic event lies on some action-causal chain *c* with *a* on it, is causally basic on *c*. I do not consider the idea of causally basic action a clear enough idea with which to work; a Feinberg accordion is not one with which any accordion player could play a convincing tune about causal basicness.

Jennifer Hornsby introduces her own notion of causal basicness based on (what I have called) action-causal chains. She claims that the correct account of more basic than depends on causation; her account[22] is that one action *a* is more basic than another iff the event intrinsic to the first causes the event intrinsic to the second. So far, we are in agreement. Her account, as I have described it, has been somewhat amended by me, but not in ways that matter for this point, since, as an austere theorist, she speaks in terms of descriptions rather than actions. Also my characterization at least allows for the possibility that it is the action itself that is a cause, rather than only the event intrinsic to the action.

She then goes on to say:

we should presumably regard any description that introduces no effect at all as even more basic than a description that introduces some effect, because descriptions become more and more basic as the effects introduced are more and more immediate, and the introduction of no effect—the introduction of the null effect, as it were—can be seen as a limiting case of this. So we should think of a description of *a* that introduces no effect as in reality a description that introduces *a* itself.

Speaking as an austere theorist, she thinks that 'my killing of the Queen' introduces an effect of my bending of my finger, namely the Queen's death, an effect that the description of the same action, 'my bending of my finger' does not introduce, and hence the latter description is more basic than the former. So the causally basic description for her will be that description of the action that does not introduce any of the action's effects.

I don't find her account of causal basicness attractive. The intuitive idea of causal basicness of an action has to do with whether the action itself has any actions or events intrinsic to actions among its causes, not whether it (or its description) introduces any effects. There could, I suppose, be an action which had no effects, or whose description introduced none, and yet it may have among its causes actions or events intrinsic to actions. Hornsby locates causal basicness in the failure of an action (description) to look forward to its effects; my account of causal basicness locates the idea in its failure to look backwards to a certain kind of cause. If it is causally basic, in my sense, it may well have causes, but none of them will be actions or events intrinsic to actions.

(G) The metaphysical distinction that I think gets confused with basicness (of any of the kinds) is the one developed in Chapter 1, between real and Cambridge action. I think that all actions that are basic on either a

---

[22] Hornsby, *Actions*, 70–2.

teleological chain or on an action chain must be non-Cambridge, but not all non-Cambridge actions are basic in any of the senses. Consider an action that is often taken to be (and usually is, in my view) teleologically basic, like an agent's bending of his finger. But it could fail to be basic. I need not bend my finger 'directly'. I can also bend my finger by placing it in a sling and turning my hand in a certain way that bends the sling, and hence my finger also bends as a result.

That is, I can bend my finger *by* turning my hand, and when I do, my basic action might be of my turning of my hand. My bending of my finger would not be, in this case, teleologically basic. But my bending of my finger, although non-basic, would still not be a Cambridge action either: it involves a real change in my finger. Unlike my killing of the Queen, it is a non-basic action that is a real action.

It follows from this example that there can be action chains and teleo-logical chains with more than one real, non-Cambridge, action on them. On the chain I discussed before, which included my killing of the Queen, only one action on that chain was real; the rest, Cambridge, in the derivative sense. (Only one action involved a real change in me.) But this sort of chain, although typical, is certainly not universal.

Even though there are or can be non-basic actions that are real, it seems plausible to hold that all Cambridge actions are non-basic. I could not ini-tiate an action chain or a teleological chain with a Cambridge action. Any of my Cambridge actions must be grounded, both metaphysically and teleologically, in some one or more of my real actions occurring somewhere earlier on the action or teleological chain. In order to Cambridge act, I must do it by doing something real. All basic actions are real. But the concepts of a real action and a basic one must be kept distinct.

The sling-and-finger example should also convince us that there is no physical action type that is teleologically basic. Basicness is not a feature of physical action types at all, but of certain of their tokens. For every physical action type, some of whose tokens are basic, other tokens of it are or can be non-basic. I can, to the delight of small children and to the embarrassment of my own older ones, directly wiggle my ears. Others can wiggle their ears only by placing their ears in their hands and moving their hands about. Both they and I can wiggle our ears, but only for me is it a basic action token. For others, the tokens are non-basic.

Are there physical action types (e.g. turning on the light, flooding the val-ley, alerting the infamous prowler), no token of which could be teleo-logically basic, or basic on an action chain? Certainly there are physical action types, no token of which is in fact teleologically basic or basic on an action chain; turning on the lights is an example. But it does not seem conceptually impossible that any portion of the physical word be under an agent's direct control. I could turn on the lights just like that, in the same way as I now bend my finger or raise my hand, without doing something else in order to get the light turned on. One might think that, if this were to happen, we would begin to think of that portion of the physical world as a non-contiguous part of the agent's body. I don't think that is right, but if it were so, then the claim here would be that given the right sort of direct control, any part of the physical world logically could be part of my body, however distant that piece of the world were from me.

Richard Swinburne discusses the distinction between God's basic and non-basic actions (presumably, His teleologically basic actions).[23] Curing someone of cancer is an action type (this is Swinburne's own example). Merely mortal doctors can non-basically cure someone of cancer. They cure cancer by doing something else—chemotherapy, radiotherapy, surgery, or whatever. But God is such that He could perform some tokens of this, and of any, action type as basic actions. Swinburne's view is that typically God produces effects in the natural world 'in a non-basic way. . . . But He could bring about any event by a basic action', and when He does, He brings about a miracle, 'for example, curing someone of cancer, when they would not get better by normal processes'.

Swinburne's thought here is not entirely clear. 'He could bring about any event by a basic action.' Which event and which action does Swinburne have in mind? Is the curing meant to be the basic action or is the cure the event, no doubt intrinsic to one of His non-basic actions, that some basic action of God brings about? I cannot quite see how, even for God, curing someone of cancer could be a basic action. Curing cancer is like winning a race; 'curing' and 'winning' are what are sometimes called 'success verbs' or 'achievement verbs'. No one can win a race as a basic action; they can only win the race by doing something else, namely running the race.

So too for curing someone of cancer. One can only cure by doing something else. Perhaps by destroying the cancer cells. God might be able to destroy the cells as a basic action, whereas doctors must destroy the cells by doing something else. But not even an omnipotent being can cure as a basic action, because curing is an achievement requiring some other action that leads to it.

[23] Richard Swinburne, *Is there a God?* Oxford: Oxford University Press, 1999: 12, and also ch. 7.

Mental and Physical Action

As an initial thought, much in the same way that it is an initial thought that persons have or are in both mental and physical states, it seems that persons engage in both mental and physical activity. I agree with McDowell regarding mental action (setting aside, for the moment, the distinction between action and free action): 'Judging, making up our minds what to think, is something for which we are in principle responsible—something we freely do as opposed to something that merely happens in our lives . . . This freedom, exemplified in responsible acts of judging . . .'.[24]

I do not mean to be begging any philosophical questions in favour of dualism; the initial thought is consistent with a large number of philosophical positions that make very different things of the initial thought, including the idea that philosophical reflection will show us that every mental action is identical to some physical event or action. I agree also with Peter Geach that, in the anodyne sense in which the assertion of the existence of mental acts is intended, 'this ought not to be a matter of controversy'.[25]

There has at least to be this initial thought, for one subsequently to make something of it. Any theory of agency, to be plausible, must offer an account both of physical and of mental action. Such a theory must explain each phenomenon, or even perhaps explain it away. But what it cannot be is merely silent on the issues. As we shall see, most philosophical effort has gone into the treatment of physical agency. Mental agency has suffered from neglect.

Examples of physical action are legion: waving of a hand, running, walking, bending of a spoon, killing of a queen. It is not sufficient for some token action a to be physical that a have physical effects. Many mental acts have physical effects.

An action type A is a physical action type if E is the event type intrinsic to action type A and E is a physical event type (my killing of the Queen is a physical action because the death of the Queen is a physical event). This characterization of physical action is partial and incomplete, since it defines the idea of physical action only for actions which have events intrinsic to them. I return to this question in Chapter 5.

What about mental action? Mental actions include such things as deciding, judging, considering, concentrating, attending, and inferring. If

[24] John McDowell, 1998, *Meaning, Knowledge, and Reality*, Cambridge, Mass.: Harvard University Press, 1998: 434.

[25] Peter Geach, *Mental Acts*, London: Routledge & Kegan Paul, 1964: 2.

judging is a mental action, as both McDowell and Geach say, it must be distinct from acquiring a belief, which does not seem very act-like.

Some nouns can stand either for mental actions or (mere) mental happenings or events. For example, thought and intention have this ambiguity about them. Thinking is an activity. Sometimes I actively order my thoughts about some subject-matter. On other occasions, thoughts may merely pass through my mind, one following another by associations of various sorts. They come and go 'of their own accord'. When I daydream or am lost in reverie, thoughts simply seem to crowd in on me, with no participation by me. Perhaps this is also what happens if I engage in the so-called free association that a psychoanalyst might ask me to 'do'. And similarly for intentions. On some occasions, intentions simply arise in me, passively. On other occasions, I form intentions. On the latter occasions, I mentally act.

Thoughts are the events intrinsic to genuine acts of thinking. I am here disputing a thesis of Hugh McCann, who says that thinking is altogether intrinsic-event-less.[26] It seems to me that at least some mental actions, and in particular, thinkings, have events intrinsic to them. When I actively think, the thoughts (more precisely: the comings and goings of those thoughts) are the events intrinsic to the active thinking. When I actively form an intention, the arising of the intention in me is the event intrinsic to the active forming of the intention. I am not asserting that all mental actions have events intrinsic to them (although they might), but that some at least do.

An action type A is a mental action type if E is the event type intrinsic to action type A and E is a mental event type (my thinking is a mental action because the occurrence of thoughts is a mental event). This characterization of mental action is similarly partial and incomplete (the 'if' cannot be turned into an 'iff'), since it defines the idea of mental action only for actions which have events intrinsic to them. In neither of the accounts that I have offered can the 'if' be converted into an 'iff'. And of course both this characterization of mental action and the one above of physical action take as primitive the ideas of mental and physical events, so they are not really very illuminating.

It is sometimes said that Descartes was entitled only to assume that there was thought, not that there was thinking, much less that he was a thinking thing. What Descartes says in his *Meditations* is that he is certain that he is thinking, that he is a thinking thing. This goes beyond the mere occurrence of thoughts. What Descartes claims to possess, I take it, is incorrigible

    [26] Hugh McCann, *The Works of Agency*, Ithaca, NY: Cornell University Press, 1998: 87.

knowledge of the existence of a certain kind of mental activity, namely active thinking, and not just incorrigible knowledge of the existence of certain mental events, namely, the coming and going of thoughts. And for there to be this activity, there must be an agent of that activity.

Are mental actions on chains, teleological or action-causal or action chains? Suppose Uri Geller bends a spoon by concentrating on it, and suppose he pleases his audience by his bending of the spoon. There is then an action-causal chain, leading from his neurones firing (event) to his mental act of concentrating and thence to the events, the spoon being bent, and to the audience being pleased. Based on that action-causal chain, there are two action chains with at least these fragments: (i) he pleases by bending and bends by concentrating; (ii) he also fires his neurones by concentrating. A part, but only a part, of at least the first action chain is a teleological chain, since he plans to reach his goal, pleasing his audience, along some of the nodes of the action chain. But agreeing that mental actions have a place on some action chains is not to agree that every action chain has a mental action on it.

If Geller bends the spoon by concentrating, then his basic action is a mental action (his concentrating), and his physical action (his spoon bending) is non-basic. But his bending of the spoon might be a basic action for him. No concentrating needed—he just does it, like I just bend my finger. So 'Agent X moved physical object o' might attribute a basic physical action to an agent, not just a non-basic physical action, even if o is no part of the agent's body, in any conventional sense.

Indeed, as far as I can see, assuming that a disembodied agent is conceptually possible, it would be possible for such a disembodied agent to engage in both basic and non-basic physical acts. (This returns us to Swinburne's speculation about God's miracles, mentioned above.) I see nothing inconsistent about the idea of an agent who is a disembodied mind (assuming that that itself is a conceptual possibility)—a Berkeleian agent, so to speak—being able to bring about changes directly in the physical world (and not just, for example, by mentally acting and bringing about the physical effect thereby). Such an agent would not even have a physical body with which he was able to manipulate his environment, but the agent would still physically act.

Some might say that, if such a thing happened, the physical object would just constitute a discontinuous bit of the agent's body, or, in the extreme case, would just count as His body. As I have said above, this sounds wrong to me. If one of God's basic physical actions is His miraculously making the cancer cells disappear, what plausible physical object becomes a part of His body thereby?

How do mental and physical actions relate? Persons as we know them engage in both kinds of actions, as a matter of deep but still only contingent fact. What different kinds of agents could there have been? Pertinent questions include these:

(1) Is it logically possible that a person mentally acts but never physically acts at all, either basically or non-basically?

(2) Is it logically possible that a person mentally acts but physically acts only non-basically?

(3) Is it logically possible that a person physically acts but never mentally acts at all?

(4) Is it logically possible that a person physically acts, but mentally acts only non-basically?

As for (1), a person might engage in mental activity, for example, actively think, decide, reason, infer, prove theorems, and so on, but never bring about any physical effects in the world, such that those effects were events intrinsic to any action of his. He could have commerce with the physical world, as long as none of those events brought about by him fell within the scope of the accordion of action. It is hard for me to imagine what this abstract possibility would be like: whatever the first physical effect was on the action chain that had his mental action on it, how could that physical effect fail to be an event intrinsic to one of his actions? If he brings about physical event e so immediately by his mental action, he has a_e-ed, and his a_e-ing would be a non-basic physical action.

Certainly, this agent would have to be disembodied. If he had a body, he would have to bring about some effects in that body, if it were really to count as 'his body' at all, and any such bodily effects are bound to be events intrinsic to some physical actions of his. If he never even brought about any effects in that body, there is no interesting sense in which it could be his.

As a limiting case of this possibility, we might consider the possibility of an agent who not only brought about no physical effects which were intrinsic to actions of his, but an agent who brought about no physical effects at all, intrinsic to his actions or otherwise. Such an agent would have no causal commerce with the physical world but he would still be an agent of sorts. Think of a group of disembodied mathematicians, each proving theorems and communicating the results to one another. One of them, A, could prove Goldbach's Conjecture (his basic action) and communicate the result to another, *B*, perhaps by telepathy, thereby convincing *B* to believe this result (convincing *B* to believe this would be a non-basic mental action of *A*'s), since *A* causes *B* to come to believe this by proving the theorem and communicating the result, by telepathy, to *B*.

As for (2), suppose, on the other hand, that when the agent mentally acts, his actions do have physical effects. If some of the physical events he brings about are events intrinsic to some of his actions, then such actions will be his non-basic physical actions. But the agent might never engage in any basic physical action; all of his physical action may be somewhere along the accordion, to the right of any basic mental action. This is, in one of its formulations, the view of volitionism, to which I briefly return later.

(3) Could an agent physically act but not mentally act at all? I think this is possible, but such an agent would be very different from us. But they would be much more than mere robots or automata. They would have an inner life, but it would not be characteristic of what we take to be human. They would have some inner life, albeit a passive one; they might have intentions, suffer pain, feel pleasure, have desires, beliefs, hopes, and wishes. But they would lack a capacity to decide between conflicting beliefs or desires, to adjudicate between different emotions or attitudes to which they were subject. They would be creatures whose mental life was badly crippled, truncated.

Indeed, the creature could have second-order desires, that is, desires about his desires, and may even have what Frankfurt misleadingly calls 'second order volitions',[27] that is, desires to have various of its desires be its effective will. As far as I can see, to have a Frankfurtian second-order volition may be an entirely passive affair, since to have such a second-order volition is merely to have yet another desire, albeit one with a special content about one's will. One could presumably have the second-order desire about one's will, without actually engaging in any acts of will at all. Such a being would have desires about his will, but would never exercise his will, since exercising the will, unlike the having of desires of any order, would be a mental action.

(4) is interesting, and I do not know the answer to it. On the accordion cause principle, some of the physical events internal to the agent may be events intrinsic to his non-basic actions, for example, contracting his muscles, firing his neurones. One might speculate whether some of the

[27] Harry Frankfurt, 'Freedom of the Will and the Concept of a Person', *Journal of Philosophy*, 68, 1971: 5–20, repr. in Gary Watson, ed., *Free Will*, Oxford Readings in Philosophy, Oxford: Oxford University Press, 1982: 81–95.

mental events mentioned above might serve the same purpose: suppose that when the agent basically physically acts, certain mental events or processes must have taken place. Why can't these be mental events intrinsic to some of his non-basic mental actions, the mental parallel to his contracting his muscles, and so on? Since these intrinsic events would be mental, the actions would also count as mental actions of his. If so, any physical actor would almost be bound to be a mental actor too, albeit a non-basic mental actor.

I do not think any of this sounds right, but I do not know why mental events do not lend themselves to being events intrinsic to non-basic mental actions, in the same way as internal physical events do lend themselves to being events intrinsic to non-basic physical actions.

Let me return the discussion briefly to (2), and to volitional theory. As I am using the expression, volitionism is the view that all basic action is mental action (or, as an austere theorist might say, action under a mental description). Volitionism says this: 'on every occasion on which a person physically acts, there is something that he wills or tries to do and he does the former by his willing or trying'. Typically, all such basic mental action was construed as acts of will, but I intend the concept of volitionism somewhat more widely, since there might be cases of basic mental action other than acts of will, like tryings or attempts, which this theory might wish to utilize.

Volitional theories of action were put forward by Bentham, Mill, and Austin, and had earlier echoes in Hobbes and others. Volitional theory became the established orthodoxy in classical jurisprudence, until the Wittgensteinian attack on it by philosophers such as Ryle. It is important to see that rejecting these volitional views does not entail that there are no mental acts, or even that there are *no* acts of will or trying. The truth might be that *some* of our basic actions are mental acts, maybe even that some of our basic acts are tryings or willings, but that we do not mentally act every time we engage in every physical action whatsoever.

I am no enemy of tryings or attempts, but I think the theory that says that whenever we physically act, we do so *by* willing or trying to act, overpopulates the mind (this is a charge that I will subsequently bring to other theories of action as well). In any event, whatever view we take of tryings and attempts, there are certainly other mental actions, some of which I mentioned above. Examples include: forming a decision, or evaluating and considering various options. All mental actions are real. It is not at all clear that the category of Cambridge action has any application in the mental realm.

3

Theories of Action and an Introduction to the Causal Theory of Action

Folk Naturalism

Agents in the sense I intend are creatures who can deliberate and choose, who have or lack rationality, autonomy, freedom, liberty, self-control, and self-determination. They can be morally appraised as good or bad. What they do, their actions, can be or fail to be voluntary, according to or against their wills, deliberate or accidental, intentional or unintentional. Those actions can be morally appraised as right or wrong.

The words, 'agent' and 'action', certainly occur in the natural sciences, but the actions and agents postulated in such assertions as 'every action has an equal and opposite reaction' and 'this bottle contains chemical agents' are not the sort of actions or agents I intend. When one speaks of human agents and their actions, different sorts of things are being spoken of. A human agent differs from a chemical one in the ways I mentioned above, to do with freedom, responsibility, self-control, moral evaluation, and so on.

Indeed, sometimes the word 'act' is used in connection with human agents and is still not the sense I require, as in 'acts of perception'. As far as I can see, a person is or may be entirely passive in an act of perception. I normally lack responsibility and control over what I perceive. The acts or actions I want are displays of genuine activity, bringing in its wake all of the other considerations I mention above.

Nor is the use of the expression 'what the agent does' of much help, even when restricted to agents in the sense I intend. Amongst the things I do might be: to hiccup, blink, bleed, and yawn. Normally, none of these are things for which I am responsible; they may be quite outside my control. But in spite of there being no acid linguistic test for the agency I intend, I believe that we can recognize cases of it and distinguish them from these other phenomena.

Perhaps most importantly, as the first paragraph indicated, agents in the sense I want can be morally responsible for their actions, subjects of praise and blame, reward and punishment. Part of seeing ourselves as morally responsible is seeing ourselves as beings who can act or can forbear from acting.[1]

The precise connection between action and responsibility, or between action and free action, is not always straightforward. I can be responsible for the actions of my young children, for example. Further, I might intentionally act, but have only diminished responsibility, because, say, of the coercion under which I have been placed. In general, the theories that I will be looking at will be theories of action, not of free action. It is important, though, for a theory of action to leave sufficient conceptual space, so that the distinction between action and free action can be marked.[2]

However complicated the connection between responsibility, freedom, and action may be, this much is true: if we could find no room in our world-view for action, we could find no room in our world-view for ourselves as morally responsible or as free agents. Even if it were true that, whenever I act, I only mentally act, so that I never physically act at all, I could at least be free when I mentally act, and responsible for my mental actions. 'Die Gedanken sind frei', as the song and saying go, and the song and saying must be speaking about mental activity, not just the passive having of thoughts that arise in me and pass away.

So agency and action seem pretty deeply entrenched in our folk, non-scientific view of the world, the common-or-garden perspective that we share when we do things or think things about the world around us. It is what we assume when we are on that famous Clapham omnibus.

The philosophical difficulty that some philosophers think they face about

[1] Kathleen Wilkes has an excellent discussion of what is involved in the idea of a person, which will be relevant here, since many agents (ourselves, for instance) are just persons who act. See Kathleen Wilkes, *Real People*, Oxford: Clarendon Press, 1999: 21–6.

[2] See Irving Thalberg's discussion of Roderick Chisholm and Richard Taylor's agent-causalist theories on this requirement, in I. Thalberg, *Misconceptions of Mind and Freedom*, Lanham, Md.: University Press of America, 1983: 167–70.

all this action-talk arises from a view that we might call 'folk naturalism'. Let me explain. Folk naturalism is a very commonly held view by philosophers. Let's begin with the naturalism. 'Naturalism' is a vague term. It is no part of my project to make it less vague. It has meant different things in different contexts. It comes in at least four versions: epistemic, ontological, methodological, and conceptual.[3]

All four versions privilege natural science in some way. On the epistemic version, only the claims of natural science, or anyway such claims as natural science can underwrite, deserve our literal, cognitive assent. On the ontological version, only the entities required by natural science, or the entities that are reductively identifiable with the former, exist. The ontology of natural science includes so-called observable entities and, on some naturalistic views, includes irreducible theoretical entities as well.

On the methodological version, the methodology of natural science (assuming its methodology is the same or similar in all branches of natural science) is the method of choice in all fields of cognitive endeavour. On the conceptual version of naturalism, only the concepts of natural science, or the concepts that are reducible to them, are legitimate in any cognitive enterprise. This statement of philosophical naturalism, in any of the four senses, is itself vague, especially in the absence of a precise characterization of what counts as natural science (psychology?), but it indicates to some extent the area of concern I wish to discuss.[4]

But what of the 'folk' in 'folk naturalism'? I count myself a friend of the folk in general, but not of folk naturalism. The folk naturalist accepts as

---

[3] The reader interested in some of the problems with naturalism might like to consult Steven Wagner and Richard Warner, eds., *Naturalism: A Critical Appraisal*, Notre Dame, Ind.: University of Notre Dame Press, 1993.

[4] What connection, if any, is there between ontological and conceptual naturalism? I do not have a criterion for concept identity, and do not intend to discuss the issue here. But what does seem true is that if one rejected the view that concept identity required some meaning or semantic relation between the two concepts, the difference between a conceptual and at least a type-type ontological form of naturalism, indeed of any reductive theory, would disappear. Imagine, for example, that on a weakened view of concept identity, two concepts are identical iff it is either a nomologically or a metaphysically necessary truth that every instance of one is identical with some instance of the other. On that view of concept identity, I cannot see any important difference between the conceptual and type-type ontological versions of naturalism. On the other hand, if concept identity requires something stronger, say a meaning relationship, the conceptual and type-type ontological versions of a reductive claim can be kept distinct. And of course there is always the possibility that the ontological version of what the naturalist wants can be expressed in some so-called token-token form. For some healthy scepticism about this distinction, see Helen Steward's excellent *The Ontology of the Mind*, Oxford: Clarendon Press, 1997: 120–34.

unproblematic only some part of our (and his) non-scientific folk talk. He may be a reductivist, and think that the unproblematic part of folk talk is reducible in principle to some natural science, or, more simply but less precisely, he may just think that the ontology of that unproblematic part of our non-scientific, folk talk is coherent and consistent with the ontology of the natural sciences. For the folk naturalist, a part of our non-scientific talk poses no philosophical problems (or relatively speaking, does not pose such problems, when compared to the other part of folk talk). As an example of this, many folk naturalists accept an ontology of events and causal relations, even if they have wildly divergent accounts of what these are.[5]

But there is, or may be, another part of our non-scientific talk that does pose philosophical difficulties for a folk naturalist, and, on one central folk-naturalist view, our discourse about action and activity poses just such a problem. In that discourse, we speak of action and agents, with all of the metaphysical commitments about self-control, freedom, rationality, autonomy, moral responsibility, and so on, and none of this (in the intended sense) has a place in the natural sciences, nor does any of the former seem to be underwritten or legitimated by it. So it is seen as problematic. It may be salvageable for the folk naturalist, but there is a problem with it, to be overcome.

There is a distinction between reduction and elimination, as two different philosophical strategies.[6] The eliminator cares nothing for the methodologies or concepts or entities or claims to knowledge made in our non-scientific, folk lives, in so far as they appear to be out of step with natural science. In those cases in which scientific progress has or appears to have superseded any of the above, the eliminator's advice is to eliminate the folksy. If everything is, for instance, merely atoms in motion, or whatever, then strictly speaking there simply are no chairs, tables, or other macro-objects. He will tell us that our folk physics, our ordinary set of views about middle-sized macro-objects (or, in another vein, our folk psychology, our ordinary set of views about our mental life), is quite simply for the birds (of course, there are no birds either, just more atoms in flight).

When it comes to action, activity, and agency, the eliminative philosophical naturalist will tell us that there simply are no such things. Not surprisingly, this is because these are not to be found within any natural science.

---

[5] Jonathan Bennett's *Events and Their Names*, Oxford: Oxford University Press, 1988, has a good synopsis of some of the leading accounts.

[6] For the distinction between elimination and reduction, see William Lycan and George Pappas, 'What Is Eliminative Materialism?' *Australasian Journal of Philosophy*, 50, 1972: 149–59.

(Clearly and trivially, they are found, and apparently in an ineliminable way, in the activity of natural science, and that is itself a problem for the eliminator.) For him, discourse about action and activity is not only within the problematic part of our folk views, but also cannot be reconstrued or reconstructed in a manner acceptable to the folk naturalist, and so is to be jettisoned.

I question whether this eliminative move is coherent, in the case of action and agency. How could I see myself as someone who is not responsible for his views and has no control over which views he holds? My view, that I am not responsible for my views, would itself have to be a view for which I would believe that I am not responsible, and so it is hard to see why I would want to regard myself as being justified or warranted in holding the view that I am not responsible for the views I hold, since I have no responsibility for the holding of it.

The position that we will be dealing with in this and the next chapter is not eliminative, but it is not really reductivist either, in the standard meaning of that term.[7] The folk naturalist might espouse a reduction of the acceptable part of folk talk to scientific talk at a later stage, but the folk naturalist move I will focus on in what follows concerns his attempt to save, rather than eliminate, the problematic part of folk discourse by reconstructing it in terms of the other, non-problematic part of folk talk.

The folk naturalist first uses his naturalism to select the non-problematic part of folk talk, the part that is consistent in his view with the ontology or methodology or whatever, of the natural sciences. (Again, it is really only relatively unproblematic, in the sense that it does not raise the issues or problems that the problematic part under discussion raises.) He then tries to understand the problematic part of folk talk in terms of the non-problematic.

A comparison here might be with Hume, understood as attempting to reconstruct causal necessity in terms of constant conjunction. Both discourse about necessity and discourse about constant conjunctions are parts of our folk views of world. For epistemic reasons rather than scientific ones, Hume thought that the former was problematic and had to be reconstructed in terms of the latter. I would say that most philosophical analyses work in this way. At one time or another, some philosophers have thought that: knowledge is problematic, relatively speaking, but belief, truth, and justification are not problematic in the same way; numbers are relatively

---

[7] For a fuller and more nuanced account of these options, see Lynne Rudder Baker, *Saving Belief*, Princeton: Princeton University Press, 1987: 11–15.

problematic, but sets are not problematic in the same way; right and wrong are problematic, but an act's maximizing the amount of happiness is not problematic in the same way; social wholes are problematic, but individual persons are not problematic in the same way.

Our protagonist, whom I will therefore call a reconstructionist rather than a reductionist, will wish to show that agency, activity, and action (like causation or numbers or right and wrong or knowledge or persons) can be retained in our overall folk understanding of the world, since they can be explicated using other folk terms, ideas, entities, or whatever, which are ultimately acceptable or available to the natural sciences. So the reconstructionist naturalist will take the puzzling phenomena of action, control, freedom, responsibility, and the rest of that family, and understand them in terms of the folk phenomena he does not regard as problematic for the natural sciences. For all the reasons I have already mentioned, the philosophical naturalist is bound to hope that the reconstructionist strategy will work and that he need not be driven to the eliminative position, in order to retain his naturalism.

Thomas Hobbes's *Leviathan* contains one of the most systematic attempts in philosophy to execute this sort of reconstructive programme for action.[8] Hobbes starts with the idea of very small beginnings of 'motion in the organs and interior parts of mans body', or 'endeavours', which later 'appear in walking, speaking, striking, and other visible actions' (part I, ch. 6). Endeavours are, I suppose, part of his and our folk discourse; they certainly formed no part of seventeenth-century science. On this basis, Hobbes attempts to account for will, deliberation, voluntary action, and liberty.

There is a grand project of naturalistic reconstruction laid out for us by Hobbes. On this grand project and ones like it, our common-sense way of thinking about human beings and what they do will be compatible with natural science after all, because it will be reconstructed in terms of that other part of our folk ways of thinking about things that is already assumed to be so. The modern philosophical folk naturalist is not likely to use endeavours as his basic building block in executing his reconstructive programme for the case of action. I will return to this later, but the standard philosophical naturalist repertoire will include, as basic building blocks out of which to reconstruct action and agency, the concepts of an event and of causation as a relation between events.

The folk naturalist in whom I am interested thinks that events and caus-

---

[8] Thomas Hobbes, *Leviathan*, part I, ch. 6, any edn.

ation are items from the acceptable part of our folk theory, acceptable because they in some way are licensed by, or found in, natural science. This may not prevent him from thinking that, at the very deepest levels of natural science correctly construed, events, for example, might be reduced to something even more fundamental: zones or portions of space-time perhaps, or some such.

As an aside, it is in this way that I understand libertarian, soft and hard determinist theories of free action. The hard determinist and the libertarian are the eliminators, although they choose different things to eliminate. The hard determinist eliminates freedom and responsibility. The libertarian eliminates deterministic causation from the realm of (some?) action.[9] The soft determinist is the reconstructor. The soft determinist tries to reconstruct the idea of free action in terms of action that is uncompelled and uncoerced. The success of that programme assumes convincing accounts of compulsion and coercion that do not reintroduce the idea of freedom. But that is, alas, a story for another day.

An Overview of Where we are Going

Central cases of action require activity, and activity itself requires change, whether real or Cambridge, so that states of affairs, like being six feet tall or desiring a pineapple, which are non-changes, cannot themselves be items which evince activity. States of affairs cannot be intrinsic to actions. Recall that we are focussing on the central cases of positive action and disregarding cases of forbearance, negative action, and inactivity.

Activity may require change, but there can be change without activity. All events are changes: the waxing of the moon, the eruption of Vesuvius, the bending of my finger, the waving of my hand. All four of these events, although they are changes, do not appear, on first inspection, to evince activity. In Chapter 2, I called the first two of these events 'mere events'. All mere events certainly are passive. When, on the other hand, I bend my finger or I wave my hand, that is, when I act, I am active. What of events like the second two on my list above: the bending of my finger, the waving of my hand? Are they passive, like the mere events, or can they, first appearances notwithstanding, sometimes evince activity as well? Part of my task will be to decide if first appearances might be misleading in this regard.

---

[9] But the libertarian might retain the thought that all action, including all free action, has probabilistic or non-deterministic causes. See e.g. Robert Kane, 'Free Will: New Directions for an Ancient Problem', in his, ed., *Free Will*, Oxford: Blackwell, 2002: 222–48.

Berkeley was certainly no naturalist. He thought that some items, namely minds, were active and that other items, distinct from the minds that had them, namely ideas, were passive. He would have included ideas of events or occurrences, if he had thought that there were such, in his list of passive items: 'All . . . the things which we perceive . . . are visibly inactive: there is nothing of power or agency included in them'.[10] 'A spirit is one, simple, undivided, active being'.[11] I disregard the connection that Berkeley drew between passivity and perceptibility. However, his view entails that no active item like an action can be identified with any passive one, like an event, and it is with this that I agree.

Aristotle thought that action or activity was one of the irreducible and distinctive categories. In *The Categoriae*, Aristotle lists ten ultimate categories of thought or predication, the ninth of which is Action.[12] To say of a man, says Aristotle, that he lanced someone, or that he cauterized someone, is to predicate something about the man that cannot be captured in any other way, by predication in any other category. The eighth and tenth categories are state ('shod', 'armed') and passivity or affection ('to be lanced', 'to be cauterized'), respectively.

In particular, on Aristotle's view, when we predicate action of an agent, we predicate of him something that is categorially different from predicating a state or an affection to him. To say of a person that he runs, walks, moves his hand, lances someone, and so on, is to say something that no philosophical theory can capture in a genuinely different way. With action, according to Aristotle, we get a fundamental category of thought.

Aristotle's and Berkeley's views would need careful setting out and distinguishing. At first glance at any rate, Aristotle's view is about the concept of action; Berkeley's is best interpreted as a view about action tokens. But my view of action or activity is anti-naturalist in a way similar to the views of both Aristotle and Berkeley that I have described above. My view is, like theirs, anti-reductionist (and anti-eliminativist) about the concept of action and about action tokens. I find naturalism about action uncongenial. I, like Aristotle, believe that the category or concept of action is an irreducible, fundamental category of thought. Moreover, I, like Berkeley, believe that actions are ontologically fundamental items, in the sense that no action can be reductively identified with any item that is 'passive', in the way the naturalist proposes. As they stand, these views of mine are vague; I intend to make them more precise in what follows.

---

[10] George Berkeley, *A Treatise Concerning the Principles of Human Knowledge*, sect. 25, any edn.

[11] ibid., sect. 27.   [12] Aristotle, *Categoriae*, ch. 4, any edn.

I appreciate that my opponent is not going to express his claim in terms of actions being identifiable with passive items, for that already seems to beg the question against him. My claim, with its reference to passivity, gains what meaning it has from my denial of specific theories of action that one finds in the literature, and which I will begin to discuss immediately below. I dispute both ontological and conceptual philosophical naturalism regarding action, but I intend to concentrate mainly on the ontological issues in what follows.

Consider this example: agent X (directly) moves his hand. For me, and for Aristotle and Berkeley, there is nothing philosophically deeper that one can say about the nature of this item, X's moving of his hand. Unlike Aristotle, who would count here presumably merely a substance and a predicate or property of the substance, I think there are actions, like X's moving of his hand. Indeed, if my aim were to explicate Aristotle, to speak of actions in a philosophically serious way would be to attribute a view to him that he did not hold. We can, for example, quantify over actions, and a true Aristotelian would deny this. But like Aristotle and Berkeley, I think we have something fundamental, for which no reductive identification is plausible.

Let me limit, for the time being, the discussion to cases of basic (on an action chain) physical action, a person's directly moving of parts of his body. A currently orthodox theory of action is the causal theory of action (henceforth, the CTA):

> (CTA) a movement of X's body, m, is X's token basic action iff m is rationalized and caused in the right way by X's mental states.

On the CTA, each token basic action can be identified with some token movement or event (its intrinsic event) that is caused in the right way by a rationalizing mental or folk-psychological state (a belief and a desire pair or perhaps an intention or an action-plan).[13]

In the case of a physical action, the movement or event in question will be

---

[13] Whose view is this? I believe that it is the standard naturalistic view of action in the literature. It is certainly the view of: John Bishop, *Natural Agency*, Cambridge: Cambridge University Press, 1989: 104; Michael Costa, 'Causal Theories of Action', *Canadian Journal of Philosophy*, 17, 1987: 831–52; Myles Brand, *Intending and Acting*, Cambridge, Mass.: MIT Press, 1984: 15–18; Alvin Goldman, *A Theory of Human Action*, Princeton: Princeton University Press, 1970: 71–6. It is almost the view of Donald Davidson, in 'Actions, Reasons, and Causes' (repr. in his *Essays on Actions and Events*, Oxford and New York: Clarendon Press, 1980), except that there is not the same sharp distinction drawn by Davidson between the metaphysical and explanatory questions, he is sceptical about being able to flesh out 'caused in the right way' in a non-circular fashion, and the characterization of practical reasoning in the opening paragraphs of that paper does not appear to be identical to the one I adumbrate here.

a bodily movement. I omit the qualification about the causation not being deviant, but refer the reader to other discussions of that aspect of the debate, which I will not discuss.[14] The CTA says that every basic action is identical to some event, namely an event with some general type of causal history. There are other ways in which to state a naturalistic reconstructive theory about action, for instance, every basic action token is identical to an ordered triple, {a rationalizing mental state, the causal relation, and a physical event}. But I shall stick with my formulation.

The CTA counts as a version of philosophical folk naturalism, a folk naturalistic, reconstructive theory about action, activity, and agency. It identifies every basic action with its intrinsic event, so (on its account) a problematic part of our folk discourse, discourse about activity and agency, gets explained in terms of another, relatively unproblematic part, discourse about the occurrence of intrinsic events and their causal history, the latter of which makes no reference to activity or agency. The CTA's view of non-basic actions is that they are events caused, in the standard way, by an agent's basic actions, or caused by other events themselves caused by the latter. (This puts the CTA view in prolific talk; I suppose that most CTA theorists are austere and would speak in terms of a single action, multiple descriptions, so the last sentence will need an austere translation.)

Despite what might first appear to be the case, on this view, there is no ontological divide between actions and events, between activity and passivity. The CTA attempts to bridge these gaps. In this chapter, I describe the CTA as fully as I can. In the following chapter, I dismiss the CTA on two grounds: (a) it has no plausible account of skilled activity; (b) it cannot deal adequately with the case of mental action.

The second theory that I shall look at, the ACT, comes in two different versions. The first, the E-ACT, says that an action, like a person's moving of his finger, is identical to its intrinsic event, the finger's moving, such that the intrinsic event is caused by the agent himself. The idea of causation used here is sometimes called 'agent causation'. It is not as easy to find compelling reasons to reject this view, beyond the strangeness of some of the ideas it makes use of. But strangeness, especially in philosophy, is not a decisive consideration.

The E-ACT is not a folk-naturalistic theory, because the idea of agent

[14] Bishop, *Natural Agency*, chs. 4 and 5. Bishop provides a useful bibliography for this issue, as well as making a distinctive contribution to it himself. I have disputed his solution in my review of his book, in *Mind*, 100, 1991: 287–90.

causation that it employs is itself so unlike the idea of causation used in natural science. It does not try to reconstruct discourse about action in terms of another part of folk talk that is thought to have the approval of natural science. However, it is important to note, and I shall return to this in Chapter 5, that, like the CTA, it identifies every action with an event of some kind.

The other version, the C-ACT, holds that an action (like a person's moving of his finger) is a *causing* by the agent of an event intrinsic to that action (in this example, the finger's moving). (There is also a corresponding version of the CTA, mentioned five paragraphs above, stated in terms of causings. I do not discuss this separately, since what I have to say about causings in regard to the C-ACT would apply, *mutatis mutandis*, to a version of C-CTA.)

On the C-ACT, the action is not identical to an intrinsic event but to a causing of such an event. (But is the causing itself another kind of event, even if not an event intrinsic to the action? The impatient reader will have to wait until Chapter 5 for my answer.) I discuss various problems with the introduction of causings into the metaphysical picture required for the understanding of action. This version is not folk naturalistic either, since causings, whatever they are, do not seem to be passive events like finger bending or arm risings. Causings also introduce agent causation into the picture of action, although in a different way than the E-ACT. On the E-ACT, the action is an event that is agent caused. On the C-ACT, the action is an agent-causing of an event.

In Chapter 5, I argue against the C-ACT, because I do not accept that there are any causings. As far as the E-ACT is concerned, I consider various problems that it raises. As always in philosophy, one man's reductio might turn out to be another's happily embraced consequence. To my lights, the E-ACT tries to explain the less mysterious by the more mysterious. But I freely admit that 'mysteriousness' is a person-relative concept, and I have nothing terribly convincing to say to the philosopher who insists that he understands agent-causation better than action and hence insists that he can illuminate the latter by the former.

Is there some assumption that all three theories share, that might account for what I take to be their failure, if they do fail? Indeed, there is; all three maintain that in the case of a basic physical action, there is an intrinsic event that occurs. That is, they maintain that when a person bends his finger (assuming that the token finger-bending is basic), a bending of his finger occurs; when he raises his hand, his hand rises. According to the three views, the basic action is either identical to its intrinsic event, which is caused by his mental states, or is identical to its intrinsic event, which is agent-caused by him, or is itself a causing of that intrinsic event, depending on which of the three theories of action on offer one embraces. I disagree. When a basic action occurs, I hold that it does not follow that any intrinsic event does. When a person bends his finger, it is *false* that his finger bends, only true that he bends it.

I try to motivate this view, and show how it can solve certain problems in action theory. I hold what might be called an exclusive disjunction theory about basic physical action: either a basic action occurs (like my bending of my finger), or an event does (like my finger's bending when someone or something bends it for me), but never both. Most writers have claimed that the occurrence of the first *entails* an occurrence of the latter (and two of the three theories I described hold, in addition, that they are identical).

Indeed, when I introduced the idea of an intrinsic event in Chapter 2, the idea was introduced via those entailment relations. I deny the entailment in the case of basic action; more strongly, I hold that when a basic action occurs (my bending of my finger), it *follows* that no event intrinsic to that action does (my finger's bending).

Of course, if one believes that my bending of my finger is itself an event, whether or not it is identical with my finger's bending (because it might be thought that actions themselves constitute a subclass of the class of events in their own right), and hence uses the term 'event' more widely than I have been doing, then if my bending my finger occurs, it does follow that some event does—namely, itself. In that sense, the assumption that whenever a basic action occurs, an event does, is an assumption I could embrace; it is quite harmless to my view. What I deny is that when a basic action occurs, an event intrinsic to that action occurs, with which the basic action is identical.

What about this wider sense of 'event'? Even if no basic physical action is identical to an intrinsic event (because it does not have one) or to a causing of one, is it true that a basic action is an event in its own right? If this is only a question of arbitrary classification, and not one of substantive philosophy, then nothing of any seriousness hangs on it. I return to this issue in Chapter 5.

If this is right, a presupposition of all three theories of action will have been shown to be wrong. I sketch out some of the consequences of my denial, and try to show that my view does not have some of the counter-intuitive consequences one might suppose.

The Causal Theory of Action: An Introduction

The contemporary philosophical folk naturalist I want to describe is not tied, as was Hobbes, to the details of the natural science current at some particular time. As I have already indicated, he finds no difficulty with the idea of an event, and the idea of the causal relation between events, because these ideas are required or licensed by natural science itself. Natural science itself deals in events and event causation; if the reconstruction of action and agency in terms of them is successful, then action and its conceptual pals add no ontological commitments beyond that required by natural science.

The contemporary philosophical folk naturalist will therefore try to convince us that first inspection of the apparent distinction between activity and passivity, actions and events, might be deceiving. His alternative approach attempts to explicate or analyse activity as, after all, a certain kind of event or change. This philosophical folk-naturalist view about action is the causal theory of action (or, the CTA, as I have already called it), a preliminary characterization of which I have already offered above.

On this view, the action, my bending of my finger is, after all, the event, my finger's bending, when that bending is (non-deviantly) caused, for example, by my desire for something and my belief that my finger bending will satisfy that desire. A token basic action just is its intrinsic event. Of course, not all bodily events are actions. But bodily events with the right rationalizing mental state causal ancestry are, on this view, actions.

The CTA must address this question: how can activity 'emerge' from, or supervene on, the apparent passivity of events?[15] This is, let us call it, 'the problem of passivity'. This is a difficulty faced by any anti-Berkeleian, reconstructionist position about action, which tries to reconstruct action using only the resources available to that part of our folk outlook in which no explicit mention is made of action and agency.

The CTA, as I have stated it, is not a theory about the meaning of the sentence, 'Agent X acts in such-and-such a way'. It does not say that action sentences can (or cannot) be translated without remainder into sentences about events, or states, and their causal relations. Think of an analogy: the fact that physical object discourse cannot be translated into sense data discourse without remainder does not by itself show that physical objects are not just sets of sense data. Physical object discourse and sense data

---

[15] An interesting discussion of this point is to be found in J. David Velleman, 'What Happens when Someone Acts?', *Mind*, 101, 1992: 461–81.

discourse might be two discourses about the same things, namely, sense data, neither discourse translatable without remainder into the other. Similarly for action and event discourse. The former might be untranslatable into the latter, but that would show nothing about the truth or otherwise of the CTA.

Is the CTA about the property of being an action, about the concept of action? If the criterion for concept or property identity is sufficiently weakened to exclude any commitment to semantic or meaning relations between the concepts or properties, then this may say nothing more than what the CTA says already, if it is understood as a type-type theory of identity (more on that issue later). If the identity criterion is not weakened to exclude the requirement for semantic or meaning relations between the properties or concepts, then a proponent of the CTA could make some further claim about the reducibility of the concept of action, or the property of being an action, if he wishes, but he certainly need not do so just in so far as he subscribes to the CTA.

Since the CTA is a metaphysical or ontological view about what a token action *is*, it is silent also on the question of the explanation of action, as well as on the question of the reduction of the concept of action. Many philosophers do not use the name 'causal theory of action' to refer to this metaphysical doctrine. Often, it is used to refer to the view that all actions are preceded, and partly explained, by rationalizing mental states. I distinguish between this latter view, which I call 'the causal theory of action explanation' (hereafter, the CTAE), and the causal theory of action. The CTA is an ontological or metaphysical theory; the CTAE, since about explanation, is an epistemological theory. What one thinks about action explanation will be partly a function of the general theory of explanation one holds, and this is a separate issue. I discuss the CTAE separately, in Chapter 6.

The CTA is not a theory about free actions, about what actions are free. It is a theory about all *basic* action tokens, free and unfree ones, if such there are.

The CTA must admit psychological states like belief and desire or intention into its scheme of things, but of course it is free at a later stage to reductively identify each such mental state with a state of the brain. Folk naturalism works in stages. In the first stage, and the only stage with which I shall concern myself, it reconstructs action and agency using the resources of other parts of our folk views, including causation, physical events of various sorts, and mental states and events such as beliefs, desires, intentions, plans, and so on (folk psychology). In a second stage, if it has one, it may wish to reductively identify all of the mental items with underlying brain or neurophysiological events or states.

I do not consider this further stage here. Since the philosophical vision that informs the CTA is a naturalistic one, the further, physicalist move that would identify mental states and events with brain states and events would be an appropriate one for the CTA. But since the naturalism is folk naturalism, it is important that it proceeds to the second stage, if it does, only after completing the first; it does not itself reduce action and agency to the purely physical, except perhaps indirectly, via the reconstruction.

I have mentioned the contrast between type-type and token-token theories. Which is the CTA, as I have explicated it? It depends on how one individuates the relevant event types. As we shall see, the CTA identifies, for example, a token, such as my bending of my finger, with the token, the bending of my finger, when the latter has a non-deviant rationalizing causal history.

The action type, my bending of my finger, can't be identified with the event type, a bending of my finger (*sans* further qualification), since some of my finger bendings (like the one that occurred when you bent my finger for me, you rascal) are not cases of my bending of my finger at all. But, if the appropriate event type can be specified rather more specifically, say as the event type, a bending of my finger with some non-deviant rationalizing causal history or other, then perhaps, one might hope, the theory can be construed as type-type.

If the event types are even more specifically identified, say, by their specific causal histories, and since many different causal histories can rationalize a finger bending (my desiring d_1 and believing that my bending will lead to d_1; my desiring d_2 and believing that my bending will lead to d_2), there are an indefinitely large number of types available, so the action type would have to be identified with an indefinitely long disjunction of event types. It is precisely in those cases that philosophers tend to embrace token-token theories as the more attractive option.

The Rationalizing Requirement

The idea of rationalization used by the CTA is the old Humean idea of reason as the slave of the passions. Suppose I desire some end or goal, g (perhaps, I want to impress you), and I believe that only by engaging in action A (perhaps, bending my finger) will I obtain g. My doing a (my bending of my finger) is thereby rationalized. On the CTA, the action, my bending of my finger = its intrinsic event, the bending of my finger. But rationalization is, as one says, 'under a description'; what gets rationalized on the CTA is the item under its action description, 'my bending of my finger', and not under its description, 'the bending of my finger', although sometimes CTA theorists say the latter and one can easily understand what they mean.

(On a similar issue, the CTA says that the rationalizing mental state causes the event intrinsic to the action. But if the intrinsic event = the action, then the rationalizing mental state causes the action. There is no circularity here; that it causes the action merely follows from the analysis.)

There is an initial ambiguity in the idea of rationalization. This ambiguity can be brought out by considering cases of weakness of the will. Suppose I desire some goal g, and I believe that B-ing is better than A-ing for achieving g. However, I also believe that one can achieve g by A-ing, but only sub-optimally. So I have some reason to A, but less reason than I have to B.

Suppose further I do an act of type A none the less, in order to achieve g. Since I desire g and believe that doing B is more effective than doing A for obtaining g (and I have no other beliefs about any other bad effects of B-ing), one might say that nothing rationalizes my token a-ing. My a-ing is not rational, because nothing rationalizes it.

But when I do action a none the less, isn't it true that I do it for a reason, or for some reason, even though I accept that I had a better reason for not doing it and doing an act of type B instead? Why is this not sufficient to 'rationalize' my doing a?

What this shows is that there is a stronger and a weaker sense of 'rationalizes': in the stronger sense, to show that an action is rational for an agent is to show that the agent had more reason to do it than any other available alternative. Perhaps we should extend this stronger sense to include cases in which I have at least as much reason to do the action as I have to do any available alternative. I surely act rationally, let's say, in the strong sense, in choosing the tin of tomatoes on the left, in the supermarket, even though I had no less reason to choose the (apparently) qualitatively identical tin on the right. In the weaker sense, to show that an action is rational is merely to show that the agent had some reason to do it, however slight or weak, in the circumstances, even if he had much more reason to do something else.

Are there actions which are not rational in each of the senses? I described a case above, in which I do not act rationally in the strong sense. If I sometimes knowingly act sub-optimally to achieve my goal, I sometimes act non-rationally in the strong sense. That is presumably one meaning of what it is to act akratically, to act with a weak will.

What about acting non-rationally in the weak sense of 'rationalizes'? I may allow time to count, *per se*, as a relevant consideration in choosing what to do. I may put off going to that painful dentist visit today and decide instead to go tomorrow, even though, let us suppose, it is equally probable that I will undergo the same degree of pain on both occasions.[16] I think nothing rationalizes my dental delay in any sense and hence it is not a rational action of mine even in the weak sense. True, I had the same reason to go today as to go tomorrow, so the making of either appointment is strongly rational, given my views on the elimination of tooth decay, but I had no reason at all to change my appointment. So this might be a case of non-rational action in the weak sense in which nothing whatever rationalizes my delay to any extent, however small.

Which sense of 'rationalization' does the CTA require, for its account of agency? None of my arguments against the CTA saddle it with the stronger requirement. But I am sceptical of this lower standard. The CTA is bound to have some difficulty with weakness of the will in any case, but allowing merely weak reasons to causally drive bodily movements increases the chance that one is not going to be able to capture the idea of full-blown agency, tied as it is to the idea of self-control, using the weaker account.

'Rationalization' is, of course, Donald Davidson's own, favoured term of art. To borrow Daniel Dennett's terminology, it is meant to be a part of the personal, rather than the subpersonal, level of discourse.[17] The literature has not, to my mind, really grappled with the question of what sorts of folk-psychological causes are rationalizing causes, or whether the various candidates all rationalize in the same sense.[18] In part, this stems from widespread confusion about the form and content of the practical syllogism. But the guiding requirement for the CTA is an affirmative answer to this question: is causation and rationalization of the bodily event by *that* sort of folk-psychological item prima facie enough to produce agency, and hence solve the problem of passivity?

John Bishop speaks in terms of the psychological causes making the action 'the reasonable thing to do'; Brand talks of the psychological causes

---

[16] Jon Elster, *Nuts and Bolts*, Cambridge: Cambridge University Press, 1989: 45. Elster has described many cases of intentional irrational action, both in *Nuts and Bolts*, in his *Sour Grapes*, Cambridge: Cambridge University Press, 1985, and elsewhere.

[17] Daniel Dennett, *Content and Consciousness*, London: Routledge, 1993: 93–6, and *passim*.

[18] See e.g. Joseph Raz's (ed.) collection, *Practical Reasoning*, Oxford: Oxford University Press, 1978.

being 'appropriate' to the action.[19] Brand's wording is in fact too weak, unless 'appropriate' just means 'rationalizes' in Davidson's sense. In one sense, if I have a benevolent character, then acting out of loving-kindness is an appropriate way for me to act, given that I have that character and that the circumstances call for this sort of behaviour. My benevolent character might be an appropriate causal condition for my so acting in these circumstances, but it might not rationalize my so acting.

Can every action be rationalized, strongly or weakly, by the agent's mental states, in the sense that the CTA requires? Changing the date of the dental appointment is already problematic for the view that all actions can be rationalized, in either of the two senses available to the CTA. The view that actions can be rationalized, if it works at all, works best for instrumental action, action for the sake of some end or goal. Does it work for intrinsic action, action done for no further purpose or reason?

Maimonides introduces the category of futile action, action 'by which no end is aimed at all'.[20] His example is that of people playing with their hands while thinking. Pacing a platform awaiting a train (not his example, as trains were in short supply in twelfth-century Cairo), or doodling, or whistling (in some contexts) are other examples. These futile actions might be considered as examples of intrinsic action, since there is no apparent end, for the sake of which they are done.

If there are intrinsic or futile actions, it might seem that the idea of rationalization could not apply to them, and the CTA would already face its first (or second, if we count the delayed dental appointment) apparent counter-example. Is there a reply on behalf of the CTA? Suppose I do futile action *a*, for no further purpose. The CTA, as I have described it, is committed to finding some belief, or anyway some mental state with appropriate cognitive content. As a degenerate case, the CTA theorist can say: the desire in question is just the desire to do an action of type *A*, and the belief is the belief that this action, the one I am now doing, is of that type (I want to play with my hands, and believe that what I am now doing is a case of hand playing).

As far as I can see, the reply is problematic. The reply, and any reply like it, to get a belief on board, will need a belief with an indexical referring to the present time or place in it—'this', 'now', or some such. But if the belief refers to the action I am *now* doing, or to *this* action, then the belief

---

[19] Brand, *Intending and Acting*, 7 and *passim*; Bishop, *Natural Agency*, 104.
[20] Maimonides, *Guide to the Perplexed*, iii, 25.

co-occurs with the action, and, since they would be simultaneous, on most views about causation, the belief could not also be the cause of that action. I return to this issue of action descriptions containing indexicals in Chapter 4.

In spite of the difficulty the CTA has over futile actions, and actions that are motivated solely by the passage of time (as in the change of the altered dental appointment), I would not wish to rest my case against the CTA on either of them. There are futile actions and I believe that they are fully intentional actions. I pace, or may pace, on purpose, and I am responsible for my pacing, and so on. But one might hold that in some way they are at the margins of action. If the only difficulty the CTA faced came from the challenge of futile actions, the challenge might not be sufficiently serious to overturn what is widely regarded as an otherwise attractive theory. And I am aware that there are strategies for dealing with, and more that can be said about, mere-passage-of-time cases.

There are at least two different senses one might give to the term, 'rationalization' (beyond the weak and strong distinction I have already made for 'rationalizes'). Like many words ending in '-tion', 'rationalization' is subject to a process/product ambiguity.[21]

Compare 'deduction' and 'explanation'. In the product sense, whether or not there is a rationalization, deduction, or explanation is an objective question about the existence of a certain kind of syntactically or semantically structured product; in the process sense, whether or not there is a rationalization, deduction, or explanation is a question about an actual (mental) process or activity which occurred on the part of a person, and which produced that product. The rationalizing or deducing or explaining activity can be dated and placed, but this is not so for what is offered in that activity, its upshot or product.

In the process sense of 'rationalization', if some action has been rationalized, then some actual process of inferring something about the action (its desirability, or that he ought to do it, or that he intends to do it, or whatever) by the actor from his reasons for it has taken place. It is true that such an inferential process might not itself be conscious; whatever we might be able to make of the idea of an unconscious or subconscious inference, the process sense might only be committed to it.

On the other hand, in the product sense, from the fact that an action is rationalized, nothing whatever follows about the actor having actually

---

[21] See Romane Clark and Paul Welsh, *Introduction to Logic*, Princeton: van Nostrand, 1962: 153–4.

gone through any kind of inferring, conscious or unconscious. Notice that the question of whether the inference is conscious or unconscious is different from the question of whether the beliefs and desires are unconscious, which I address in the next chapter. The beliefs and desires might be consciously held but the inferring from them still be unconscious, although it would be hard to make any sense of the idea of consciously inferring from unconsciously held beliefs and desires.

What exactly does the product sense of 'rationalization' require? In that sense, whether or not a mental state rationalizes some action is an *objective* fact about the existence of a practical syllogism with sentences describing the contents of those mental states as its premises and a sentence to the effect that the action is done, or about the desirability of doing it, or that it ought to be done, or that it is intended that it be done, as its conclusion. In Popperian hyperbole, it's a fact about the Third World, just like facts about whether there is an explanation for something, or a deductive argument or proof for some conclusion, and so on.

For any ordered set of n sentences, whether there is a valid practical syllogism with the first $n - 1$ sentences as its premises and with the nth sentence as its conclusion, is a structural fact that 'supervenes' on the semantic or syntactic properties of the n sentences and their order. The existence of such a practical syllogism will by itself provide no information concerning the actual processes, conscious or unconscious, which the agent undergoes.

I say nothing about the nature of such practical syllogisms. Are their conclusions actions, as Aristotle seems to have said, or statements about the desirability of actions? Are the premises about beliefs and desires, as the above tends to suppose, or about intentions, as von Wright argues?

Does the CTA require the process or the product sense of rationalization? If the former, the CTA would be committed to the view that at least an unconscious actual process of inferring has occurred, in every case of action. Of course, as a separate requirement, the CTA must also say that, in every case of action, the belief and desire must *cause* the event which is an action (that is part of what the CTA explicitly asserts). But the commitment to a, perhaps unconscious, rationalizing process going on in every case of action seems problematic, in a way in which the causal commitment does not.

Problematic, and, I think, unnecessary. What I think the CTA must say is that: (1) there must be appropriate beliefs and desires (or whatever); (2) the beliefs and desires must rationalize the action in the product sense; and (3) the beliefs and desires must cause the action. There is no need to postulate

(4) a further rationalizing process that connects the beliefs and desires on the one hand and the action on the other, no need to postulate any connecting process beyond the causal one.

Divesting the CTA of (4) is good ontological sense, just because (4) would commit its proponent to far too many goings-on in the agent. Further, if (4) were retained, one might doubt that the CTA was really giving a reconstructive account of all action, rather than just physical action, since it would be using the idea of a rationalizing process, which is or seems to be a type of mental activity, in the analysans.

On the other hand, I suspect that divesting the CTA of (4) makes dealing with the problem of passivity that much harder. If the agent had actually to have gone through a process of rationalizing or inferring, there is an obvious source of agency available, namely, the rationalizing activity. Without (4), the sense that the components (1) to (3) cannot really add agency to events becomes that much sharper. The problem with taking the rationalizing requirement in the product sense alone is that it is hard to see how it would be sufficient to really deal with the problem of passivity. How could an event appropriately caused get 'upgraded' into an action, simply because there existed some 'valid' practical syllogism, that had the appropriate premisses and had something about that action as its conclusion?

One might approach this issue differently. Standard presentations of the CTA assume that the causation and rationalization requirements are logically distinct. Perhaps an unconscious rationalizing process just *is* the causation that the CTA needs. Are unconscious rationalizings and causings really distinct, as I have been assuming? It might be that all we can make of the idea of an unconscious inferring is the idea of such a causal process. Such a result would ensure that, in every case of action caused by beliefs and desires, there was an actual, albeit usually unconscious, inference, but then the rationalization requirement, taken in this process sense, would not really be adding anything beyond the causal requirement after all.

As I said earlier, rationalization is 'under a description'. Suppose I reach for a glass. According to the CTA, the cause of the reaching must include rationalizing beliefs with contents about reaching, no more and no less. No more, because if the reaching was of a certain kind (say, one done with a gloved hand), the belief does not need to be about a reaching of that kind, if one is attempting only to rationalize the reaching rather than a reaching of that kind. But also no less, because the reaching might be a case of an arm moving, but the belief cannot only be a belief about an arm moving, if it is to rationalize the reaching rather than just the arm moving.

The reason for requiring this of the CTA is clear. The CTA must provide some story for why that act, namely, the reaching, occurred. If *that* story were not to be found in the belief's contents, then the story would be non-rationalizing for that action. It would be at best a rationalizing story about some other action, or about that action under some different description.

On the causal theory of action, action requires rationalizing mental states. Even if ultimately mental events like beliefs and desires were in turn to be reduced to physical ones, the CTA is committed to finding, in the first instance, and at the level of folk psychology itself, some mental occurrences that cause and rationalize each token action. Assuming that we engage in a great deal of genuine activity, the demands of the CTA will also require of agents an implausibly rich mental life, overfull of reasons, acts of rationalizing, beliefs, and desires, even intentions. The CTA must inflate the mental, as a precondition for reducing action. Its slogan might be: no (action) reduction without prior (mental) inflation.

In this way, the CTA is engaged in dramatic mental overpopulation. It overintellectualizes action. I count myself amongst the friends of mind and action. In my view, the friendliest thing one can do in the case of action is to prune (but not, of course, to eliminate) the mind's contents. If the CTA can be said to inflate the mind, in order to reduce action, I prefer to deflate the mind's contents, to preserve action's integrity. So, as a friend of action, I wish to practise some form of mental birth control. Mental life, on my view, is simply not rich enough to ensure that there are sufficient mental states on hand to meet the requirements for the reduction of action, like those advanced by the CTA.

In the next chapter, I turn to the task of substantiating that claim.

Why I am Justified in Focussing on this Formulation of the CTA

As I know from experience, a common response to my project has been, and is likely to be, the claim that the view I am focussing on is overly narrow and that many views, rightly also called 'a causal theory of action', escape my criticism entirely. The version of the CTA I have been discussing is sometimes called 'the standard causal story'. That something is wrong with the standard causal story is not an observation that is original to me. Several non-standard CTA stories have been developed. Neither I, nor my opponent, is of course worried about the correct use of the name, 'CTA'. The question is whether much philosophical purpose is to be served by my focussing on a doctrine so narrowly circumscribed, as I have done. I believe that this restriction can be justified. I discuss this below and also at the end of Chapter 4.

Two restrictions in my account may leap to mind: (1) Often, desires, or emotions, cause actions without beliefs (so it might be said, and I agree). The doctrine I attack is too narrow, in light of this observation. There are two possible ways in which to use this observation as a rejoinder to my account of the CTA. (1a) Desires or emotions may rationalize as well as cause actions, on their own and without beliefs. (1b) Desires or emotions do not rationalize without beliefs, but rationalization is itself not necessary in the formulation of a CTA.

(2) The second restriction concerns the dependence of my formulation on beliefs and desires alone. What of intentions? Might not intentions—or indeed some other mental states or events—cause and rationalize? It is true that my formulation of the CTA above allows for intentions, since my formulation only refers to 'mental states', but in fact the whole of my substantive criticism in Chapter 4 is about a doctrine that requires beliefs and desires. I discuss (2) in the section following this one.

Let me take (1a) and (1b) in reverse order. First, (1b). Could the CTA dispense with rationalization altogether? I think not. Events, mere events like the eruption of Vesuvius and events intrinsic to actions like the bending of my finger, are or anyway appear to be passive, since they merely happen or occur. How can some events be actions, which are of course active? How can activity 'emerge' from, or supervene on, passivity? This is the problem of passivity that I mentioned earlier.

The rationalizing requirement is intended to help with this problem. The requirement that the mental states rationalize is added by the CTA to the requirement that they cause the event, and is intended to solve the problem of passivity. Causation alone cannot solve this problem. So there is no chance at all of locating action or agency simply in bodily or other events, as and when driven by just any old psychological cause or other, a desire or an emotion or anything else, if the latter is non-rationalizing. My eyelids flutter, and the fluttering is caused by my desire for something or by my irascible temperament or by a wave of anger that comes over me. This is not simply a case of deviant causation and curable if deviancy is. My desire for something or my current emotional state may cause my eyelids to flutter in a perfectly non-deviant way.

I can't always get agency (my fluttering of my eyelids) out of the passivity of events (the fluttering of my eyelids) and their psychological causes (the desire for something or my irascibility or the anger). The fluttering of the eyelids might only be a reflex effect of that desire or emotion, as the dilation of my pupils is to the absence of light. What is missing in these examples, according to the CTA, is that such psychological causes (irascibility; anger; a fleeting, embarrassing thought; desire-without-belief) don't rationalize as well as cause.

Aquinas's example (my failing memory tells me that this example is used by Arthur Danto somewhere and that he attributes it to Aquinas) can serve to make the point: a man has an erection, as a causal consequence of a desire. But mere causation by the desire does not 'make it into' an action of his.

(1a) Might desires, or emotions, at least sometimes rationalize actions without the need for beliefs to accompany them? If desires or emotions on their own can both cause and rationalize actions, then my arguments against the CTA that focus on beliefs might still leave a version of the CTA formulated in terms of desires intact. The examples I gave above regarding the causation of bodily movements by desires or emotions (like the case of the erection or pupil dilation) were not cases in which the desire or emotion rationalized as well as caused that bodily movement. But are there other cases in which they do, on their own, rationalize actions as well as cause them?

Let me focus on desires, or 'pro-attitudes', as Davidson called the genus that includes desires, wants, urges, promptings, lusts, and so on, as they are the more promising candidate of the two as rationalizers of action on their own. We need two distinctions: (i) that between desires for objects and desires to act; (ii) that between basic or underived desires and non-basic or derived desires.

(i) In the discussion so far, I have understood the desires required for rationalization as desires to have objects, to achieve valued ends, or to obtain goals. 'To have' should be understood rather widely, so as to include the case in which one simply wants to be with someone or something. These are not, or are not immediately, desires to do anything. An agent desires to have g and believes that if he does an action of type A, he will obtain g.

In Davidson's well-known discussion of the matter, desires are taken as desires to act: 'Wants and desires often are trained on physical objects. However, "I want that gold watch in the window" is not a primary reason and explains why I went into the store only because it suggests a primary reason—for example, that I wanted to buy the watch.'[22] Putting the point in my prolific terminology, rather than Davidson's austere one, an agent wants to perform a token act of type *A* (kill the Queen), believes that by performing a token act of type *B* (pulling the gun's trigger), he will perform an action of type *A*, so he performs an action of type *B*. (If the reader thinks that desires are always desires that a certain proposition be true, this talk of desires to possess and to do can be translated into the corresponding talk about the desire for two different sorts of propositions to be true.)

(ii) Some desires of an agent are given and fixed, at least in the circumstances, in the sense that there is no further desire that the agent has that explains why he has the first desire. Those desires are the agent's basic desires at the time. Most of the desires we have are not like that; they are derived desires; why an agent has a derived desire can be explained by its being a consequent of his having some other, more basic desire. In Kantian terms, he who wills the end wills the required means. If the agent desires to pull the gun's trigger, it is only because he desires to kill the Queen and believes that he will kill her if he pulls the gun's trigger. I think that one needs to be careful not to multiply derived desires beyond necessity. In a teleological chain like the ones we discussed in Chapter 2, I do not think that one needs to invoke a distinct desire to do every action on the teleological chain. But still, surely there are some cases of derived desire.

Basic and non-basic desires can be desires either to act or to have objects. It might just be a fact about an agent that one of his desires, derived or non-derived, is his desire to have, own, or posses something. On the other hand, it might be one of his desires, derived or non-derived, that he sail a boat, race in a certain car, overthrow the monarchy, or take a trip around the world.

Maimonides' category of futile action, mentioned above, provided cases of what I called intrinsic action. I noted the apparent absence of belief in such cases. The person who plays with his hands might desire or want to play with his hands. If so, the desire to play with one's hands will be a basic desire to act. No other desire the agent has explains why he has that desire. An intrinsic action, in the sense I was using it, is an action, the desire to do which is a basic, underived desire. In that sense, the action has no further end in view.

Since the CTA requires rationalization, derived desires to have or to do are not going to help the CTA avoid the need to invoke beliefs, as

---

[22] Davidson, 'Actions, Reasons, and Causes', 6.

Davidson's account of primary reasons for action itself makes perfectly clear. Why did the agent *b*? His desiring to *B* does not rationalize his *b*-ing. Rather, what will rationalize it, if anything does, is his desire to do *A* or his desire to have *g*, and his believing that his *B*-ing is a good way, or the only way in the circumstances, to do *A*, if he *B*s in order to *A*, or to obtain *g*, if he *B*s in order to get *g*. Moreover, all cases in which an agent has a non-basic or derived desire to have or possess something will require a belief, if an instrumental action to obtain that thing is to be rationalized. The cases I shall be examining in Chapter 4, as counter-examples to the CTA, will be of these kinds. If the CTA were a correct account of them, it would still need beliefs as well as desires.

What of basic or underived desires to do something? Do they at least weakly rationalize actions? This is an interesting question, although my criticism of the CTA does not depend on the answer to it. Does an agent who plays with his hands really desire to do so, and, if so, does that underived desire, in the absence of any relevant belief, rationalize his hand playing?

Wayne Davis distinguishes between volitive and appetitive desire, and separates what Davidson tended to lump together.[23] I find the distinction very helpful. A volitive desire is akin to a want; an appetitive desire is akin to a longing, urge, craving, and so on. Whenever an agent genuinely acts, on balance he does what he wants; he has a volitive desire to do what he does. But he may not be acting on an appetite, for he may do what he does out of a sense of duty, commitment, loyalty, or whatever. He may not desire (in the appetitive sense) to do what he does.

An agent can have volitive desires without corresponding appetitive desires, and appetitive desires without corresponding volitive desires. Conflation between these two senses of desire gives rise to endless confusion, and is what sometimes makes the thesis of universal egoism seem more attractive than in truth it is.

Even if an agent believes that he has more reason to do something else, so that he has a weak will when he acts, or even if has no reason at all to do what he does, or even if he does what he does only because of the presence of coercion, he has a volitive desire, because he does do what on balance and all things considered he wants to do. (If he has a weak will, he may not do what he thinks on balance is the best thing to do in the circumstances,

[23] Wayne Davis, 'The Two Senses of Desire', in Joel Marks, ed., *The Ways of Desire*, Chicago: Precedent Publishing Company, 1986: 63–82.

but he still does what he most wants to do.) Were an agent 'to do' even what he does *not*, on balance and all things considered, want to do, then he is not really acting at all. In such a case, his body is simply the plaything of another agent. In this sense, to act against one's will is not to act at all. It is to lose control of what one's body does or is made to do.

Appetitive desires do provide reasons for actions. My urge to do *A* gives me some weak reason to do *A*. But there will be many cases of intrinsic action in which the agent does not act out of appetitive desire at all, as I claimed above. Typically, the agent who plays with his hands has only a volitive desire to do so. In that sense, that he desires to play just follows from the fact that it is he who is playing with his hands. But in such a case, he has no reason to play with his hands, so nothing rationalizes his hand playing. He just plays with his hands, like that.

Now of course the agent might have an appetitive desire to hand play— he may have a strong urge or yearning to hand play. In a case in which he has that sort of desire, does the urge cause and rationalize the action? It seems to me that it does, although I do think there are some theoretical limits on the urges that we can count as basic and underived rationalizers of action. There is a literature on whether we could really understood an agent's claiming, of any desire whatever, that it was a basic desire for him, with no further story to be told. In such a case, his action may quite simply be irrational and utterly puzzling.[24]

But in the case of an urge like the urge to hand play, or for that matter an urge to scratch an itch, I do think that desires of the appetitive sort can rationalize and cause actions, in the absence of beliefs. I repeat, however, that my counter-examples to the CTA will not be of this kind.

Let me also say here, again, that the items, in order to rationalize, must appear at the level of folk psychology. There are loads of motivational mechanisms that are implicated in action but that do not appear at that folk level: what we might call psychic turbulence of various kinds that participate in causally driving action. But none of these are relevant to the problem of action as I conceive it. 'Appetitive' or 'motivational' brain states (Hobbes's endeavours), perceptual mechanisms, physical dispositions of various sorts, do not rationalize an action, even if they (help) cause it. Rationalization, at least in the cases I shall be discussing, requires beliefs and desires, states with propositional content.

[24] See e.g. Philippa Foot, 'Moral Beliefs', *Proceedings of the Aristotelian Society*, 59, 1958–9: 83–104; Peter Winch, 'Understanding a Primitive Society', *The American Philosophical Quarterly*, 1, 1964: 307–24.

So we need rationalization for the cases I will focus on, and desires or emotions on their own won't do the job. But what about intentions? Might an intention rationalize?

Intentions as Causers and Rationalizers?

Is the account of the CTA which I discuss too narrow, by not allowing intentions to replace beliefs and desires as causers and rationalizers? Many philosophers do not think that intentions have a simple content, since they are self-referential; there is also a distinction that some philosophers draw between a future-directed intention and a present-directed intention, and between a long-standing and an immediate intention.[25] But I do not think any of these sophistications will alter the argument below, so I continue to think of intentions *sans* qualification, introducing these distinctions only as and when I find them useful for my argument.

I want to say as little about this topic as I can, focussing what I have to say on how intentions might or might not alter the arguments I use against beliefs and desires in the next chapter. I return briefly to the question of intentions as explainers in Chapter 6. There is a lot to be said about intentions, and many views which place them at the heart of action in various ways. I am not necessarily opposed to all of those views. I stress that my interest in intentions in this section is solely focussed on their unsuitability for use in a variant version of the CTA, which might replace its standard causal story.

There are four points I wish to make:

(1) at best, intentions might replace desires in the account that the CTA requires, but that account would still need beliefs along with those intentions, so that the arguments in the next chapter which focus on belief still work even if intentions are introduced into the CTA;

(2) what is an intention? On many analyses of intention, intentions themselves are or require beliefs. So arguments about belief in the next chapter may well apply to intentions anyway, depending of course on which beliefs intentions are said to be or to entail;

[25] See e.g. Michael Bratman, *Intentions, Plans and Practical Reasons*, Cambridge, Mass.: Harvard University Press, 1987, chs. 7–9; Alfred Mele, *Springs of Action*, New York: Oxford University Press, 1992; and of course John Searle, *Intentionality*, New York: Cambridge University Press, 1984, esp. chs. 1–3; J. David Velleman, *Practical Reflection*, Princeton: Princeton University Press, 1989, esp. ch. 4.

(3) intentions are unavailable in sufficient numbers to co-cause or co-rationalize all the actions the CTA must account for;

(4) unlike the case of belief, I can find no clear sense in which an intention might rationalize an action.

(1) There is a literature on long-standing intentions, and their role in guiding and monitoring stretches of ongoing activity, like that of buttoning a shirt, that might be thought to be of help in stating a plausible version of the CTA.[26] It is said that a representation of the goal of action must continue to exist throughout the motion and must play a continuing causal role in shaping the action. If there are these long-standing intentions which monitor and guide our activity (and I do not necessarily dispute that), will they not provide the mental state material we need, to cause and rationalize that activity, in the way in which the CTA requires?

A long-standing intentional state could of course in principle be part of the cause of an action, when some triggering event is added to the causal brew, just as fragility can be part of the cause of the glass breaking, when a thrown stone is added to the causal conditions of the breaking. But remember that the CTA looks for the causal conditions of the action at the level of folk psychology, because the cause needs to be a rationalizing cause. It is insufficient for the CTA to just find the remainder of the causal brew that includes the long-standing intention somewhere or other, perhaps at the level of the physical; the 'somewhere' must be at the level of folk psychology.

'Monitoring' and 'guiding' are causal ideas, but the difficulty I raise is a difficulty for both the thought that long-standing intentions cause and that they rationalize actions. Suppose I have a long-standing intention to clean the house. Does that long-standing intention cause or rationalize the vacuuming, the polishing, and the scrubbing? If it does, it could only do so in the company of certain beliefs, like the belief that polishing, and so on, is a part of house-cleaning (and maybe only in the company of some additional desire as well). Specific house-cleaning beliefs must be on hand, to mediate between the level of the general, long-standing guiding intention to clean the house and the specific house-cleaning actions, the polishing, vacuuming, and so on, that are to be caused and rationalized. So we are certainly not going to evict beliefs from the causal picture by importing long-standing intentions.

[26] See e.g. Mele, *Springs of Action*, 136–7, 221–2; Brand, *Intending and Acting*, 153–9, who draws a very different conclusion from the absence of belief than I have. See also Searle, *Intentionality*, and Velleman, *Practical Reflection*, 22.

In fact, some of the relevant literature on intentions, rather than offering the material for a plausible variant of the CTA, seems to me to be making a point that is unfriendly to it. An agent's long-standing intention is associated with a plan of action, itself available to his consciousness, and must include beliefs of various sorts about his behaviour. But if there were no appropriate beliefs in these cases about the various actions that make up the whole stretch of ongoing activity, it could not be long-standing intentions which, via an action plan, are doing the monitoring and guiding. Action plans and long-term intentions need specific beliefs to 'get to' the level of specific actions.

Of course, without the beliefs, the guiding and monitoring may be going on at a subpersonal level, 'below' that of folk psychology. But that is to tell a different story than the one to which the CTA is committed.

(2) On some analyses, having an intention, long-standing or immediate, entails having a belief.[27] Yet stronger analyses attempt to reduce intentions to beliefs (plus, perhaps, desires). But, even if intentions are non-reducible to them, it is plausible that intentions still entail the holding of beliefs (and desires), and that may give us enough purchase to argue their unsuitability for a version of the CTA, if I can show, in the next chapter, that the beliefs they entail are unsuitable.

To take just one example that I do not discuss further in Chapter 4, it is sometimes said that if I intend to A, I believe that I will do A. If so, I would argue that there must be actions preceded by no intention, since I sometimes act without having believed beforehand that I would so act.

(3) I am sceptical that whenever I act, or even whenever I act intentionally, at t', there is an intention at t, where t is earlier than t', long-standing or immediate, future-directed or present-directed, which causes, or is part of the cause of, my action. Rosalind Hursthouse claims to be explicating Professor Anscombe's view in *Intention* when she claims: 'In particular, "intention" does not refer to a mental event (or state) which precedes or accompanies an intentional act and makes it intentional; there may be mental events which immediately precede intentional actions but there need not be'.[28]

---

[27] Does intending that p entail believing something to be the case? See e.g. Mele, *Springs of Action*, ch. 8; Bratman, *Intentions, Plans and Practical Reasons*, 5–9 and *passim*; Robert Audi, *Action, Intention, and Reason*, Ithaca, NY: Cornell University Press, 1993, ch. 2.

[28] Rosalind Hursthouse, 'Intention', in Roger Teichmann, ed., *Logic, Cause and Action: Essays in Honour of Elizabeth Anscombe*, Royal Institute of Philosophy Supplements, vol. 46, Cambridge: Cambridge University Press, 2000: 83–105.

I am not clear from this whether Hursthouse thinks that 'intention' never refers to a mental state or only that it does not always do so. I would in any case prefer to put the point in this way: when an agent acts intentionally, it does not follow that the act was preceded by his having an intention to act. (Nor does it follow, on my view, that there was no such intention.) Perhaps 'intention' always does refer to a mental state or event if it refers at all, the point being that there may fail to be something to which the term refers in the case of some intentional actions.

But even when there is a long-standing intention at t, that is an intention to engage in the whole activity, the relevant cause for each bit of the activity must be, not the whole of the long-standing intention, but some part of the long-standing intention, that occurs at a time just preceding that bit of activity. Speaking of intentional states guiding what an agent does is loose and imprecise. On the assumption that a cause is temporally contiguous to its effect, such theories will always have to postulate some bit of activity caused by some prior bit of the guiding intentional state. We would need to 'decompose' a long-standing intention into a multiplicity of relevant parts. So we would require a multiplicity of present-directed intentions, or present-directed relevant parts of a long-standing intention, or whatever we are to call them, not just the one temporally extended long-standing one.

This is a question of the ubiquity of intentions. In the next chapter, I shall argue an unavailability thesis for beliefs: I don't think, on any understanding of 'belief', that there are enough of them around to do the causal or rationalizing job that the CTA requires to be done. I don't really believe they are as ubiquitous as many other writers think. I do not believe that a causing intention, long-term or immediate, precedes every action either, even when the action is done intentionally. So I think that intentions, like beliefs, are non-ubiquitous in the context of actions.

Of course, from the fact that there is no folk-psychological intention available to guide and monitor, it does *not* follow that there is no monitoring and guiding going on at all. The monitoring and guiding that goes on may not go on at the folk-psychological level at all. Mele speaks of the role of 'intention-external representational states' in this connection, and Brand, following Stich, talks in terms of 'subdoxastic states'.[29] This fits in well with the view I wish to develop.

The monitoring and guiding of the agent through such stretches of activity depends on a whole host of informational and quasi-perceptual

---

[29] Mele, *Springs of Action*, and Brand, *Intending and Acting*.

mechanisms, and 'executive' mechanisms as well, none of which may surface, as it were, as folk-psychological items which are states of a person with conceptual or propositional content in principle available to that agent. It is these mechanisms, whatever they may be, that play a role without requiring the mind to be populated with corresponding action plans or long-standing intentions, or a myriad of one-off short-term intentions.

So, if one requires intentional states to be folk psychological, as the CTA must require, there are not enough of the intentions around to do the causal or rationalizing job; if there are simply monitoring and guiding mechanisms, unavailable to folk psychology, then they are not useful for the purposes of the CTA at all.

My remarks in this section have made several assumptions about activities and their parts. I return to that issue in the next chapter.

(4) Are intentions rationalizers of action? What mental states are rationalizers? However ubiquitous intentions might or might not be, they cannot be rationalizers on their own and hence cannot replace belief-and-desire pairs in a statement of the CTA.

Intentions might be thought to figure in an account for rationalizing action in one of two ways. For von Wright, for example, intentions simply take the place of desires.[30] The intention is not an intention to act, but an intention to gain an end or make a certain proposition true.

My intention to gain goal g, and my belief that, by doing A, I can obtain g, together rationalize my doing a. On this first view, beliefs are still required, along with intentions, and my arguments in the next chapter against the existence of beliefs in some central cases of action will still stand, even if they are accompanied by intentions rather than desires. But on the von Wright view of intentions, in those cases in which there are beliefs and intentions, I have no reason to resist the idea that they can together rationalize action.

On the other type of proposal, intentions replace both beliefs and desires, and are meant to serve as rationalizers of actions on their own. It is this second type of proposal that I would resist. In the simplest case (there are more sophisticated ones), an intention to do A might be said to rationalize (by itself) token action a.

There are two reasons that fuel my resistance to allowing intentions to rationalize action on their own: (a) the existence of intentional actions that

[30] See G. H. von Wright, 'On So-Called Practical Inference', in Raz, *Practical Reasoning*, 46–62.

are not rational; (*b*) a failure to see how intentions could rationalize actions even when those actions are rational.

(*a*) Since some intentional actions can be irrational, or anyway non-rational, in both the strong and weak senses, when an agent intends to *A*, and even when that intending non-deviantly causes his *a*-ing, his intending leaves it open whether his *a*-ing was rational at all. The case of the dental delay above was of this kind. Suppose his delaying of his appointment was preceded by an intention to do so. This shows, I think, that intentions by themselves can't rationalize an action.

Some of the cases I mention in Chapter 4 for another purpose, due to Rosalind Hursthouse, and other cases like them, seem to provide additional examples: a man kisses the picture of his loved one; a person knocks on wood. These are or can be actions that a person intends to do and so, on the theory being discussed, they will be caused by a preceding intention. But the intention that causes them does not rationalize them; in fact, they are not rationalized by anything, since they are at best non-rational actions. Kissing a loved one's picture is not irrational, but it does not seem to me to count as rational action either, in either the weaker or the stronger sense. I do it because 'I feel like it', but that is not to give any reason for doing it.

The agent not only fails to have more reason to do that action than any other available alternative, he fails to have *any* reason whatever to do the action. He has volitive desires to be sure, but no reasons. (An agent surely might not have any reason to act just because he has the appropriate volitive desire to act in that way.) Yet the action is one he intends to do. It may be that akratic actions, discussed briefly above, which are intentional actions, also count as counter-examples under (*a*), depending on which sense of 'rationalize' the CTA requires.

(*b*) Finally, suppose that I raise my arm, and that its rising is caused by my intention to raise it. Moreover, suppose that this is not a case in which the causation is in any way deviant. The intention to *A* causes my doing *a* non-deviantly.

I simply have to register my inability to understand what sort of rationalizing this causation-by-intention-alone might provide. The idea of rationalization is that the agent has at least some, or perhaps the best, reason to do something. I cannot see how the fact that an action was caused by an intention shows that the agent had any reasons whatever to do what he did, even when he did have reasons. There may be some deep connection between an intention and an intentional action when the former non-deviantly causes the latter, but that connection, whatever it might be, does not, I think, include any rationalization of the action by the intention.

Frankfurt's Intentions

Harry Frankfurt, in his very insightful 'The Problem of Action', tries to make intention the key to action in a way quite different from the CTA, a doctrine that he rejects.[31] Does Frankfurt succeed?

To begin with, why does Frankfurt dismiss the CTA and other, similar views? Frankfurt observes that any theory that distinguishes between actions and mere movements by their differing causal histories, like the CTA does, is improbable on the face of it (I agree). 'And he is not performing an action . . . even if he himself provided the antecedent causes—in the form of beliefs, desires, intentions, decisions, volitions, or whatever—from which the movement has resulted.'

There are two, non-equivalent ways in which to make Frankfurt's case against the CTA: a temporal way and a way that involves essential or intrinsic properties. The two are connected, if one assumes that historical, including causal, properties cannot be intrinsic, but the points are distinguishable none the less.

The temporal way in which Frankfurt argues against the CTA is this. According to Frankfurt, what should distinguish an action and a mere movement is something that is present or absent at the very time that, during or while, they are happening or occurring. But their different causes occur only at earlier times, not at the times at which the action and mere movement occur.

But a defender of the CTA might reply to Frankfurt by claiming that, on the CTA, there is *a* feature of the action that occurs at the very time that the action occurs, namely, the property of having been appropriately caused, and which is not a feature of a movement that is not an action. An action is so caused when it occurs, not at some earlier time. The action has, at the time of its occurrence, a certain tensed property that the mere movement fails to have.

I think that what Frankfurt should employ, in order to make this point, is a distinction between historical and non-historical properties. The tensed property of having been appropriately caused may be a property that the

---

[31] Harry Frankfurt, 'The Problem of Action', repr. in *The Importance of What we Care about*, Cambridge: Cambridge University Press, 1988: 69–79. Subsequent quotes in the text from Frankfurt are from ibid. 73–4.

action has at the very time at which it occurs, but it is an historical property of the action. An item has its historical properties, like its non-historical ones, when it occurs (assuming that we are not posthumously predicating). So what Frankfurt should say is that the difference between an action and a mere movement cannot be located in their differing historical properties.

The second way in which Frankfurt might word this argument against the CTA concerns the natures of the two sorts of items. On the CTA, there could be a qualitatively identical action and mere event, as far as their intrinsic or essential features are concerned. On the CTA, an action and a mere movement or event could be intrinsic doppelgangers. The property of being caused in some way is not an intrinsic feature of an action. Contrary to the CTA, there must be some difference between an action and a mere movement that is an essential difference between them. I evaluate the non-historical and intrinsic property arguments at the end of Chapter 5.

On both of these two ways in which Frankfurt could make his point, prior causation of the movement by an intention fares no better than prior causation of the movement by a belief-and-desire pair, or prior causation by anything else whatever.

What view does Frankfurt propose, as a replacement for views like the CTA, that locates the difference between action and mere movement in non-historical or essential properties? What is simultaneous with the action, says Frankfurt, is the presence of guidance or direction, by the agent, of the movement. To fill in the missing part of the quotation above: 'And he is not performing an action if the movements are not under his guidance as they proceed . . .'.

Guidance does not require actual causation. A driver who is allowing his car to coast downhill may be satisfied with its performance and do nothing. Yet it is under his guidance in the sense that he is prepared to intervene if necessary. 'Let us employ the term "intentional" for referring to instances of purposive movement in which the guidance is provided by the agent. We may say, then, that action is intentional movement.' In this sense, guidance and movement can co-occur. That a movement is being guided counts for Frankfurt as a non-historical property of the movement. Is it an essential property? Could the numerically same movement that is guided have failed to have been guided, or vice versa? That seems to me to be unclear and Frankfurt does not further discuss this point in the article.

I do not believe that the intentional states that guide and direct, even were they ubiquitous and folk psychological, can solve the problem of action in which I am interested. Frankfurt and I agree that they cannot solve the action problem by serving as prior causes.

But does Frankfurt's alternative use of the category of the intentional, explicated as movement guided by the agent, help with the problem of action? He notes that there are many systems for the guidance of purposive movement in a person such that those movements do not count as action: the dilation of the pupils of the eye as response to changes in the light 'is a purposive movement; there are mechanisms which guide its course'. But the movement is not 'under his guidance'.

But what is it for a movement to be 'under the agent's guidance', rather than just guided by some subpersonal system in the agent? Doesn't the contrast sound awfully like the problem of the distinction between action and movement restated? Is a movement to be under the guidance of the agent just for the agent to guide the movement? If so, Frankfurt's account of action is circular, since guiding is itself an action. To be told that a person's movement is an action iff the person guides the movement is no help at all, in getting at the essential difference between action and movement.

In one paragraph of the paper, Frankfurt tries to defend himself from this charge: 'Our guidance of our movements, while we are acting, does not similarly require that we perform various actions . . . Otherwise action could not be conceived, upon pain of generating an infinite regress.' So Frankfurt says that an action's being under an agent's guidance is not a matter of the agent doing something, or presumably even a matter of something he could do if necessary (e.g. when the car is coasting downhill), since even the latter qualification would reintroduce action into the analysans.

We are left pretty much in the dark as to what it is for an agent to guide a movement, if it does not involve action, actual or possible. Frankfurt only provides this cryptic remark: 'It is a characteristic of the operation at that time of the systems we are'. So Frankfurt leaves us with an unexplained primitive idea of an agent guiding a movement, without any idea of what that means or comes to, save that it cannot be given an actional analysis on pain of infinite regress.

In the next chapter, I will discuss the CTA, in a formulation that requires belief and desire. I hope I have justified in this chapter my neglect of the alternative that would employ intentions to replace beliefs and desires.

4

The Causal Theory of Action

Beliefs of Various Kinds

For my action to be rationalized, it may not be required, as I argued in the last chapter, that I consciously or even unconsciously engage in such practical or instrumental reasoning. However, it certainly is required, at the very least, that I do actually have the rationalizing belief and desire (or action plans) in question, if they are to be causes of my behaviour and be responsible for 'upgrading', as it were, the finger's bending, to the level of an action, my bending of my finger.[1] So, the CTA needs beliefs, and a very large number of them at that.

'Belief' is capable of something akin to the process–product ambiguity that I described in the case of 'rationalization'; the word 'belief' sometimes refers to psychological states; at other times, to abstract objects that are the contents of those states. In the first sense, it can also refer either to a type of state or to a token state. In what follows, when I speak of beliefs, I am using this merely as shorthand, and I intend to be talking about the token states of believing in which believers find themselves, rather than about beliefs as abstract objects or about belief state types. 'Desire' is also ambiguous, having both state and content senses, and type and token senses, but I focus on 'belief' in what follows.

It is sometimes said that there are different senses of 'belief', or different kinds of belief, and that once we note the different senses, it becomes more plausible to hold that we hold many beliefs, in at least one of those senses,

[1] For the purposes of this discussion, I treat beliefs and desires as categorically different phenomena. This is certainly controversial. Especially in the absence of an agreed analysis of desire, it is not clear that desires are not a subtype of belief. See for example I. L. Humberstone, 'Wanting As Believing', *Canadian Journal of Philosophy*, 17, 1987: 49–62, and Huw Price, 'Defending Desire-As-Belief', *Mind*, 98, 1989: 119–27.

in all those myriad of cases in which the CTA would appear to require a belief. We need to be clear about this, before we can assess the plausibility of the CTA.

The clearest, most central, kind of belief is what is often referred to as occurrent, or episodic, or, as Braithwaite somewhat less happily called it,[2] actual belief. I know of no plausible characterization of what is intended by these terms, except the one that ties it to present awareness or consciousness. So understood, to say of a belief that it is occurrent is elliptical; more fully, it is a person's token state of belief that may be occurrent at a time, since the very same belief state may not be occurrent to that person at a different time.

This assumes that a person can be in numerically one and the same token belief state, whether the latter is or is not occurrent. If I consciously believe today that the earth is approximately round (today, I am thinking about the question of the roundness of the earth) and yesterday I also believed it but without thinking about it, I am in the numerically same state of belief yesterday and today, but today I am in it occurrently, yesterday not. (One could just as well assume that the occurrent and non-occurrent states of belief are different token states, but that only the belief as abstract object is the same in both states. I shall use the former assumption, but what I say in criticism of the CTA could be said using the other assumption as well.)

Putting matters this way suggests that the distinction between occurrent beliefs and non-occurrent ones is not really a distinction about belief itself at all. I think that that is right. The distinction has to do with the kind of access the believer has to the state of belief he is in. An occurrent belief is really a state of belief (a holding of that belief) to which the believer has current access. As Tim Crane says, and I agree: '. . . although there is such a thing as being conscious of one's belief, that does not mean that there is such a thing as consciously believing. "Occurrent belief" is a myth.'[3]

I will henceforth use 'occurrent' in the following way: a token belief b is occurrent for person X at time t iff X is aware at t that he holds belief b. As my terminology presupposes, I am using 'aware of' and 'conscious of' as synonyms. Obviously, I do not mean by '. . . is aware of', '. . . believes'.

If I did, my account of occurrent belief would be: a token belief b is occurrent for person X at time t iff X believes at t that he holds belief b. Such an account would leave us with the question: in what sense of 'belief' does the

[2] R. B. Braithwaite, 'The Nature of Believing', repr. in A. Phillips Griffiths, ed., *Knowledge and Belief*, Oxford: Oxford University Press, 1968: 28–40.
[3] Tim Crane, *Elements of Mind*, Oxford: Oxford University Press, 2001: sect. 32: 105–8.

person believe that he holds an occurrent belief *b*? If occurrently, the account would be both regressive and circular; if non-occurrently, we are owed an account of this non-occurrent belief.

I do not have an account of 'conscious of' to offer, but I am hardly alone in that non-possession. I do not deny that there is an empirical connection of some sort between belief and consciousness. Typically, a person who is conscious of something has certain beliefs about the thing, as a consequence of his being aware of it. But I do not think there is an entailment from the fact that *X* is aware of *o* to *X*'s having an *o*-involving occurrent belief. If there were, the account would still be unsatisfactory for the reason mentioned in the paragraph above.

So, for example, someone might ask me if I believe that the world is approximately round. With this belief now salient to me, as a result of having been explicitly asked the question, I reply that I do believe this. When asked, I am thereby currently aware that I believe that the world is round; I am conscious that I hold that belief.

Both 'actual' and 'occurrent' can be misleading, since there may be another, less technical sense in which unconscious or subconscious beliefs are both actual and occurrent (if there are any such beliefs at all, they do, after all, actually occur). In this less technical sense, both 'occurrent' and 'actual' seem pleonastic, for if there are those beliefs, then there actually are those beliefs, and that is the end of the matter. But some beliefs are not available to consciousness at particular times, and hence are not occurrent in the technical sense I have indicated. Using 'occurrent' in the way I propose at least provides us with a distinction that distinguishes something.

The CTA requires beliefs to be rationalizing causes of action. Since we are dealing with causation of token actions, it is token belief states that are at issue, not types of belief states. We are discussing singular causal statements about actions, not causal generalizations about them. One issue we should lay to rest at the outset. There are, of course, widely differing views on the analysis of causation. One view, held, for example, by J. S. Mill and John Mackie in his earlier writings, makes the whole cause of something a set of conditions, states, events, and so on: 'The cause, then, philosophically speaking, is the sum total of the conditions, positive and negative taken together . . .'.[4] Another view, attributed to Davidson and others, makes the

---

[4] J. S. Mill, *A System of Logic*, London: Longman, 1970, bk. III, ch. V, sect. 3: 213–18. Quote from p. 217. J. L. Mackie, 'Causes and Conditions', *American Philosophical Quarterly*, 2, 1965: 245–64. In his *The Cement of the Universe*, Oxford: Clarendon Press, 1974, ch. 3, Mackie accepts a view like Mill's for the analysis of causal regularity, but not for singular causation.

whole cause a single event.[5] On this second view, the causal relevance of conditions and states is preserved as causally relevant descriptions true of the single event. So, for example, on the first view, when a match is struck, its striking (an event) and the presence of oxygen (a state) are both part of the whole cause. On the Davidson view, the striking is the whole cause, but of course that striking is a striking done in the presence of oxygen. I will use the language appropriate to the Mill–Mackie view, but anything I need to say could, if one wished, be translated into the language of the second view.

What kinds of beliefs can be (parts of whole) causes? In the beginning, the CTA was a crisp, clear thesis: every action is an event caused by a rationalizing belief-and-desire pair, where that belief, and indeed that desire too, are conscious states (a belief state of which a person is aware, when he acts). Some early proponents of the CTA worked with the dichotomy of dispositional (or standing) versus occurrent (or episodic) mental states, and thought that the causing and rationalizing mental states required by the CTA had to be of the latter sort. Many, like Alvin Goldman, thought of 'occurrent' as I do, as elliptical for 'occurrent to present consciousness'.[6] Goldman, although he was arguing specifically for the CTAE (a view about action explanation) rather than for the CTA (for this distinction, see Chapter 6), held that 'It appears, then, that the role of causing action must be assigned to occurrent [and hence, conscious] wants and beliefs, not standing [subconscious or unconscious] ones'.[7]

Why did Goldman think that dispositional beliefs and desires (ones of which the agent is unaware when he acts) could not be causes of actions? Goldman gave two cases in which the presence of an agent's dispositional or standing belief or desire, even in the right circumstances, fails to lead to action because the standing states are not 'activated', that is, do not become occurrent. Goldman's conclusion was that the beliefs and desires have causal powers, at least in so far as actions are concerned, only if and when they become occurrent.

Goldman's argument is, though, inconclusive: it shows that dispositional or standing beliefs and desires could not constitute the whole of the cause of action, because they need activating by something else, but it does not show that they cannot be any part of the cause (or, alternatively, does not show that they cannot figure in the causally relevant description of the

[5] Donald Davidson, 'Causal Relations', Journal of Philosophy, 64, 1967: 691–703. See esp. sect. 3.
[6] Alvin Goldman, A Theory of Human Action, Princeton: Princeton University Press, 86.
[7] ibid. 88. See ch. 4: 86–125.

activating event cause). The whole cause might be constituted by the belief, the desire, and the activating or triggering event, whatever it might be. The requisite triggering event might be only neurophysiological, invisible at the level of folk psychology. It is only the belief or desire that must be folk psychological.

In any case, even if Goldman's argument were valid, it could not be sound. The problem with Goldman's conclusion is that it just seems false. In very many cases of action, careful introspection, or retrospection, fails to provide any evidence of such conscious beliefs and desires, ones of which I was aware at the time of action. What better criterion for the presence of conscious mental states do we have than introspection of this sort?

I proceed to the buffet table and heap some rice on my plate. What conscious, explicit beliefs did I have about rice, its ability to assuage my hunger, and so on? I was hungry, saw the rice, and so, alas for my waistline, just heaped away. Introspection may not, in general, have much probative force in philosophy, but when the question is: are there these beliefs, present to consciousness, to one's awareness, introspection seems to have just the right methodological credentials.

Bruce Vermazen,[8] among others, pointed out that the phenomenological evidence did not appear to support Goldman's thesis: the thesis ascribed to the agent many more conscious or occurrent wants and beliefs than the agent seemed to possess. It requires more awareness on the agent's part than he in fact has. Goldman himself was aware of the difficulty posed by this requirement, although he was addressing the questions of wants rather than beliefs: 'A difficulty for the view that acts are always caused by occurrent wants arises in the question of whether there are really enough of these occurrent wants to account for all action.'[9] The same problem arises for beliefs as it does for wants.

In response to these difficulties, one obvious move on the part of supporters of the CTA is to accept, *pace* Goldman's explicit denial to the contrary, that dispositional or standing mental states or events, rather than just occurrent ones, can be parts of the requisite rationalizing causes for actions. Our difficulty seemed to arise only because Goldman insisted on the rationalizing mental states being occurrent or conscious. No occurrent mental states may figure at all in the causal story. But dispositional ones, in this way, might so figure, along with the triggering event, even on an events-only

    [8] Bruce Vermazen, 'Occurrent and Standing Wants', in *Bowling Green Studies in Applied Philosophy: Action & Responsibility*, Bowling Green, Oh.: Bowling Green State,University, 1980: 52.   [9] Goldman, *A Theory of Human Action*, 88.

view of causation. So let's count dispositional states too, as part of the causally relevant action story and hence available to the CTA.

What might these dispositional wants and beliefs be? Goldman said that a dispositional want (of kind K) is a disposition to have occurrent wants (of that kind). (As we shall see, this may be a necessary condition for dispositional belief or dispositional desire, but cannot be a sufficient one.) Davidson himself spoke of 'fixed purposes, standards, desires, and habits'.[10] 'Fixed' might plausibly be construed as 'dispositional'. Dispositional beliefs of some kind are said, similarly, to be dispositions to have occurrent beliefs of that kind.[11]

And let's be liberal and give the CTA even more resources on which to draw. One might even add unconscious or subconscious beliefs and desires to this stock of occurrent and dispositional beliefs and desires. Presumably, even in the case of an unconscious or subconscious belief, it must in principle be available to consciousness, however difficult the discovery process might be (Chat to a friend? Counselling? Extensive psychotherapy? Lifelong analysis?).

How do subconscious beliefs differ from just plain dispositional beliefs? Ordinary dispositional beliefs, although the agent won't be currently aware that he has those beliefs, are readily available to recall, whereas subconscious or unconscious ones, although ultimately recallable as well, are actively blocked from easy recall by some mental mechanism. They can actually be recalled only when that mechanism is bypassed in some way.

In so far as this category of belief has entered folk psychology (as it surely now has) from psychoanalytic modes of thought, such beliefs are ones that would be available to consciousness, but for some identifiable mechanism that suppresses them and keeps them from entering the conscious arena. Such mechanisms include: repression, fantasy, wish fulfilment, various forms of denial, self-deception, projection, displacement, and so on. So let us not be niggardly in giving the CTA all the beliefs we can muster: occurrent, dispositional, unconscious, and subconscious beliefs are all available to the CTA in making its case. If one were, contrary to my views in the last chapter, running the story with intentions rather than beliefs and desires, no doubt one would want to avail oneself of the same extended range of intentions.

[10] Donald Davidson, 'Actions, Reasons, and Causes', in his *Essays on Actions and Events*, New York and Oxford: Clarendon Press, 1980: 13.

[11] I have no doubt that this analysis is utterly inadequate. I am merely repeating the literature here.

Now, one might speculate that if Goldman's currently-available-to-consciousness criterion is relaxed, so that we have a much wider range of beliefs available, we would have enough mental material to fulfil the requirements of the CTA. Of course, the CTA still requires an awful lot of beliefs and desires, but in the relaxed sense of 'belief' and 'desire' we are now using, we do in fact have an awful lot of them. The only restrictions on the beliefs and desires employable by the CTA are: (a) that they must in principle be available to consciousness, for otherwise it is not easy to see what content could be given to the thought that they exist at the level of folk psychology; (b) that they must possess both causal and rationalizing powers.

However, there will still be insufficient mental material, whether episodic or dispositional, conscious or subconscious, to make the CTA plausible for many cases of action. Why do I think this?

Dispositions to Believe

Before I turn to my argument proper, we need to be clear about another category of so-called belief (and desire). Do I believe that doctors wear underpants? That elephants do not carry umbrellas? That 845.765 is larger than 845.764987? That estate cars are inedible? Do I desire to maximize my long-term self-interest? Do I want to do what I have decided to do? Do I desire to conform to the norms of practical rationality? I am thinking of the rather extensive literature on tacit or implicit belief (and, by extension, desire).[12]

The point being made by some of this literature is, I take it, also made by Robert Audi in his helpful articles in which he carefully distinguishes dispositional belief from mere dispositions to believe (and, we can add, dispositions to want).[13] Audi argues, convincingly in my view, that there is a difference between having a dispositional belief, for example, that the earth is round, and merely having the disposition to believe something if one considers the matter.

[12] William Lycan, 'Tacit Belief', in Radu Bogdan, ed., *Belief: Form, Content, and Function*, Oxford: Oxford University Press, 1986: 61–82; Mark Crimmins, 'Tacitness and Virtual Beliefs', *Mind & Language*, 7, 1992: 240–63; John Searle, 'Consciousness, Unconsciousness, and Intentionality', *Philosophical Topics*, 17, 1989: 193–209; John Searle, *Intentionality*, Cambridge and New York: Cambridge University Press, 1984: ch. 5. A related discussion by Stephen Stich, 'Beliefs and Subdoxastic States', *Philosophy of Science*, 45, 1978: 499–518, fights the tendency to fit too much into the category of unconscious belief.

[13] Robert Audi, 'Dispositional Beliefs and Dispositions to Believe', *Nous*, 28, 1994: 419–34. Also see Robert Audi, 'Believing and Affirming', *Mind*, 91, 1982: 115–20.

In the earlier of the two articles, Audi's case is that of an overexcited man, who considers whether he is speaking too loudly. If and when he considers the matter, he will assent to the fact, but he did not believe it all along, before he considered the matter, not even dispositionally. All along, he only had the disposition to believe it, but did not believe it dispositionally.

Audi explicates the difference using a computer analogy. What is actually or occurrently believed is on the computer screen. On the other hand,

[w]hat is dispositionally as opposed to occurrently believed is analogous to what is in a computer's memory but not on its screen . . . By contrast with both of these cases . . . propositions we are only disposed to believe are more like those a computer would display only upon doing a calculation, say addition: the raw materials, which often include inferential principles, are present, but the propositions are not yet in the memory bank or on the screen.[14]

The difference, as Audi explains it, is, in the case of dispositional belief, accessibility of a proposition by a retrieval process (from the memory bank) and, in the case of a disposition to believe, accessibility to a proposition by a belief-formation process, by the latter of which a person comes to believe something for the first time that he never actually believed before, not even dispositionally. Yet, though he did not dispositionally believe it, in virtue of the 'raw materials and inferential principles' that he does have, he was disposed to believe it all along.

As I explained above, dispositional belief and occurrent belief are merely different epistemic modes of access that a believer has to his belief states; one can be in one and the same belief state and at one time have occurrent access to it, and at another time not have occurrent access to it. A dispositional belief state is dispositional only in the sense that, in that state, one is disposed to occurrently believe something in the right set of circumstances, *and* to do so without undergoing any further inferential process. If a person dispositionally believes something, then he is disposed to gain occurrent epistemic access to a belief state he is already in, in the right circumstances. Belief states are not dispositional or occurrent *per se*.

But dispositions to believe are not epistemic modes of access to existing belief states at all. If a person is only disposed to believe, then there is no state of belief he is in, and hence no kind of non-inferential access that he could have to it. Dispositions to believe are just what their name implies that they are: dispositional states of a believer, in a strong sense of dispositional. Of course, having dispositions to believe something may cause one

---

[14] Audi, 'Dispositional Beliefs and Dispositions to Believe', 420.

to dispositionally believe that thing (they may cause him to occurrently believe it as well), but they are distinct. It is not always easy to tell which of the two states a person is in. A person may be in a belief state (including a state of dispositional belief) or a mere dispositional state to believe, but, whether it is easy or not to tell the difference, there is a categorical difference between them.

Suppose a person is such that, if he were to be asked, he would say that he believes that p. On some views, the truth of such a subjunctive conditional is sufficient for dispositional belief. But even if necessary, the truth of the subjunctive conditional cannot be sufficient, since the subjunctive conditional is true in the case of being disposed to believe as well.

Audi's computer analogy is suggestive, but in the end the distinction between dispositional belief and dispositions to believe should be made without reliance on it. That analogy with a memory bank in the case of dispositional belief might suggest that, to believe something dispositionally, I had once to believe it occurrently, and that it is now available to memory recall. This does not seem to be true.

In the ordinary case of perceptual belief, I acquire many beliefs as I move about and am subjected to the vast amount of perceptual input that I receive. I thereby come to believe things dispositionally that I never believed first occurrently. As I walk down a street that I have never seen before, I may come to believe dispositionally that it is tree-lined, without ever believing occurrently that it is tree-lined. The belief is really 'there' in some sense, although I may not be aware of it when I acquire it, and may never be aware or conscious of it, if I ever am, until some later time.

It is, I think, Audi's idea of a belief-formation process that is essential for drawing the distinction we want. We can draw the distinction between believing dispositionally and being disposed to believe on an intuitive basis, but in the end the distinction must be buttressed by an empirical hypothesis. In the case of dispositions to believe, the relevant beliefs will only be present once the agent has gone through a belief-forming process, but not so in the case of dispositional beliefs. With the latter, no further belief-formation process is necessary, because the relevant beliefs are already there.

In the case of being disposed to believe, the belief-forming process will typically not itself be conscious. We noted in Chapter 3 that there may be no difference between an unconscious inferential process and a certain kind of causal process. But such processes would need to be identified, and in the case of being disposed to belief, some such inferential or causal process— whether conscious or not—must take place, but not so in the case of believing dispositionally. It is the absence or presence of these processes that underpins the distinction we need.

Let us suppose that yesterday I did believe dispositionally both that all men are mortal and that Tom Jones is a man. In truth, yesterday I may only have been disposed to believe that he is mortal, disposed to so believe, in virtue of the beliefs I truly did have. I did not then believe that he is mortal. It does not matter that we may say, as a piece of ordinary language, that yesterday, when not thinking about it, I believed that Tom Jones is mortal. The important point is that, in the case we are envisaging, at t there are two things we believe (dispositionally or occurrently): that all men are mortal and that Tom Jones is a man, and at t there is a disposition to believe that Jones is mortal. There is no further, distinct belief at t, that he is mortal. After t, I may come to believe that he is mortal, by drawing out that implication from what I do believe at t.

The importance of the distinction that Audi draws lies in the questions both of causal powers and of rationalization. Let me deal first with causal powers. Believing something occurrently has causal powers. Even if only events are causes, believing something occurrently, which is a state, has causal powers, just as the presence of oxygen has causal power, even though not itself an event, powers which it evidences whenever a match is struck in its presence. And believing something dispositionally can have causal powers, since it is the same state of belief that one is in when one has an occurrent belief; it is just that one has a different mode of access to it.

But, when I am only disposed to believe, say, that Tom Jones is mortal, my believing that Tom Jones is mortal has no causal power in such a case. It can't have, because there is no such belief that I have, either occurrent or dispositionally accessed. Of course, being disposed to believe that Jones is mortal can have causal powers if any dispositions can. Some maintain that dispositions supervene on their non-dispositional basis; others hold that they are identical to them. I remain neutral on that point. Presumably, even if dispositions only supervene on their bases, the disposition has the same causal powers as does whatever is its non-dispositional basis.

If dispositions to believe have the causal powers of their bases, surely that explains why, when hungry, I do not try and eat estate cars. I act just as if I believed this, or just as if I believe that Jones is mortal, because the non-dispositional bases on which these dispositions supervene or with which they are identical have causal powers that lead me to avoid eating estate cars or treating Jones as if he is immortal. Or, put it another way. My belief that all men are mortal and my belief that Jones is a man have causal powers, and together those causal powers normally lead me to act just as if I also believed that Jones is mortal, even though I do not actually believe this.

The case is clear when the belief I am disposed to have follows logically— and indeed fairly straightforwardly—from the beliefs I really do have. In cases in which the dispositions to believe rest on more complicated deductive inferences, or on non-deductive inferences, I may not act just as if I had the beliefs that I am only disposed to have. For example, I may have had a number of similar singular experiences. On their basis, I may be disposed to believe some inductive generalization which I will come to believe once I engage in an actual inductive-belief-forming process. But until I do, I may not act as if I believed that inductive generalization; acting as if it were true may require my actually moving from being disposed to believe to really believing, unlike the cases of Jones's mortality and the inedibility of estate cars.

There are three 'powers' of something that need to be distinguished: causal power, power to explain, and power (ability) to rationalize (more on this just below). Suppose the case is one in which I do in fact act just as if I had the belief. If I am disposed to believe that estate cars are inedible, that disposition, or its non-dispositional base, can cause my non-consuming-estate-cars behaviour. As I go on to claim in Chapter 6, all causes explain their effects (under some description of the cause), and so dispositions, if they cause behaviour, also explain that behaviour.

But a disposition's causing and explaining behaviour still falls short of rationalizing it, in the sense of 'rationalization' under discussion. My irascible temperament might cause and hence explain some inappropriate outburst of mine, without that irascible temperament, which is a disposition, rationalizing what it causes and explains. My behaviour, caused and explicable though it is, might yet be utterly non-rational or irrational, in the circumstances.

Beliefs, dispositional or occurrent, can co-rationalize actions (with desires). Dispositions to believe are really no more than physical states that confer on a person certain of the abilities that he may have, to believe various things if he subsequently undergoes certain belief-forming processes. They have no place within common sense, folk psychology, nor are they personal states of the agents that are candidates for explicating the rationalization that the CTA requires. Dispositions to believe do not rationalize the actions that the beliefs would rationalize, were the agent to have them. The upshot of this is that our liberality with the CTA has theoretical limits. The CTA can include, in the scope of its claim about the rationalizing causes of action, dispositional, unconscious, and subconscious beliefs. But it cannot include mere dispositions to believe as rationalizing causes of action, for dispositions have a location in the agent's underlying mechanisms, not in his folk psychology.

Hard Cases for the CTA

Let's turn now to the cases on which I think the CTA shipwrecks. Others have pointed out alleged examples of action for which the positing of causing and rationalizing mental states (especially, beliefs) seems to be implausible. Brian O'Shaughnessy distinguishes between what he calls sub-intentional acts, like tapping one's feet to music and moving one's tongue in one's mouth, on the one hand, and intentional actions done for no reason, on the other, like drumming one's fingers out of boredom (this last is similar to Maimonides' case of futile action that I mentioned in Chapter 3).[15]

In actions of both kinds, the faculty of reason, especially beliefs, plays no part in their causation, so, if there really were such cases, both would be counter-examples to the CTA. The difference between the two cases seems to be, for O'Shaughnessy, that in the sub-intentional case, the actor typically does not know that the act is occurring when it occurs but can come to discover that it is (p. 60); in the case of intentional action done for no reason, the actor does know that the act is occurring, when he is doing it, and so no discovery about its occurrence is possible (p. 62). (To put it in the terms we have been using, perhaps in the sub-intentional case, the agent is disposed to believe that he is so acting but has no dispositional belief that he is acting.)

My counter-examples to the CTA are actions that are intentional, so are not like his sub-intentional cases. Like his case of intentionally drumming one's fingers on the table, in my cases too, one's faculty of cognition, at the level of folk psychology, has played no rationalizing part in their origin. But I think my counter-examples are far less peripheral to action than O'Shaughnessy's (or Maimonides') examples. In the cases I cite, the actor may know, and hence believe, that they are occurring, or may only be disposed to believe that they are. It makes no difference which.

Rosalind Hursthouse has also offered examples of action in which she claims that the relevant belief is missing. Her examples are cases in which

---

[15] Brian O'Shaughnessy, *The Will: A Dual Aspect Theory*, ii, Cambridge: Cambridge University Press, 1980, ch. 10.

the action is explained only by the presence of emotion(s).[16] In her examples, no rationalizing is going on, since the actions she focuses on are said by her to be arational. But what is important from my perspective is simply that these are claimed as actions but with no relevant belief to cause or to explain (or to rationalize) it.

One of her examples is that of a person kissing the picture of a loved one. One can always manufacture some sort of belief in her examples: the person wants to mitigate his loneliness, and believes that by kissing the picture, he will feel less lonely. With such 'ad hoc hypotheses' about belief, the CTA begins to look empirically empty. The ascription of such beliefs to the agent seems implausible and motivated only by the desire to save the theory.

Responses to Hursthouse differ. I have heard criticism advanced of her cases, on the lines that she considers only the thesis that belief-and-desire pairs are rationalizing causal mental states for actions, but that she does not consider intentions for this role. It might be less clear that, in her examples, even when a belief seems to be missing, an intention is missing as well. The man who kisses a picture of his girlfriend certainly has the intention to kiss the picture, and it is sometimes said that the intention to do so rationalizes and causes the kissing, whether the belief is there or not.

I do not myself find this a devastating reply to Hursthouse, partly because, as I explained in Chapter 3, I do not really understand the sense in which intentions could rationalize the actions they cause. A person's intending to do A does not necessarily make his doing of A the strongly rational thing to do in the circumstances, if, for example, his intentions are at variance with his beliefs as to what is best and his desire to do what is for the best. Moreover, there are cases that I discussed in Chapter 3, in which a person's intending to do A might not even make his doing A the weakly rational thing to do, for instance, in the case of the postponed dental appointment. So even if there is an intention present in all of her cases of action, the intention can't play the same role that the belief-and-desire pair was meant to play. The actions would remain arational, even if intentions were present.

Alfred Mele also argues against Hursthouse's examples. His view is that, whereas Hursthouse may have shown that her allegedly 'arational' actor has not acted for reasons in the sense of a belief–desire pair, it does not follow that she has shown that the actor has acted for no reason at all. Perhaps

[16] Rosalind Hursthouse, 'Arational Action', *The Journal of Philosophy*, 88, 1991: 57–68.

the arational actor acted for bad reasons, or for intrinsic reasons, rather than no reasons.

Mele suggests that a reason can be simply an intrinsic desire, like 'showing one's gratitude to a friend for its own sake' (p. 359), and can even be 'constituted by an irrational intrinsic desire to drink the paint' (no beliefs required) (p. 360).[17] In terms of Wayne Davis's distinction, introduced in Chapter 3, if the desires are to rationalize as well as cause the action, such desires have to be appetitive desires rather than volitive desires. If there are appetitive desires-as-reasons that rationalize actions in these cases, even if these reasons are not belief–desire pair reasons, then the CTA might survive her criticism: a movement m is an action iff m is non-deviantly caused and rationalized either (1) by a desire-and-belief or (2) by an appetitive desire to act, on its own.

Unlike O'Shaughnessy's examples, the cases I have in mind for discussion in this chapter are uncontroversially non-peripheral cases of action, and, unlike Hursthouse's, are cases in which there is no special reason to think that an appetitive desire (or an emotion) will always be available and on the mental scene. Even if Mele is right and the urge to drink the paint can weakly rationalize a person's paint drinking, the cases I introduce below are ones in which a belief would still be required, if the action is to be rationalized. They will be instrumental cases in which an agent acts only because of some further or larger action that he desires to do (recall my discussion of this in Chapter 3). I also need my cases to meet the following criteria: (1) they are genuine cases of intentional action; (2) the agent has no rationalizing mental states (in particular, no beliefs) whose propositional content matches the action description.

The main idea is that one finds cases meeting these criteria in so-called routine action, various kinds of skilled activity, and in displays of technique.[18] I use these terms rather interchangeably; neither philosophers nor psychologists (as far as I am aware) have a well-developed vocabulary to distinguish various nuances between various kinds of cases. This is, I think, itself quite telling. Contemporary philosophers, especially action theorists, have concentrated on what is often called efficient rationality: taking efficient (or sometimes, the only available) means to desired ends. An older

---

[17] Alfred Mele, 'Acting for Reasons and Acting Intentionally', *Pacific Philosophical Quarterly*, 73, 1992: 355–74.

[18] For a good introduction to issues of practical skills, see Robert Sternberg *et al.*, *Practical Intelligence in Everyday Life*, Cambridge: Cambridge University Press, 2000.

philosophical tradition, represented in Greek philosophy, focused on crafts: sculpting, shipbuilding, potting on a wheel, and so on.

These craft-related activities bring to the fore different problems and considerations for action theory. However, engaging in crafts is not itself something many of us do for much of the time (not after attending summer camp at any rate). But once one sees the similarity between some of the craft activities (not all) and routine activities and exercise of certain kinds of skills, I believe that the sorts of activities I want to focus on can be seen to be ubiquitous in our lives. Most of us for much of the time engage in activities for which the CTA is implausible as a theory of action.

Using the distinction I drew in Chapter 2, I want to concentrate on activities that are made up of a large number of individual actions. Judith Jarvis Thomson's example of house-cleaning is, one might say, a meta-activity, since each of its parts is itself made up of further individual action parts. For example, one of the parts of my house-cleaning is vacuuming the floor, and the vacuuming of the floor is itself an activity made up of various actions, like moving my hand forward, then backward, then bending over, and so on, each of which is itself an action. The individual actions in this case are not themselves activities, although one could imagine other, somewhat stranger, examples, in which they might be.

A child is born with the ability to do a few things (sucking is an example, grasping with his toes when suspended off the ground is another), but not many things. In the course of a person's life, he gains the vast majority of his abilities. The abilities in question are abilities to do various things; as such, they are behavioural dispositions. There seem to be at least three ways in which these abilities can be acquired: by being taught, by emulation and imitation, and as a natural by-product of growth and development. In the acquisition of most skills, the three are typically combined in varying degrees. (There is reason to think that the importance of imitation and emulation has been understated in many past accounts of ability acquisition.) Even when one method of acquisition of some skill dominates for one person, a different way may dominate in the case of another person: what one person acquires mostly by explicit instruction, another may acquire by observation and imitation.

One may be taught how to drive, how to swim, how to read and write, how to shave, how to play various competitive sports, how to ride a bicycle. The teaching is typically verbal, although it may have some nonverbal elements. For example, the teacher may guide my hand as I learn to form certain of the letters, as well as by issuing verbal instruction.

One clear case of ability learning by imitation or emulation is learning to speak one's mother tongue. In many cases, this too may have some taught element, but first languages can be learnt purely by imitation and emulation, and surely sometimes are. In learning to shave, I may simply watch someone else shaving and 'catch on'. Or, I may watch someone brushing his hair and then proceed to do it myself. Much grooming is learnt by imitation, both at the human and the animal levels.

Finally, some abilities can be acquired simply in virtue of the process of maturation itself. A child can acquire the ability to walk or to eat almost as an automatic by-product of growth, plus a bit of initial trial and error, even in the absence of any teaching or imitation. Animals typically learn things in this way; baby birds learn to fly 'automatically', as we might say, at a certain stage of their development.

Within these activities, there is a distinction between technique and strategy.[19] A skilled golfer, for example, displays both skill in his strategic thinking and skill in his technique. Technique is a matter of knowing how to do various things, and is non-propositional; strategy involves propositional knowledge or belief. In some skilled activities, there is a large element of strategic thought. Someone who has the skills of golf must know not only how to swing the club (technique), but also must think out which club to use in certain conditions, how to hit the ball in the particular circumstances, where to hit it to best advantage, and so on (strategy).

Golf and many other competitive sports are skilled activities that typically require a great deal of strategy. There is some strategic thought in most activity, although less in some than in others. I want to concentrate either on those activities that minimize reliance on strategy, or at any rate concentrate on the purely technical aspects of those activities that have both technique and strategy.

I want to consider abilities that are relatively strategy-less displays of technique. Many of them demand an ability to improvise. Let me list several examples:

(1) shaving;
(2) ice-skating around a pond;
(3) painting a picture, especially non-representational or abstract art;
(4) dancing. Especially think of 'modern' dancing where the person does more or less what he feels like, rather than the highly ritualized dancing in which there are set steps in a determinate order;

---

[19] I owe this distinction to Andrew Pyle.

(5) kissing, hugging, embracing another person.

(I agree that (5) is somewhat different from the others, and hardly counts as a display of technique, at least not in the normal case, unless one is Don Juan.)

(6) Riding a bicycle.
(7) Eating and drinking (minus, perhaps, the overlay of learned etiquette).

In these cases, (1) to (7), the CTA does not seem to have much trouble with the whole stretch of activity. I desire to be clean-shaven. I believe that if I shave, I will be clean-shaven, so I shave. I want to enjoy myself, and I believe that if I dance, I will enjoy myself, so I dance away. I want to show you affection and I believe that if I hug you, I will show this, so I hug away. So far, so good (although even here, in the example of the hugging and embracing at least, the CTA stretches my credulity).

But the CTA is a theory that is meant to apply to all our actions, even to those actions that are parts of other actions. In painting a picture, or shaving, or dancing, or riding a bicycle, for example, I perform many such actions. I move different parts of my body in many and varied ways. How will the CTA deal with these actions constitutive of the whole activity of painting or shaving or dancing or riding?

Consider the shaving example. In shaving, I make many movements, all of which are my actions. I pull the electric razor vertically down my face, from cheek to chin. I desire to rid myself of my whiskers, and if I believed that by pulling the razor in some particular way, I would rid myself of some of my whiskers, that belief and desire would rationalize my so pulling the razor. Or, in dancing, I twist this way and that. I desire to dance, and if I believed that by twisting in some particular way, I would be contributing to my dance, that belief and desire would rationalize the twisting. But of course I may not have, and typically will not have, any such beliefs. The CTA founders, I think, on many of these actions that are the parts of longer stretches of activity requiring technique.

Now, suppose someone agrees that I have no such occurrent beliefs, but steadfastly holds that I have such beliefs dispositionally. Don't I believe, at least dispositionally, that pulling my razor from cheek to chin will lead to the elimination of some whiskers, or that twisting my body in some particular way is part of a dance? I think that the reply confuses what Audi carefully distinguished. If I am asked whether I believe that by twisting in some particular way, I would contribute to the overall dance, or whether I believed that if I pulled my razor from cheek to chin, I would rid myself of some of my whiskers, I would reply that I did. But that is because, when asked, I form those beliefs on the basis of other information I have stored, and not because I had those beliefs stored before being asked. These cases seem very much like the man who believes that he is talking too loudly, but only after his attention is drawn to it.

Might these beliefs be subconscious or unconscious ones? The difficulty with that suggestion is that there is no obvious blocking mechanism, like denial or self-deception or whatever, that serves to prevent them from appearing to consciousness. The important point with the idea of subconscious or unconscious belief is to prevent its unprincipled expansion to include anything a theorist wishes to conjure into existence.

It would be too uneconomical to attribute to me all these means-ends beliefs. I should have to store too many of them. I would have to hold a great many beliefs about whisker-elimination being brought about by a large number of hand movements, beliefs that may never even have occurred to me before; I would have to believe that many different and varied bodily gyrations, some quite novel, would contribute to the dance, or to my hugging and embracing, or to my bicycle riding. Improvisation allows me to do many things that I hold no beliefs about, at least not before I do them.

It is far more plausible to believe that I am in receipt of a store of general information about dancing and body movements, about shaving and hand movements, about bicycle riding and balancing techniques, and, only if and when appropriate, I can form particular beliefs about the specific types of gyrations and hand movements and balancing motions in which I am engaging. On the basis of the general information, I am disposed to believe these things, but don't actually believe them, even dispositionally, until and unless I am required to do so. No doubt, it is also in virtue of these information states that a person has whatever dispositions he has to believe things about efficient means to desired ends. The abilities he acquires by this information are abilities to do, but they probably account for, so we might speculate, his Audi-like dispositions to believe as well.

What sort of general information does the agent possess? As I claimed, the information is about how to do various things, how one performs certain sorts of activities. In the cases I have mentioned, I must learn or in some other way acquire the techniques or abilities involved in dancing, shaving, painting, bicycle riding, and ice-skating. When I learn to do such things, the specific guidance that directs these stretches of activity certainly has to be hard-wired in, in some way. Moreover, the hard-wired guidance must allow for variation, improvisation, since it must allow for my ability to dance a pattern I may have never engaged in before, or to shave with strokes I never used previously, or even to hug in a way that is novel and responsive to the perhaps unusual way in which the other person might be hugging me.

So I am not claiming that any of these activities can dispense with complicated brain-goings-on. None of us is, after all, the Straw Man from the Wizard of Oz, who lacked a brain but could still walk, talk, or whatever. But this general information about how to do various things, which also accounts for the agent's dispositions to believe things if and when appropriate, is really no more than a physical state that confers on a person certain of the abilities that he may have, dispositions to do various things or to believe various things. They are indeed essentially implicated in the control of an agent's behaviour. What these brain-goings-on provide for us is knowledge-how, as it is sometimes called. I may know how to do these things, to shave, to dance, to hug, to ride a bicycle, to eat, without having any specific beliefs of the sort that the CTA requires.[20]

The connection between knowledge-how and knowledge-that is a disputed issue. Jason Stanley and Timothy Williamson argue (a) that knowledge-how is a species of knowledge-that.[21] They also argue (b) that 'ascriptions of knowledge-how do not even entail ascriptions of the corresponding abilities' (p. 416).

Let's take (b) first. What is their argument for (b)?

It is simply false, however, that ascriptions of knowledge-how ascribe abilities. For example, a ski instructor may know how to perform a certain complex stunt, without being able to perform it herself. Similarly, a master pianist who loses both of her arms in a tragic car accident still knows how to play the piano. (p. 416)

What these above two examples demonstrate is that having know-how is not a sufficient condition for being able to do what one knows how to do. For instance, certain physical conditions (use of one's arms for the pianist, and whatever it is that prevents the ski instructor from performing the complex stunt) have to be in place as well as the know-how. However, the examples certainly do not show that having know-how is not necessary for the ability to do something. When the claim is made that knowledge-how is an ability, that should be read as the claim that know-how is one essential component in being able to do something. With this understood, I shall continue referring to knowledge-how as an ability.

[20] Gilbert Ryle, *The Concept of Mind*, Harmondsworth: Penguin Books, 1963, ch. 2.
[21] Jason Stanley and Timothy Williamson, 'Knowing How', *Journal of Philosophy*, 98, 2001: 411–44.

Regarding (a), what Stanley and Williamson argue is this: Hannah knows how to ride a bicycle iff 'for some contextually relevant way w which is a way for Hannah to ride a bicycle, Hannah knows that w is a way for her to ride a bicycle' (p. 426). So, 'Hannah knows how to ride a bicycle' 'requires Hannah to stand in the knowledge-that relation to a . . . proposition containing a way of riding a bicycle (along with other objects and properties)' (p. 427).

Stanley and Williamson make it clear that someone who stands in this relationship to the requisite proposition might be able to refer to the way in which to ride a bicycle only in indexical terms, say as 'that way or perhaps "this way"': 'that John possesses propositional knowledge about a way does not entail that he can describe it in non-indexical terms' (p. 433).

So, if Hannah knows how to ride a bicycle, all that might be true on their account is this: 'Hannah knows that that way (pointing to the way in which someone else is riding a bicycle) is the way for her to ride a bicycle' (p. 428). This will be the case with the hugger, shaver, ice-skater as I envisage them; they can certainly say, of themselves, that they know that this is the way (pointing to what they are doing) to hug, shave, ice-skate.

Contrary to what they must be supposing, an agent might know how to do something at t, without ever having been related to a proposition about a way of doing that thing, indexically indicated, at or before t (let's take for granted that the agent is unable to produce a non-indexical description of the relevant way). He might not be able to refer to the way as 'this way', because he may never actually have done the thing himself, at or before t. If he has never seen anyone else do it at or before t, he might not be able to refer to the way as 'that way' either. And yet he may still know how to do it. Such a case of know-how seems perfectly possible. A socially isolated child who can't give any non-indexical description of the way in which to walk might still know how to walk, even if circumstances are such that he has never walked before or seen anyone else walk either. True, he might not know that he knows how to walk, but he may know how, none the less.

Let's suppose, on the other hand, that the agent can produce a proposition that is about the way in which to do the thing in question, with the way indexically indicated. Permitting the beliefs to contain indexicals presents a problem for the CTA. 'This', and 'that', the latter said as one points, must refer to something occurring at the time of the utterance, or belief, which contains the indexical. If these indexicals occur as part of the content of the belief or utterance, the believing or uttering must be simultaneous with the action that 'this' or 'that' refers to in that context. If so, then the belief state cannot cause the action as well as rationalize it, as the CTA requires, since causes precede their effects.

Given these observations, I have no reason to resist Stanley and Williamson's analysis of know-how as a species of knowledge-that, at least for the purposes of this chapter. Accepting their analysis would not disturb my criticisms of the CTA, since the indexical propositions that might be the only ones available to the agent will not help the CTA (for the reason given above). But is their analysis finally convincing? It is plain that Hannah might know that *that* is a way to ride a bicycle (pointing to John's riding) without her knowing how to ride a bicycle. She can see that John knows how to ride and she can see that that would be a great way or the right way for her to ride too, but she still might not know how to ride a bicycle. The authors themselves point this out. What bridges the gap between the two? What more does Hannah need, in order to know how to ride, beyond knowing that that is a way for her to ride?

Stanley and Williamson reply to this difficulty is to claim that for Hannah to know how to ride a bicycle, she must be related to the relevant proposition 'under a practical mode of presentation' which 'undoubtedly entails the possession of certain complex dispositions' (p. 429). We are left in the dark as to what that means. They are clear that there must be such practical modes of presentation; 'one can provide an existence proof for such modes of presentation . . . there is a sound argument from . . . [their propositional analysis of know-how] . . . to the existence of practical guises of propositions' (p. 429). I think this means that there must be such modes of presentation, if their own propositional analysis of know-how is to succeed.

Without knowing what a practical mode of presentation is, I do not think that one can fully evaluate their propositional analysis of knowledge-how. The worry is that the analysis of the idea of a practical mode of presentation of a proposition might reintroduce into their analysis reference to knowledge-how. The issue is one of the potential circularity of their account. Because of the specific way in which they express this objection to their view (pp. 433–4), their reply is that their account is not reductive, not that it is not circular.

Reductive or not, if their account is circular, if in order to understand what a practical mode of presentation of a proposition is, we were to have to reuse the idea of knowledge-how, their account would not show that knowledge-how was a species of knowledge-that. In that case, it would be just as plausible to conclude that a certain kind of knowledge-that, namely that which is presented to an agent under a practical mode, is a species of knowledge-how. Given all of this, I shall, in what follows, feel entitled to continue talking of know-how, in spite of what they say.

This knowledge-how that agents have consists in dispositional states of an agent, realized somehow in his hardware. There may need to be lots of other beliefs or other folk-psychological states on the scene to make the dancing-shaving-ice-skating-bicycle-riding stories plausible. The issue is only over whether there need to be these rationalizing beliefs on the part of the agent.

Intentions, beliefs, desires, emotions, are states of a person. The concepts contained in the contents of these personal states are concepts belonging to that person; they are in principle 'available' to him, available to his thought, to his reasoning, to his inferential powers, at least under favourable circumstances. They must be accessible to the agent; the beliefs which contain them are either retrievable because stored in memory, or retrievable although currently blocked by a psychological mechanism.

Even though there will be elaborate brain-goings-on, there might fail to be any appropriate rationalizing beliefs at the level of folk psychology. We can describe the difference between hard-wired guidance and belief by using a distinction due to Daniel Dennett that we have mentioned before, between personal and subpersonal states of a system.[22] Jennifer Hornsby similarly distinguishes between the personal and subpersonal levels.[23] Her point is that much goes on at the subpersonal level, in skilled activity, but much of it will not make its appearance at the folk-psychological level, where it could manifest itself as belief.

Control is one thing; it is a causal idea. Rationalization is quite another. Neither the ability to do A, nor the disposition to believe something about A-ing, can rationalize doing A; mere physical abilities and dispositions have no place in the folk-psychological arena that includes mental states and rationalization. These dispositional states of know-how are not even candidates for rationalizing what the agent does. Such neurophysiological states may encode information about various matters, but the information they encode may not be accessed or retrieved by the agent in any of the ways in

[22] Daniel Dennett, *Content and Consciousness*, London: Routledge, 1993: 93–6, and *passim*. See also Christopher Peacocke, *A Study of Concepts*, Bradford Books, Cambridge, Mass.: MIT Press, 1992, ch. 3.
[23] Jennifer Hornsby, *Simple Mindedness*, Cambridge, Mass.: Harvard University Press, 1997: 165.

which occurrent or non-occurrent beliefs are, except perhaps in the index-ical form that I have already conceded.[24]

And without rationalization, the case for the CTA offering an adequate analysis of action simply collapses. It is consistent with my argument thus far that the agent *could* form beliefs (that he does not already hold, in any sense) about what he is doing, how he does what he does, if he tries hard enough. He may be disposed to believe as well as be disposed to do. My argument is only that he can do what he does in the absence of the (non-indexical) beliefs. But could his information states contain information that was, in principle, closed to the agent, which he could not bring to the level of 'personal' belief, no matter how hard he might try, save perhaps in the indexical form described above? Might the information be unretrievable rather than only unretrieved, inaccessible, rather than only unaccessed?

I claimed in Chapter 2 that an agent may act in an ungrasped way; agents might be truly said to do all sorts of actions, the concept of which they do not grasp either in general or as applying to their particular case. The agent need have no concept of the activity in which he is engaged, other than being able to say, 'this', as in 'I know how to do this', thereby demonstrating the activity. In the next section of this chapter, I shall argue that it is logically possible for there to be a case in which the hardwired information that drives an agent's activity be closed to that agent, even in principle.

Stanley and Williamson insist that the proposition that a believer believes, when they have so-called knowledge-how, must be retrievable in some 'favoured circumstance': 'The favoured circumstance may include sitting on a bicycle, and Hannah can retrieve the proposition without being able to express it in nonindexical words'.[25] So all that Hannah might be able to retrieve is the proposition we described above in discussion of Stanley and Williamson's views: 'This is the way for me to ride a bicycle', said as she is riding. With the standard for retrievability set this low, I have no reason to resist their claim. The descriptive information will still be unretrievable by the agent, at least in the case I will describe in the next section.

I find it curious that I find myself in agreement with Ryle about any topic in the philosophy of mind and action. Ryle was a behaviourist, or, to put the matter with more circumspection, his philosophy had strong behaviourist

---

[24] A case similar to mine is made by Wakefield and Dreyfus, who claim that there are cases of action preceded by no representational states of any kind whatever. Their examples, like mine, are of skilled activity. See Jerome Wakefield and Hubert Dreyfus, 'Intentionality and the Phenomenology of Action', in E. Lepore and Robert van Gulick, eds., *John Searle and his Critics*, Oxford: Blackwell, 1992: 263–6.   [25] Stanley and Williamson, 'Knowing How', 441.

tendencies. To exaggerate and simplify, Ryle wanted to depopulate the mind. But since, in the case of the CTA, I find that it overpopulates the mind, perhaps it is not so surprising that I find myself quoting his account of knowledge-how. I certainly do not agree with his mental depopulation strategies generally, but on the specific matter of the presence of beliefs in action, he and I find ourselves engaged in the same sort of transfer of populations out of the territory of the mental.

Stanley and Williamson conclude their article with this gibe at Ryle: 'All knowing-how is knowing that. Neglect of this fact impoverishes our understanding of human action, by obscuring the way in which it is informed by intelligence.'[26] But the reply to them seems to me to be this: activity can indeed be intelligent, or fail to be such, but what Ryle pointed out is that there is a kind of intelligence in human affairs, one that he called know-how, that differs from the kind of intelligence that is to be found in more theoretical endeavours. One can shave, hug, ride a bicycle, dance, ice-skate, intelligently, without being able to produce any propositions that describe in any significant detail how one does these things, save, 'I am doing this' or 'I am doing that (namely, like he does)'.

It is as subpersonal neurophysiological states that I understand the effective and receptive representations of Kent Bach's theory.[27] He claims that, in the case of many actions, there will be these 'representations', but the agent may have no beliefs about that which is so represented. I take Bach to be speaking of non-conceptual, representational states, unlike beliefs.

Bach says that these representations are characteristically 'not conscious' (p. 367). Indeed, in spite of Bach thinking of them as unconscious sensuous awarenesses, nothing is lost if one merely thinks of them as subpersonal representational states, neurophysiological states which have no place in folk psychology itself. I assume that, given an acceptable, principled fixing of the extension of 'folk psychological' by the CTA, Bach's effective and receptive representations will fall outside that extension, in the same way in which I have argued that subpersonal neurophysiological representational states do.

Some Entertaining (I Hope) Science Fiction

I want now to introduce a piece of utter science fiction. I am not claiming that the story I now wish to tell is empirically cogent in the slightest; we sim-

[26] Stanley and Williamson, 'Knowing How', 444.
[27] Kent Bach, 'A Representational Theory of Action', *Philosophical Studies*, 34, 1978: 361–79.

ply do not know enough about the parts of the brain which control action to know whether or not this is so. But I believe that my story is logically or metaphysically possible, and as such helps us to appreciate the conceptual links, or lack thereof, between belief and agency. The story shows, I think, that it is logically possible for a person to act, even in the absence of any access in principle to the subpersonal informational states of know-how that make his actions possible.

Suppose that I do not know how to ice-skate, shave, paint a picture, ride a bicycle, or dance. A famous ice skater, or a veritable Picasso, or a talented Argentinean Tango teacher, or a Tour de France cyclist, sells a software programme, and a piece of hardware which straps onto one's back. That ubiquitous friendly neurophysiologist (well known from his recent successful work with the brain-in-the-vat on Alpha Centauri) wires the hardware in the backpack into my brain in an appropriate way.

With the device operational, I can ice-skate or paint or dance or ride as well as he can. My technique is as good as his, and unsurprisingly so, since I am utilizing the backpack information that he provided on how to do what I am doing. I can turn the device on and off.

There is no doubt that, in these cases, I am acting. Action must be under the agent's own control. Although I utilize the software programme someone else provided, what I do is under my control. I control the backpack module. What I do is also under my control, in the sense that were I to stop desiring to skate, I would cease skating. But given that I do have my desire, and the pack on my back, now I too can ice-skate or paint or ride the bike or dance professionally, by tapping into these informational states. I could find myself riding or skating or painting professionally, surprised at my marvellous technique, and unable to say precisely what I am doing, or how or why I do what I do.

I may have no conscious access to the software programme states in the backpack, even in principle. The software states that I make good use of are informational states that encode a great deal of useful know-how. But they do not result in my having any beliefs, items with conceptual content that I can grasp. They allow me to make use of information that I cannot myself even understand.

One critical response that might be made to the story is this: the story may leave a person in overall control, just in so far as he can turn the switch off and on, so that he can stop and start what he is doing. But the story involves a lack of control over the parts of what he does. The phenomenology of such a case leaves the person a stranger to, and with no sense of control over, the details of what he is 'doing', and as such there is reason to doubt that this is genuine agency at all.

I think that such a critical response would be misguided. A way in which to imagine what agency would 'feel like' in the science fiction story is to imagine some skill that is innate but which develops only at a specific time in the life cycle of an organism. Imagine that you are a large bird living in your parents' nest, and one day you suddenly want to flap your wings. Before you know it, you are flying. You seem to know just what to do—how fast to beat your wings, how to position yourself for take-off and landing, and so on. All of this comes as a surprise to you. You would be in control of all of what you did, and feel yourself in control, even if you had no idea of what to do next or why you were doing it. You would be no stranger to what you were doing; you would feel that sense of intimacy with the details of your flying that is characteristic of agency.

There is no reason to think that agency in my science fiction case would feel any differently than this. How could the difference of where the hard-wired information is stored make the phenomenology of agency different in the two cases?

So here is an extreme, albeit science fiction, case of an agent whose actions are driven by informational states of know-how to which he has no conscious access whatever, even in principle. The information is inaccessible to him. He does what he does, in the presence of (perhaps, only volitive) desires, but in the absence of anything else with conceptual content, in the absence of anything that might, with any degree of plausibility, be called belief.[28]

Responses by the CTA

There are a number of responses that the CTA might make to the argument that certain instances of activity arising from technical ability can proceed without belief. My argument from technical ability assumes that these stretches of activities are composed of actions, that for the CTA these actions must be rationalized, and that there are no beliefs (or intentions for that matter) with propositional content that contain the rationalizing descriptions of these actions. All three assumptions might be disputed by

---

[28] One might try making out a case similar to the one I am arguing, by using the case of animal action rather than science fiction about the actions of persons. See Susan Hurley, 'Animal Action in the Space of Reasons', *Mind and Language*, forthcoming. Hurley's argument is not dissimilar to mine. For her, animals who act may lack conceptual abilities.

the CTA, which might argue (1) that my cases are not ones of action at all, or (2) that there are appropriate mental states that are available, sufficient for the CTA's rationalizing requirement to be met. Moreover, the CTA might argue (3) that, by a slight alteration to the CTA as I have stated it, it is not, after all, required to find beliefs that rationalize all the actions I have mentioned.

Let me take each response in turn.

(1) It might be disputed that the activities are composed of actions, in the way supposed. So, the idea might be that although shaving, or painting, or dancing, or bicycle riding, are activities, the parts of the activities, the various movings of the bodily parts that make up the activities, are not themselves actions.

Not all the parts of activities or actions are themselves actions, let alone intentional ones. But by every common-sense test of intentionality that I can think of, the bodily movements that make up these activities are not only actions, but also intentional ones. First, there is this simple test: ask the putative agent if the specific movement is something he meant to do, did on purpose, did intentionally. Did you bring your razor from cheek to chin on purpose? Did you do gyrate your hips intentionally? Did you mean to place the yellow circle over the black background on the canvas? The answer will be in the affirmative, unlike the cutting of his lip (while shaving) or the wearing down of the blade of his ice-skates (while ice-skating) or stumbling (while dancing).

Second, there is the test of responsibility. I typically have no responsibility, or reduced responsibility, for the movings of my body that are not actions. If my knee jerks when tapped by the doctor's hammer, and if there were a law against knee jerking, I would not be prosecuted under that law (although the doctor might, since it occurred as a direct causal consequence of something he did). On the other hand, if there were a law against bringing one's razor from cheek to chin, or gyrating one's hips, or painting yellow circles on black backgrounds, or steering a bicycle to the left, and this happens, it seems clear that it is something for which I would be fully accountable.

Finally, there is the test of control. Of course I control the whole shave, but the proponent of the CTA might claim that there is a lack of control over the parts of what one does, over the individual shaving or painting movements or gyratings, for example. If so, there might be reason to doubt that this is genuine agency. We have already discussed this issue above. I don't think this claim of lack of control over the detail is right at all. There is a

characteristic phenomenology of control and exertion of effort that per-
vades these cases too (as in my imaginary case of Big Bird). In shaving,
painting, dancing, bicycle riding, the control and effort extend all the way
down. The parts of the activities are actions too; the parts instantiate agency
in the same way as does the whole activity.

(2) The prolific theory to which I adhere is not necessarily the most prolific theory one could imagine. In Chapter 1, I entertained the thought that
there can be some cases in which two non-equivalent descriptions pick out
the same action, if at least the times, places, and subjects of the actions are
identical: my bending of my finger and my giving of the signal (by so doing),
or my saying 'I promise' and my promising (by so doing).

Where there is a series of action descriptions that run from the very general to the very specific, the action descriptions in the series might, as far as
my theory goes, refer to numerically one and the same action. Examples are
ones in which there are more and less general descriptions of an action: my
doing something, my doing A, my doing A in context c. These three might
be descriptions of one and the same action token. If so, rationalization will
have to have some degree of description-relativity, even for a prolific theorist, since there can be cases of two or more descriptions of the same action.
If and when this is so, to rationalize my action under some description may
not be to rationalize it under a more or under a less general description.

So, a variant of this response by the CTA argues that, although the parts
that compose the activity are actions, the actions requiring rationalization
are not to be described in the way in which I have assumed. For example,
the token action that is my moving of my finger from left to right = my token
doing something with my hand = my token moving of my finger left to right
on a cloudless day. Now, if my action is described merely as my doing of
something with my hand, then it might be easier to find the missing belief: I
desire to paint a picture, to become clean-shaven, and I believe that by doing
something or other with my hand I will accomplish my goal, so I do something with my hand. So my action, described as my doing something with
my hand (and *not* described as my making some specific hand movement),
is rationalized.

Under what description do we require the action to be rationalized?[29] I

---

[29] There surely is some microphysical description, M, of the mere event that underlies the
action. But that will not typically provide us with the item to be rationalized, since an agent may
have no beliefs or desires with any M-content. Because of the requirements of rationalization,
what gets rationalized will almost always be an item that is visible at the level of folk psychology
(unless of course the rationalizer happens to be a microphysicist out to prove a point and refute
my claim!).

discussed this briefly in Chapter 3. I think the action needs to be rationalized in all and only its intentional detail, and I have already suggested some
informal tests for checking at which level of description the intentional
detail we require figures. If what I do intentionally is to move my finger left
to right, then it is insufficiently specific to find a doing-something-with-my
hand belief that will rationalize my action only as a doing something with
my hand. So this is the important point: a desire or belief whose content is
less specific than the action's full intentional description cannot rationalize
that action under that more specific description.

And there is a similar lesson with regard to overspecific descriptions. If I
do not intend to move my finger on a cloudless day—it just happens that the
day is cloudless—then I do not need to find a belief with cloudless-day content. An overspecific content can arguably rationalize a less specifically
described action (see Chapter 6 for a parallel problem about overspecific
properties in explanation), but contains redundant, and potentially misleading, content.

So what I conclude is that even if we were more likely to find beliefs by
making their content less specific for example, they would not be the beliefs
we need in the rationalization story we require. True but not sufficiently
specific for the CTA that, when I hug you, I believe that I am putting my
arms somewhere or other. The propositional content of the rationalizing
beliefs must include the most specific detail, but no more, that still provides
a description of the intentional action being rationalized.

(3) The third type of rejoinder on behalf of the CTA introduces an alteration to the CTA as I have formulated it. This line of defence (I call it 'the
whole–part strategy') is suggested by remarks by Mele and by Adams and
Mele, made in several places. Adams and Mele treat an issue related but
somewhat different from the one I am discussing (in one place, they call this
'the status of subsidiary actions'), and their proposal follows the outline of
an earlier suggestion by Alvin Goldman.[30] In his 'Acting for Reasons and
Acting Intentionally', Mele is concerned with intentional action, not just
action, but the strategy is again the same: 'The various strokes may be intentional in virtue of their particular relation to a "larger" intentional action
(swimming a lap, say) that is done for a reason.'[31]

As Goldman argued, my mental states can rationalize my taking twelve
steps in all, without a separate and distinct mental state rationalizing every
single step included in those twelve. Goldman's and Mele's view may reflect

---

[30] Goldman, *A Theory of Human Action*, 88–91. Frederick Adams and Alfred Mele, 'The
Role of Intention in Intentional Action', *Canadian Journal of Philosophy*, 19, 1989: 511–32.

[31] Mele, 'Acting for Reasons and Acting Intentionally', 356.

welcome common sense, and I fully accept the view, but I do not believe that
it is a view that is available to the CTA.

Let us distinguish between actions and their parts. If the actions which
are preceded by no belief or desire are such that they are parts of larger
actions which are so preceded by a suitable desire-and-belief pair, and hence
which are rationalized, then it may be that the former qualify as being
rationalized and as being actions simply in virtue of being parts of 'larger'
actions which qualify in their own right. So, the idea would be that there
may be action parts for which we have no relevant beliefs or desires, but
these are merely parts of larger actions, and we can always find relevant
beliefs and desires for the latter.

I must have, let us suppose, a relevant mental state whose content concerns the whole stretch of activity, painting, shaving, tying a knot, embracing a person, dancing, riding a bicycle, but, the reply might continue, I
surely need not have a distinct rationalizing belief whose content concerns
only lifting my left arm to the canvas, or bringing my razor from cheek to
chin, or gyrating my hips, or balancing myself, and so on. The idea is that
the rationalizing is of the whole action, and spreads inward, as it were, to
the action's parts, in virtue of their being parts of the whole action. What is
it, it might be asked, to rationalize a whole action unless so doing just is to
rationalize all of its parts? The parts are rationalized by a belief and a desire
because the whole of which they are parts is rationalized by that belief and
desire; the parts are actions because the whole of which they are parts is an
action.

What is this reply proposing? The idea must be that a basic action, like
my waving of the hand or my lifting of my arm, is either a movement or
event that is *itself* rationalized, or it is a movement or event which is a part
of a larger activity, and it is the latter that is rationalized. Presumably, the
account of action now proposed is disjunctive:

> (CTA′) a movement of X's body, m, is X's token basic action iff *either*
> (a) m is rationalized and caused in the right way by X's mental states,
> *or* (b) there is some activity or larger action y (where y is a whole made
> up of such movements), y is itself rationalized and caused in the right
> way by X's mental states, and m is a part of y.

Call this 'the amended CTA'. If this is the proposal, then immediately a further difficulty arises. If actions can have parts that are not actions, then the
disjunctive account is too permissive. It would wrongly convert some non-
actions into actions. Do actions have at least some non-action parts?

A logically prior question is whether some or all actions have any parts at all. Judith Jarvis Thomson assumes that at least some do, and uses at least two quite different sorts of examples.[32] One type of example includes items we would naturally think of as activities, in terms of my distinction in Chapter 2; house-cleaning is her example. Her other, and perhaps more famous example, is Sirhan Sirhan's assassination of Robert Kennedy.

The latter example is controversial. Since she regards SS's pulling the trigger as only part of, and hence not identical to, his assassination of RK, the latter must have, she says, some further part that the former lacks. Indeed, she regards RK's death as just that additional part of SS's assassination of RK. Some will dispute whether an event like someone's death can be a part of an action. Austere theorists will reject this, but so too will some versions of prolific theory. (A prolific theorist might say that an event intrinsic to an action might not count as a part of that action.) But her parts thesis might be right about the house-cleaning and not about the assassination. So let me restrict the discussion to the first sort of example.

Recall the discussion of activities in Chapter 2. Surely Thomson is right that activities like house-cleaning have parts: vacuuming the floor, dusting the mantelpiece, polishing the table, washing the dishes. In turn, those actions can also be thought of as activities with further action parts. The activity of washing the dishes is not itself a single bodily movement, but is made up of many different bodily movements. So, many activities and actions are not identical with any single movement of the body, even if they are merely ordered sets of such movements. On any plausible theory of action, there will be some actions or activities with parts. House-cleaning, then, shows two things: that at least some actions have parts; that some parts of actions are themselves actions.

Since at least some actions and activities have parts that are also actions, we are faced with the following trilemma: either (a) every action has parts, all of which are actions, or (b) some actions have no parts at all, or (c) some actions have parts, at least some of which are not actions. I discuss each of (a), (b), and (c), and dismiss the first two. If (c) is true, then the disjunctive account cannot save the CTA, since the disjunctively amended CTA, (CTA'), entails (c)'s falsity.

(a) Suppose every action has parts, all of which are themselves actions. This would lead to an infinite regress, but the regress does not seem to be a vicious one. There is no viciousness in the regress that between every pair of

---

[32] Judith Jarvis Thomson, *Acts and Other Events*, Ithaca, NY and London: Cornell University Press, 1977.

points, there is another point, or that every physical object has parts, all of which are themselves physical objects. If there is something wrong with (*a*), it is something further. I have two arguments against (*a*).

(*a*1) The most well-behaved sense of 'whole' and 'part' that we have is the mereological sense, governed by various definitions and axioms, including the theorem of universal summability.[33] The theorem of universal summability tells us that any two things can be summed. The things are the parts of that sum.

I assume that the is-a-part-of relation is transitive (if *x* is a part of *y* and *y* is a part of *z*, then *x* is a part of *z*). Consider an action *a* with two action parts, *b* and *c*. Either *b* and *c* will have further parts which are actions or not. If not, the parts of *b* and *c* are not actions, and then not all the parts of *a* are actions. *a*, *b*, and *c* would all be actions with parts which are not actions, contrary to (*a*).

Suppose, on the other hand, that the parts of *b* are actions *d* and *e*, and the parts of *c* are actions *f* and *g*. So far, all the parts of actions are actions, as (*a*) claims. But summability allows us to consider the gerrymandered entities, {*d,f*} and {*e,g*}. These are not actions, any more than gerrymandered people are people (half of you or your mental states, plus half of me, or my mental states).

Yet {*d,f*} and {*e,g*} are parts of *a*. *d* is a part of *a* by transitivity and *f* is a part of *a* by transitivity. There is a sum, {*d,f*}, by summability. {*d,f*} is neither a part of *b* or of *c*. But it is a part of *a*. If all the sum's parts are parts of *a*, then the sum is itself a part of *a*, at least in the sense of 'improper part' (like 'improper subset'), the sense which allows a thing to be a part of itself.

So not all the parts of *a* are actions; (*a*) is false. I follow Judith Jarvis Thomson (but not for her reasons) in thinking that many acts with parts have both act-parts and parts that are not themselves acts: '. . . it must surely be granted . . . that a person's acts may have among their parts events that are not acts of his'.[34]

(*a*2) Perhaps it might be felt that the above result only shows that we should be using a more natural sense of 'part' than the rather technical one provided for us by mereology, that allows for this strange summability. And it might be hoped that in this less technical sense of 'part', all the parts of actions are themselves actions. If so, (*a*) might be vindicated.

---

[33] Nelson Goodman, *The Structure of Appearance*, Indianapolis: Bobbs-Merrill, 1977, ch. II, sect. 4; Nicholas Rescher, 'Axioms for the Part Relation', *Philosophical Studies*, 6, 1955: 8–11.
[34] Thomson, *Acts and Other Events*, 52.

There are indeed more natural, less technical, senses of 'part', but none that I know that render (*a*) true. Some hold that an event like the death of the Queen or of Robert Kennedy can be a part of an agent's action like his bending of his finger or his pulling of the trigger. If so, some actions certainly have parts that are not themselves actions. But let me eschew such controversial examples and restrict the argument to cases that only involve action parts which are also movements of or changes in the agent's body.

I act and, when or while I act, parts of my body merely move and change. The latter may occur as parts of my activity, in one very natural and ordinary sense of 'part'. But the latter are not actions, and yet, if (*a*) were true, they would wrongly come out as actions. For example, dilation of the blood vessels is a crucial part of exercising. Salivation is a part, indeed an essential part, of eating. One can't eat unless it occurs. And perhaps the best example of all, mentioned earlier: essential to and a part of (a male's) engaging in sexual intercourse is the occurrence of his erection.

Once one gets the hang of it, examples making the same point can be produced endlessly. It is obvious that lots of activities or 'large' or extended actions have non-actional parts, many of which are quite essential to them, in any reasonable sense of 'part' I can think of. So (*a*) must be wrong.

(*b*) Perhaps some actions have no parts at all. (*a*) asserted that all actions had parts, all of which were actions. Denial of (*a*) is consistent with the view that some actions have no parts at all, but the actions that do have parts have only actions as their parts. (Of course, one would then not wish to deny (*a*) by using the cases I have used above, since they are cases of actions with non-actional parts.) Is there anything to be said against the view that some actions have no parts at all?

How could there be partless actions? Surely actions at least have fractional parts, like moving a finger a half-inch, or a millionth of an inch, or whatever. In Chapter 2, I canvassed different possibilities about these fractional movings of some small but determinate distance *d*: that they are not actions at all, that they are actions but not basic, because of an infinite regress in the by-relation regarding them, that they are basic actions because they are not done by doing anything else at all, or that they are basic actions because they were not done by doing anything else disjoint from them.

But whichever option is chosen, every physical action has such parts. We can demonstrate that any spatially situated action whatsoever has parts, by making ever-finer spatial discriminations. And this is enough of a basis on which to reject (*b*). That all actions have fractional parts must be the case at least for physical actions, since any physical action will be spatially situated. Whether they are actions or not in their own right, they are parts of an action.

I believe that there are also mental actions, like thinking, deciding, and judging. If there are such things as temporal parts, and if actions have them, we can show, in a way analogous to the spatial parts of physical actions, that all mental acts, since they occupy some finite amount of time, have temporal parts. And if mental actions have temporal parts, physical actions surely have them too.[35]

So, if we reject (a) and (b), (c) must be true: some actions have parts, at least some of which are not actions. Examples were offered above. But I do not see how to distinguish between acts that are proper parts of the shave and non-actional, perhaps gerrymandered, events that are also proper parts of the shave, unless we already have the distinction in place between actions and non-actional items. We can't read off which parts of an action are themselves actions merely from their being parts of the whole action, as (CTA′) supposes; we must already know which of the parts of an action are themselves actions and which are not, independently of their being those parts, and so (CTA′) is of no help in providing a criterion or definition of actionhood.

I want to stress, so that there can be no misunderstanding, that it is not my view that we do need to postulate beliefs that specifically involve each of these sub-acts of a larger act; such a view would be clearly absurd. That view would overpopulate the mind in such a way as to make the original version of the CTA look quite abstemious in that regard. I do not doubt in the least that, in many cases of action, the action I perform can be broken up into smaller action units, concerning which I have no specific beliefs.

But the point, to repeat, is this: this perfectly acceptable thought is of no help to the CTA, since those smaller actions do not acquire their status as actions by being parts of the large action of which they are parts, which is what the amended CTA that we are imagining would require. On my view, they are actions, in spite of the absence of beliefs that rationalize them, and in spite of their not inheriting their actional status from their being parts of larger actions.

My argument is that, if the CTA were to be taken seriously, it could not rely at this point on the distinction between acts and events but must

---

[35] For the question of whether events, states, continuants, and so on, have spatial or temporal 'aspects', see Helen Steward, *The Ontology of Mind*, Oxford: Oxford University Press, 1997.

explain that distinction. Therefore, what the CTA would need to maintain is that, since it is an action, the lifting of my left arm from chin to cheek is rationalized by the mental events that cause it (and not just caused by those same beliefs and desires that cause and rationalize the large act of which it is a proper part). So we are back, on the CTA, to the need for left-arm-lifting beliefs after all, and not just whole-shaving-involving ones. Since there may not be, and typically will not be, any of the former, the CTA, amended or not, fails as an account of actionhood.

I conclude that there is no way available to the CTA of getting the parts to inherit the property of being an act from the action wholes of which they are the parts. Actionhood does not spread from the whole into the parts; on the contrary, it is the actional status of (some) parts that spreads outward and makes the whole an action or activity.

Mental action

In the remainder of this chapter, I want to discuss how the CTA might deal with certain cases of mental action. I defined what I meant by the CTA in the previous chapter in terms of a view about basic physical action. If there are cases of basic mental action, the CTA will owe us an account of them as well (and it will also have to produce a plausible story about non-basic mental action, if such there be). And I think there are cases of basic mental action: if I do form an intention, there is no action I do such that I form that intention by doing it.

I believe that I initiated discussion of the difficulty the CTA encounters with mental action.[36] (Pardon the arrogance.) I considered the case of mental action. I called such mental actions 'spontaneous'. A spontaneous mental action is not one that has no causes, for if there is universal causation, there is nothing like that. (I take no stand in this book on the issue of universal causation, one way or another.)

Nor is a spontaneous action one which has no causes internal to the agent, whether neurophysiological or psychological, since a causal pathway to a mental action must surely go through some neurophysiological mechanism of the agent, and often also does go through some of his mental life, mental events or happenings or whatever. Spontaneous mental actions neither pop up in us altogether uncaused, nor pop up uncaused by any of our internal goings-on.

[36] In 'Mental Overpopulation and the Problem of Action', *Journal of Philosophical Research*, 20, 1995: 511–24.

A spontaneous mental action, if such there be, is one that has no ration-alizing mental cause. That is,

> Token mental action *a* is a spontaneous mental action iff there is no cause of *a* which also rationalizes *a*.

A spontaneous mental act could have mental as well as neurophysiological causes, as long as the former do not rationalise the act they cause. Thus, 'spontaneous', as I use it, is really elliptical for 'spontaneous relative to rationalizing mental states or events'. I think that there are spontaneous physical as well as mental actions, but I concentrate only on the latter here.

If there are such acts, the CTA is false, for the CTA analyses actions as events with non-deviantly rationalizing causes. If the CTA is a thesis about all action, whether physical or mental, and if it is false in the case of some mental action, then the CTA fails.

Consider these examples: we are confined to a small room, in which someone shouts 'Fire!', and I begin to evaluate different escape routes and I decide how I shall escape. Or, in response to a question about the identity of the twelfth president of the United States,[37] I search my memory for his name. Finally, in a job interview, I am asked a difficult question about my work, so I consider as rapidly as I can the plausibility of alternative replies before responding to the question.

In such case, I am likely to have standing desires that may figure in my current mental landscape. No doubt, I desire to stay alive in the first ex-ample, desire to name the twelfth president in the second, desire to give a plausible reply to my questioner in the third. Had I not had the desire in question, I would not have engaged in the mental activity in which I did engage. The standing desires are (part) causes, motivators, and explainers of my subsequent mental action. But they cannot, on their own, rationalize the mental actions they cause, motivate, or explain.

What is uncompelling, in these examples, is the idea that such mental activity is the outcome of any strategic plan, a plan which would require a belief, even a dispositional one, as well as the standing desire. It is the absence of a plan that justifies the title of 'spontaneous' for such mental actions. When I evaluate means of escape, or decide my escape route, or search my memory for the name, or consider replies to a question, I do not normally have the belief, occurrently or dispositionally, that such metal activity is an efficient means to some further end, namely, the ends of escap-ing, recalling the name, or giving the appropriate reply. I just evaluate,

---

[37] Ah, so you want to know? Zachary Taylor.

search, and consider spontaneously, naturally, in response to my circumstances and situation.

Nature has no doubt wired me up, just as it does in the case of the skilled physical actions that I have already discussed, so that what I do in these cases is just as good, perhaps better, than what I would do if I did have such a plan. In the *Groundwork*, Kant asserts that the purpose of reason cannot be the achieving of human happiness, since human happiness is better achieved by instinct rather than reason. He says: 'Let us take for a principle that in [an organic being] no organ is to be found for any end unless it is also the most appropriate for that end and the best fitted for it'.[38]

In similar vein, whether or not Kant was right in general, it is so with mental action and belief. In the case of some mental action, given the desires, spontaneity is more effective than belief. Spontaneous mental action is action better taken without a plan. That I evaluate, decide, memory-search, and consider, all these have great survival value. But to say that is certainly not to concede that some actual belief, occurrent or dispositional, must precede and cause that mental activity. In particular, I do not have the belief that, by evaluating escape routes, and by deciding on one, or by searching my memory, or by considering alternative replies, I would be better positioned to save my life or recall the name of the twelfth president, or give an adequate account of myself in the interview.

I evaluate and decide upon an escape route. I have a standing desire to live, and I surely have a belief that I am in great danger. No doubt, those motivate and cause my considering and escaping. I have no doubt that the spontaneous mental activity is exactly in what I should be engaging in those circumstances. But without some instrumental belief, there is no rationalization in the sense required by the CTA. Without the instrumental belief, the standing desire and belief about danger don't themselves determine what course of action is rational for me in the circumstances.

Very often, one catches oneself engaging in mental activity, almost unawares. For example, I may be working on a crossword puzzle that I cannot solve. I realize that I have devoted more time to the project than it warrants, and so I resolve to stop thinking about the puzzle. But in a few moments, when that firm resolve is no longer before my mind in a salient manner, I find myself back at it, trying to solve the puzzle. Or, I go to a classical music concert, wishing to concentrate on the music. Before I know it, my mind has wandered, as we say, and I realize that I am actively thinking

[38]   I. Kant, *Moral Law*, ed. H. J. Paton, London: Hutchinson, 1969: 60–1.

about something else, some mundane affair of the day. These are all cases, it seems to me, of spontaneous mental action.

In a Humean vein, nature takes over where reason is wanting. I am naturally, but not rationally, caused to engage in these examples of mental activity. There may be other cases of mental activity for which the account offered by the CTA will work, but it does not work for the cases I have introduced. Since so much of characteristically human action is caused by the agent's own plan of action, it is forgivable if one forgets that quite a lot of action does not have such a plan (and instrumental beliefs) amongst its causes. The mental activity may be objectively purposeful, in the sense that it has or serves some sort of purpose, but it does not follow that it is part of the agent's own action plan, and hence it does not require the existence of the sorts of beliefs that would be required if it were part of his plan.

Higher-Order Beliefs and Intentions

John Bishop, using some of David Velleman's interesting ideas, has attempted to deal with my counter-examples to the CTA that involve mental actions.[39] If the CTA holds for mental actions, says Bishop, this will be true: every token mental action (say, an agent's forming the intention to purposively wiggle his ears) is identical to its intrinsic event (say, the formation of an intentional state with the appropriate content) that is rationalized by its causes. (Unlike my statement of the CTA for mental action, Bishop's is not neutral on the mind/body issue, and says that the action's intrinsic event will be 'constituted' by a certain neural state.)

What might the rationalizing cause be in this example? As Bishop says: 'we must supply this event with a causal history involving mental states which constitute Jimmy's reasons for forming his intention to wiggle his ears'. Bishop's own solution to the mental events that rationalize the mental activity they cause uses the idea of higher-order mental states: 'In order to do this, we have to be prepared, I believe, to posit higher-order intentions' (p. 260). Velleman himself spoke of higher-order desires, and in particular the desire to act in accordance with reasons.

The idea, in brief, is that one has 'certain higher-order intentions classifiable generally as intentions to act in accordance with the canons of practical rationality'. Examples cited by Bishop include: the intention to form

[39] John Bishop, 'Naturalising Mental Action', in Ghita Holmström-Hintikka and Raimo Tuomela, eds., *Contemporary Action Theory*, 1, Dordrecht: Kluwer Academic Press, 1997: 251–66. Quote from p. 260.

intentions consistently with one's all-things-considered judgements about what it is best to do; the intention to make reasonable judgements about what it is all-things-considered best to do; the intention that conflicts amongst his desires should be settled somehow.

In the last chapter, I gave voice to doubts about whether there is any real sense in which intentions can rationalize actions. These concerns, if well founded there about ordinary intentions, should apply *mutatis mutandis* to higher-order intentions. In fact, the case here seems to me even stronger: Bishop offers no example of a higher-order intention, as far as I can see, which would rationalize an agent's forming an intention to wiggle his ears, in the sense of 'rationalize' that we have identified as available to the CTA. His higher-order mental states do not provide premises for a 'valid' practical syllogism that has something about the mental action to be rationalized as its conclusion. There appears to be some sort of conceptual 'gap' between all the higher-order intentions in the premises that he mentions and the mental action (forming an intention to purposively wiggle his ears) to be rationalized in the conclusion, with no indications of the beliefs, desires, intentions, or whatever that would be required to bridge that conceptual gap between those (alleged) premises and conclusion.

What I want to do here is to repeat the argument from unavailability that I have used elsewhere, and to question the existence of these higher-order intentions, and other higher-order mental states as well, at least in the abundance the theory would require, and hence their availability to do the task Bishop attributes to them. My scepticism here is much like my scepticism about the ubiquity of intentions or beliefs that I have already expressed.

Harry Frankfurt introduced the idea of higher-order mental states, namely desires about one's desires, into the contemporary philosophical literature.[40] I certainly agree that there are many higher-order mental states: desires about desires, preferences about preferences, beliefs about beliefs.[41] Frankfurt introduced the idea as a way of explicating something essential in our concept of a person. But now it seems that the general strategy has got entirely out of hand. I am extremely sceptical about many of the higher-order states that Bishop, and others, introduce when their theory needs them. They seem to be part of the problem of mental overpopulation.

But one might ask: isn't it the case that I do have these sorts of desires, and

---

[40] Harry Frankfurt, 'Freedom of the Will and the Concept of a Person', repr. in his *The Importance of What we Care about*, Cambridge: Cambridge: University Press, 1988.

[41] See e.g. Richard Jeffrey, 'Preference among Preferences', *Journal of Philosophy*, 71, 1974: 377–91.

intentions, even if they are standing desires and intentions? Don't I *intend* to be continent (intend to form intentions consistently with my judgements about what it is overall best to do), don't I *want* to settle conflicts between desires somehow, and so on? It seems odd to deny that I have these higher-order dispositional mental states. But I think Audi's distinction between believing dispositionally and being disposed to belief can be used once again, now applied to higher-order desires and intentions as well as to beliefs.

The oddity of denying that agents have these higher-order mental states arises because, if asked, an agent would reply that he does so intend or want. But these are higher-order mental states that the agent comes to have when asked (in virtue of his dispositions to have them), not states that he already has and on which he is merely reporting. Just as agents have dispositions to believe, they also have dispositions to intend and to desire. But these are not the same as (higher-order) desires or intentions.

But if the reader has doubts about the above argument, resting as it does on Audi's distinction, there is a different way to argue the case, focussing on my specific examples above. Even if Bishop's higher-order intentions worked for his example, I see no way in which to harness them for my examples. What higher-order intentions or desires will rationalize my conjecturing of solutions to the puzzle, my searching of my memory for the presidential name, or my thinking about mundane affairs at the concert? There seem to be no high-falutin canons of continence or practical rationality that have any part in the story to be told here. There is nothing on offer to bridge the gap between the higher-order mental states that Bishop cites and the spontaneous mental activity I have described. Simply put, unlike Bishop's case of forming intentions, the high-falutin canons do not appear to have anything to do with the mental activity in my cases.

Others have variations on the same higher-order theme. Another example is Michael Bratman.[42] I am not proposing to undertake a general view of Frankfurt's work, to which Bratman is in large measure responding, or of Bratman's response, but I do wish to make a few observations. First, I am not entirely clear that I understand what the problem is that Bratman (and Frankfurt, in some passages) is addressing; Bratman calls it the problem of 'full-blown agency' or 'agential authority'. I do not know if this is the same problem as the one that I have been discussing: the analysis of what it

---

[42] Michael Bratman, 'Two Problems about Human Agency', *Proceedings of the Aristotelian Society 2000–1*, n.s., vol. 101, London, 2001: 309–26.

is for some token movement to be an action. But let me suppose it is, although I am not at all confident about this supposition.

Construed in this way, Frankfurt's idea would be to make higher-order desires crucial to agency (and not just to personhood). In response to criticism that a second-order desire was just another desire among others, and therefore could not introduce the idea of agency if ordinary desire could not, Frankfurt responded in two different ways, in order to give the second-order desires some special significance. First, he said that the agent will be satisfied with his second-order desires, but might not be with his ordinary desires. Second, he claimed that the second-order desires have a 'volitional necessity' for the agent, in a way in which first-order desires may not have, that second-order desires have a categorical quality for the agent, a quality that may be lacking in ordinary desires.

Bratman dismisses both suggestions, rightly I think; the first is too weak, and the second too strong, a requirement, in order to account for full-blown agency. The first is too weak because 'Frankfurtian satisfaction with a desire may itself be rooted in a background of enervation, depression, exhaustion, or the like' (p. 314). Call this agent, who is less than a full-blown agent, 'the merely satisfied agent'. Satisfaction is insufficient for full agency, according to Bratman's criticism of Frankfurt, whether the desire is ordinary or higher order.

The second requirement is too strong, because many full agents don't feel that there is no alternative to their being driven by their second-order desires, if that is what 'volitional necessity' is meant to indicate. Second-order desires may not present themselves in this categorical way to agents, just as first-order desires may not do so. It is possible for an agent to take or leave acting on his desires, of the first-, or second-, or n-order variety.

Bratman's suggestion is meant to move beyond Frankfurt's two criteria for the centrality of second-order desires in accounting for full agency. His proposal is that a is an agent's token action iff (roughly) a is a product of the agent's 'higher-order intentions, plans, and policies' (p. 320). Bratman connects these plans and policies with the crucial feature of the temporal extendedness of agency. It is, says Bratman, when an agent's long-term intentions, plans, and policies about his activity drive the action that the action is fully his.

I cannot see how Bratman's solution improves on Frankfurt's at all; if the latter fails, so too, I think, does Bratman's. Frankfurt said that second-order desires were special because the agent will be satisfied with them. Bratman argued that such satisfaction might be 'rooted in a background of enervation, depression, exhaustion, or the like', and hence that satisfaction with higher-order desires had no special significance in understanding full-blown agency.

But might the same be said for long-term plans and policies? If agents are satisfied with them, can we not paraphrase Bratman's own point: might not their satisfaction with such long-term plans and policies be 'rooted in a background of enervation, depression, exhaustion, or the like'? Many people may wander into a way of life, out of lack of imagination, inertia, and so on. For example, someone may become an accountant, simply because his father and grandfather were. He may develop long-term plans and strategies connected with this way of life. His satisfaction with his long-term plans and policies will have the same insignificance for the problem of agency as Bratman argues that satisfaction with higher-order desires has. If satisfaction fails regarding second-order desires, it is going to fail when added to plans and policies too. In so far as the agent is satisfied with his long-term plans and policies, it may only be the same passive satisfaction that we encountered in the agent satisfied with his second-order desires. He may not be the full-blown agent of what he does, may not fully identify with his actions, any more than the first satisfied agent was.

Of course, I do not claim to have exhausted the resources of Bratman's theory, let alone that of others, in establishing a case for the centrality of higher-order mental states to agency. There is indeed much more to be said. Let me conclude my very short discussion on this topic by merely reiterating my scepticism about the strategy. In many cases, the attribution of these higher-order mental states seems to me to be merely the attribution to the agent of certain kinds of dispositions to form mental states. Even in those cases in which it is plausible to attribute any such higher-order mental states to agents, and not just dispositions to form such, the argument remains overly sketchy about how, in the company of what else, they are meant to rationalize anything.

Finally, it is not clear that Bratman intends for their centrality to agency to be via rationalization at all. The requirement that Bratman proposes (at least in the paper of his that I am discussing) seems to be merely causal: that the activity be the product of the agent's long-term plans, higher-order intentions, and so on. But that cannot be right: unadorned causality won't do the job by itself (any more than it could with belief–desire pairs and actions). There must be some conceptual match between the content of the higher-order intentions or long-term plans and the activity. And that will place rationalization, or something close to it, back on the agenda.

5

More Theories

The second theory of action that I want to discuss is the Agent Causalist Theory (hereafter, the ACT). The ACT has received several different formulations. Two of its earlier contemporary exponents were Richard Taylor and Roderick Chisholm.[1] Irving Thalberg's 'How Does Agent Causality Work?' presents a detailed examination of the views of both authors, and especially of some of the many changes in its different presentations by Chisholm.[2] I refer the reader to Thalberg, and will not attempt to reduplicate what he says here. Recently, the ACT has had newer exponents. Three of these are Timothy O'Connor, John Bishop, and Randolph Clarke.[3]

O' Connor, in *Persons and Causes*, proposes to give an account of action in agent causalist terms. He also provides an analysis and discussion of Taylor's and Chisholm's positions, as well as a statement of his disagreements with Clarke on various matters. Clarke, on the other hand, offers an analysis of free action, and not of action *tout court*. Clarke says that 'Agent causation is a relation, the first relatum of which is an agent or a person and the second relatum of which is an event'. What event might that be?

---

[1] e.g. Roderick Chisholm, 'Freedom and Action', in Keith Lehrer, ed., *Freedom and Determinism*, Random House, New York, 1966: 11–44; Richard Taylor, *Action and Purpose*, Prentice-Hall, Englewood Cliffs, NJ, 1966.

[2] Irving Thalberg, 'How does Agent Causality Work?', in M. Brand and D. Walton, eds., *Action Theory*, Dordrecht: Reidel, 1976: 213–38. A rethought version of Thalberg's article occurs as ch. 7 of his *Misconceptions of Mind and Freedom*, Lanham, Md.: University Press of America, 1983: 153–84. It is from this revised version that I shall mainly be quoting.

[3] Timothy O'Connor, *Persons and Causes*, Oxford and New York: Oxford University Press, 2000; Timothy O'Connor, 'Agent Causation', 173–200, and Randolph Clarke, 'Toward a Credible Agent-Causal Account of Free Will', 201–15, both in Timothy O'Connor, *Agents, Causes, Events*, Oxford and New York: Oxford University Press, 1995; John Bishop, 'Agent-Causation', *Mind*, 92, 1983: 61–79. Quotes in the paragraph below are from Clarke, 'Toward a Credible Agent-Causal Account of Free Will', 207.

Clarke says: 'What is directly caused [by the agent] is her acting for a particular ordering of reasons'.

I am unclear about the metaphysics of Clarke's account. What sort of event, or entity, is acting-for-a-particular-ordering-of-reasons? It seems itself to be neither an event nor an action, but a fact: the fact that the agent acted for such and such an ordering of reasons. However, be that as it may, I shall not consider Clarke's account further in this chapter, since it is an account of free action and not just of action.

I will present two composite versions of the ACT, each extracted from the writings of more than one writer, and each of which overlooks many of the differences between them. Given the variety of views that have gone under this label, and the different nuances between them, it is, I think, easy to get so lost looking at each tree that the philosophical woods become quite invisible. I am aiming to get an overview of the woods.

The Agent Causalist Theory is intended to be an alternative to the CTA. On this view, my bringing about an event must be sharply distinguished from my brain state bringing it about, or even my belief and desire or intention bringing it about. 'When I believe that I have done something, I do believe that it was I who caused it to be done, I who made something happen, and not merely something within me, such as one of my own subjective states, which is not identical with myself.'[4]

According to the ACT, in action, I, but no proper part of me like a brain or mental state, am causally responsible for the event. The ACT does not have the problem that the CTA has in explaining activity on the basis of the apparent passivity of events; the idea of an agent making something occur is intended to capture the idea of activity and hence to dispose of the problem of passivity.

ACT theorists differ over the question of whether event and agent causation embody two distinct concepts of causation, or whether event and agent causation are merely two different applications of a single primitive concept of causation. I suppose that there could even be an agent causalist who argued that *all* causation was, basically and irreducibly, causation by a substance (including persons as a type of substance) of an event. But the action causal theorist in whom I am interested wants to draw a contrast between event and agent causation, as a way of marking off actions from non-actional items, so for him causation will come in two sorts, whether these

---

[4] Richard Taylor, *Metaphysics*, Englewood Cliffs, NJ: Prentice-Hall, 1992: 48.

are two concepts of causation or two applications of a single concept: agent causation and event causation.

So, perhaps most characteristically, the ACT disputes a central contention of most views about causality, and certainly a view embodied in the CTA, namely, the thesis of event causation:

(TEC) the causal relation always relates events (or facts about events, this difference being unimportant in the present context).

Of course, even the event causation thesis can accept that statements like the following are meaningful: 'John caused me to leave the party'; 'The brick broke the window'; 'The rain rusted the iron'; 'God created the Universe'. These four statements seem to attribute causal efficacy or powers to physical substances or to agents.

What the event causation thesis requires is that such statements be equivalent to some statement which asserts that some event involving the substance or agent (perhaps, John's obnoxious behaviour, the brick's striking the window, the rain's oxidizing the iron, God's saying, 'Let there be light') caused the party leaving, the window breaking, the iron rusting, and the creation of the Universe, respectively.

Many philosophers have asserted the truth of the TEC. C. J. Ducasse is one such: '. . . nothing can, in strict propriety, ever be spoken of as a cause or effect, except an event . . . objects themselves . . . never can properly be spoken of as causes and effects . . .'.[5] Ducasse also adds that 'by an event is to be understood either a change or an absence of change . . .'. It is common for proponents of the TEC to understand 'event' sufficiently widely to include what are sometimes called unchanges or non-changes as well as changes.

And well they might, for it may have been the presence of helium in the balloon (a state) that caused the balloon both to rise (an event or process) to the ceiling and to remain there (a state), or it may have been the humidity in the room (a state) that brought about a person's asthma attack (an event), or a second person's not replying to a first person's question (an omission or forbearance) that caused the first to become so infuriated with the second (an event).

For the ACT, on the other hand, there is, in addition to event causation, even when expanded to include unchanges, another quite distinctive kind

---

[5] C. J. Ducasse, 'On the Logic and Epistemology of the Causal Relation', in Ernest Sosa and Michael Tooley, eds., *Causation*, Oxford: Oxford University Press, 1993, 126.

of causation, the very sort that Ducasse was at pains to deny in the above quotation, namely, agent causation: a person can directly cause or bring about something, in a sense irreducible to event causation. The ACT asserts that there are, or can be, true assertions which attribute causal efficacy to persons, and that such assertions cannot be understood in the reductive way which the TEC requires.

What will the ACT say about assertions that appear to attribute causal efficacy to substances other than agents? Even for the ACT, don't chemical agents cause various reactions? Chemical agents are not agents in the sense of 'agent' I explained at the beginning of Chapter 3. In order to obtain the contrast it needs, between *agent* causation and event causation, the ACT itself will also claim that, in the case of objects which are not truly agents in the specified sense, like chemical agents, all causal assertions *can* be wholly reformulated in terms of event causation. Only those assertions that are truly about the causal powers of agents in the specified sense are the ones that must be, for the ACT, incapable of such reformulation. If causal assertions about chemical agents and persons were both irreducible to event causation claims, we would not have any contrast between event and agent causation that would be at all useful for a theory of action.

The idea of agent causation has its roots in various remarks about causation by both Plato and Aristotle. For example: 'A staff moves a stone, and is moved by a hand, which is moved by a man' (*Physics* 256ª). However, this is not a bona-fide version of the ACT as I understand it. In Aristotle, there does not appear to be a contrast between agent and event causation; the efficient cause, for Aristotle, seems always to be an 'agent' in the wider sense that includes staffs, stones, hands, and persons. The ACT requires the narrower sense of 'agent' for its formulation, which excludes these things, chemical agents, and so on. Perhaps the earliest clear statement of an Agent Causalist Theory in the sense that I intend here is by Thomas Reid, in his *Essays on the Active Powers of the Human Mind.*[6]

Do any statements about the actions of non-human animals equally employ an idea of causation irreducible to event causation? For the ACT, does 'the dog caused the complaint' behave more like 'ammonia caused the explosion' or more like 'Abraham caused the destruction of his father's idols'? About this, I take it, the ACT has some room for manoeuvre. I once thought that only persons were agents. The case of non-human animals

[6] Thomas Reid, *Essays on the Active Powers of the Human Mind*, repr. by Cambridge, Mass.: MIT Press, 1969.

gives me pause, in making that claim. Animals might qualify as agents who act, but it would not be plausible to regard all of them as persons. Maybe some are persons, but certainly some which might plausibly be thought to be actors are not.

Although persons need certainly not be of our species (think of Mr Spock for example), personhood seems to require higher standards than mere (simple)[7] agency: moral capacity, for example, and perhaps certain basic conceptual abilities beyond the repertoire of non-human animals. The question here does not really concern the nature of action, but whether any non-human animals count as agents, and on this the ACT could in principle decide either way.[8]

Is the ACT, like the CTA, a 'naturalistic' theory in any interesting sense? On the one hand, its postulation of agent causality is not naturalistic, since no such causal relation can be found in any of the sciences. But, as we proceed in our analysis, we shall find other ways in which there are very strong similarities between the CTA and the ACT. I gave the reader a preview of this in Chapter 3.

So, for the ACT, there are irreducible statements of causal relation, whose first term at least is an agent rather than an agent-involving event, or rather than a fact about such an agent-involving event. It is the whole agent who is a cause, where this is not just shorthand for a more accurate statement that takes happenings or occurrences involving the agent (be they mental or neurophysiological) as the cause.

The ACT, as I interpret it, only offers an account of basic action (or, for readers unconvinced by Chapter 1, action under its basic description), often understood as the movements of the agent's body or motions in the agent's brain, and I will confine myself to such in what follows.[9] I agree with John Bishop: '. . . the dispute between event- and agent-causalists properly emerges with the analysis of basic action . . . it is here that the agent-causalist professes to find an irreducible causal relation between agent and event'.

It is this restriction to basic action that is caught by the qualification 'direct', in the idea that an agent can be a direct cause in a way irreducible to event causation. For the ACT, every basic action is or involves a *direct* moving of a part of the body or a direct bringing about of a brain or mental

---

[7] I am not thinking of Frankfurt's full agency, but only agency which makes statements of the form '*P* did *a*' sometimes true. These may be different, but I can't be sure because I have never fully understood what full agency (or whole-heartedness) is meant to be. See the end of Ch. 4 for some remarks on these issues.

[8] See Ch. 4 n. 28.   [9] Bishop, 'Agent-Causation', 62.

event by the agent. There are many cases in which an agent indirectly causes an event, even when such events include a moving of the agent's own body, for example, when I get my left hand to rise by pulling it up with my right hand, and no one would confuse my indirectly causing the rising of my left hand (and hence my indirectly raising my left hand) with my directly raising my left hand.

Such direct movings or bringings about will have increasingly distant effects in the world, and the relationship between the basic action, whatever it might be, and its worldly effects will be the ordinary sort of event causation. So, for example, the ACT theorist will, or could, treat my killing of the Queen in the same way as does the CTA theorist: my killing of the Queen requires that her death (an event) is caused by the event intrinsic to my shooting her (namely, the gun's discharge).

The difference between the two theorists is only noticeable at the level of basic action, my bending of my finger, or whatever other action the ACT theorist designates as basic. How shall we understand my bending of my finger? For the CTA, my bending of my finger is my finger's bending, when caused in the right way by rationalizing mental states or events. Hence, his analysis of basic action is fully compatible with the TEC. This is not so for the ACT. For the latter, I bend my finger when I, rather than any proper part of me, directly cause my finger's bending. To distinguish this kind or application of causation from event causation, I shall refer to it in what follows as 'agent causation'.

So I do not think of the ACT as a 'maximal' theory about the logical form of all action sentences; I restrict it to being a 'minimalist' theory about the analysis of statements of *basic* action in terms of what the agent directly causes. Sometimes Chisholm adds 'on purpose' to exclude cases of unintentional action: directly causing on purpose. For ease of exposition, I do not always add these qualifications.

There are problems enough for the minimalist theory. If the reader wants to understand the theory in the way that Chisholm himself did, as a maximalist theory, he is free to add to my statement of it. But I do not, unlike Davidson, ask it to deal with examples like: 'Alice broke the mirror'; 'He carved the roast'; or 'The doctor removed the patient's appendix'.[10] Although Chisholm does present his theory as a general analysis of action

---

[10] Donald Davidson, 'The Logical Form of Action Sentences', in *Essays on Actions and Events*, Oxford and New York: Clarendon Press, 1980: 105–48 (repr. with comments on various earlier criticisms). See pp. 112, 128.

sentences, I don't here take ACT to be playing in the same ballpark as Davidson's 'The Logical Form of Action Sentences'.

It is, of course, true, as Davidson says, that, whenever a man walks to the corner, there is some way he moves his body, but false that there is some way he moves his body every time he walks to the corner. I am not clear just what agent-causalist target Davidson thought this criticism was to intended to hit, but this is not, as far as I can tell, a criticism of the minimalist theory I am discussing.[11]

In agent causation, it is the agent who agent-causes something (on purpose). The relation is the relation of agent-causing. The domain of the relation is the set of agents. What is in the relation's range? That is, what is it that the agent agent-causes? What is the second relatum of the agent-causal relation?

On the ACT, when an agent (basically) acts, an agent directly causes or brings about an *event*. Different versions of the ACT differently identify that event: the event might be a movement of the body, or a brain event or a mental event. So, the domain of the relation is a set of bodily or brain movements, or mental events.[12]

But what is *the* action? On this, various ACT theories seem to differ. On one version of the theory, event-ACT (E-ACT), the action *is* the event or the sum of events that the agent agent-causes; that is, the action is to be identified as the second relatum of the relation. On another version of the theory, causings-ACT (C-ACT), the action *is* the agent-causing of the event or events. On E-ACT, even if there are agent-causings, they are not the same as actions. Of course, it would be a strange and unmotivated view that held that there were both agent-causings and actions, not to be identified, but below I will argue that E-ACT does not have to accept agent-causings as entities at all, at least not simply on the grounds that agents cause events.

If the agent agent-causes an event (as the E-ACT proposes) and if his action is that event, then does it not follow that the agent agent-causes his action? If the causal relation is extensional, this does indeed follow. I noted a similar sort of implication in my discussion of the CTA: if a belief and desire cause a movement intrinsic to an action and if the action = that movement, then the belief and desire cause the action. I do not think that this introduces any circularity into either the CTA or the E-ACT. Both

---

[11] ibid. 128.

[12] There is a complication, as Chisholm does not think that events are a fundamentally basic ontological item, but I will not go into this complication here.

non-circularly analyse an action as a movement of a certain type (one that is agent-caused by an agent; one that is caused by a belief and a desire). It simply follows, as a consequence of those analyses, that agents agent-cause actions or that beliefs and desires cause actions.

Donald Davidson appears to think of the ACT as accepting causings and hence as a C-ACT theory. Davidson is presumably thinking that the agent causalist holds that the event that 'x makes it happen that p' describes is the causing. Either the causing, he says, is identical to the basic action or it was distinct from the basic action.[13] I will not trace out Davidson's argument for the second horn of the dilemma, because that implausible combination gives us actions as well as agent-causings. If there are any agent-causings at all, surely it is they which are actions. If agent-causings do not even purport to solve the problem of agency, it is hard for me to see why anyone should favour their introduction.

Bishop and O'Connor also understand ACT as C-ACT: 'Since what constitutes a basic intentional action is the obtaining of an agent-causal relation . . .'; 'The theory is that actions consist in the causing by their agents of certain events or states of affairs';[14] S's causing e 'is intrinsically a doing'.[15] On C-ACT, there is but one item, referred to both as a basic action and as a direct causing by an agent, the latter description being used to illuminate the former.

So, the two versions of the ACT differ as to what exactly actions are. The E-ACT, rather like the CTA, makes basic actions events of a certain kind; the C-ACT makes basic actions *causings* of events. Both versions have tended to claim that they offer a solution to the question of the causation of basic action that is, in some way, distinctively indeterministic.[16] (I use 'indeterminism' as the name of the view that some events have no cause of any kind. I think of 'non-deterministic' as a type of causation, sometimes referred to as 'a probabilistic causation', and contrasted with deterministic causation. Clarke, for example, rejects indeterminism but thinks that the causes of free action are non-deterministic.[17]) Although I will say a few

[13] Donald Davidson, 'Agency', in his *Actions and Events*, 43–61. See 52–3.
[14] First quote from Bishop, 'Agent-Causation', 71. Second quote from John Bishop, *Natural Agency*, Cambridge: Cambridge University Press, 1989: 68. I suppose that the obtaining of the causal relation is a causing, but anyway Bishop is more explicit about this in his later book, from which the second quote is taken.
[15] O'Connor, 'Agent Causation', 186.
[16] But not Bishop. See his 'Agent-Causation', 76–7.
[17] Clarke, 'Toward a Credible Agent-Causal Account of Free Will'.

things relevant for understanding the extent to which either version of the ACT is committed to indeterminism, this is not an issue I examine in any depth.

So now we can distinguish between the (mere) event of my finger's moving and my moving of my finger. According to the E-ACT, the latter, but not the former, is an event, my finger's moving, such that I (and not just one of my rationalizing mental states) directly bring it about. According to the C-ACT, the latter, but not the former, is my direct causing of an event, my finger's moving. The ontology of the E-ACT includes: bodily or brain movements or mental events, agents, and the agent-causal relation. The ontology of the C-ACT includes: bodily or brain movements or mental events, agents, and causings ('the holding of the agent-causal relation', as O'Connor puts it).

Causings and their Causal Properties

Once C-ACT theories reify causings, causal properties are attributed to them: either causings cause certain events or causings are the effects of certain events, or both. Commitments to their causes (if any) and commitments to their effects (if any) need to be carefully distinguished. Also, commitments to their event-causes, if any, need to be distinguished from commitments to their agent-causes, if any.

As Chisholm put it, when we act freely, 'we cause certain events to happen, and nothing . . . causes us to cause those events to happen'.[18] He means by this that nothing so *event-causes* him. The idea would be that when an agent agent-causes an event, then, there is a causing of the event by the agent, and that causing event itself has no prior event cause. Taylor thinks that agent-causings do or can have event-causes; when they do, such agent-causings are not free.[19]

Chisholm does say at one point that, although not event-caused, the agent-causing is itself agent-caused: 'what we should say, I believe, is that . . . if a man contributes causally to the occurrence of . . . *e*, then he contributes causally to his contributing causally to the occurrence of [*e*]'.[20] And, in 'Agency', he accepts that 'if *s* does something that contributes causally to *p*, then *s* contributes causally to his doing something that

---

[18] Chisholm, 'Freedom and Action', 23.

[19] O'Conner, *Persons and Causes*, 52–5, where O'Connor tries to show that any ordinary talk of an event event-causing a causing cannot be taken as illuminating Taylor's claim.

[20] Quoted in Thalberg, *Misconceptions of Mind and Freedom*, 171.

contributes causally to p'.[21] Chisholm seems committed to an infinite regress of agent-causings. O'Connor, on the other hand, rejects the regress by claiming that causings have no cause of any kind; 'A's causing of e' is uncaused, that is, has no event-cause or agent-cause.[22]

Chisholm's infinite regress of agent-causings seems unattractive. Is it vicious? Probably not, since I may well do an infinite number of things any-way when I act, quite apart from the issue of agent-causings. It was no part of my argument in Chapter 2 against an unrestricted accordion effect that, were it true, it would have this implication. What would be a vicious regress would be a commitment to an agent's doing an infinite number of things, each of which requires extra effort on his part, and Chisholm is not com-mitted to that. But even if not a vicious regress, it seems to me unattractive none the less.

On the C-ACT, the action *is* the agent's agent-causing of e, which is itself supposed to be an event, call it e^*. We might accept, let us suppose, that e^* is, or may be, event-causeless (whether or not it is also agent-causeless). I want now to raise a difficulty different from that discussed by O'Connor, and others, regarding the causes of an agent-causing. My concern, rather, is with *what effects*, if any, can be attributed to agent-causings. What do agent-causings cause, rather than what causes might they themselves have? Surely agent-causings are not effectless; they must cause something.

Might one simply insist that e^* (an example of an agent-causing) has no effects? Might e^* cause nothing? If so, we could have an event, like e^*, which had no effects, no event-causes, and perhaps no agent-causes either. I can't really see, if such is the case, why e^* would qualify as an event at all. It would stand outside the event-causal order, lacking as it would not only causes but also effects. Moreover, the causing, on the C-ACT, *is* the action. So to hold that the causing has no effects is to hold that actions never cause anything! If there is anything we know about our actions, surely it is that sometimes at least they are causally responsible for bringing about certain results. So let's assume that e^*, which is the action on this version of the ACT, must cause something or other, that e^* must have some effect. But what effect might that be?

Consider first the analogous case for event causation. Suppose c event-causes e and suppose there were a distinct event, e^*, c's causing of e (distinct from both c and e, for otherwise there is no point in positing it). What could

[21] Roderick Chisholm, 'Agency', in *Person and Object*, London: Allen & Unwin, 1976: 53–88. Quote from p. 71.
[22] O'Connor, 'Agent Causation', 186; *Persons and Causes*, 58.

e^* itself cause, in this case? Whatever effect is a plausible candidate for what e^* brings about will involve us in overdetermination.[23] And I think that this problem is the same, whether e^* is the alleged event, c's event-causing e, or the alleged event, agent X's agent-causing of e.

Suppose we think that e^* causes e, where e^* is c's causing e. But c causes e, so e will be overdetermined, event-caused both by c and e^*. If e^* causes e, e^* and e must be distinct events. Since c and e^* are, by hypothesis, said to be distinct events, and since c also causes e, this is a genuine case of causal overdetermination.

Suppose, on the other hand, that we say that e^* does *not* cause e, but that e^* causes whatever e causes, say f. Again, that will be indirect causal overdetermination, now of f, by both e and e^*. I confronted overdetermination issues in previous chapters, but I cannot see how any of the ways in which I dealt with them there would work here. If there is some other candidate for an effect of e^*, other than e itself and/or whatever else e may have caused, it behoves the C-ACT theorist to tell us what it might be.

The case will not be different if we turn from event causation to agent causation, in which e^* is the agent's (and not c's) causing of e. There is nothing plausible for the event, e^*, the agent's causing of e, itself to cause that escapes overdetermination. If e^* (now, agent X's causing e) caused e, e would be oddly overdetermined, both event-caused by e^* (for e^*'s causing e would, presumably and somewhat amazingly, be merely an example of event causation), and agent-caused by X. (e^* and X are certainly not identical.)

And the same would apply, if what e^* caused was whatever e caused (say, it is f); f would then be event-caused both by e^* and e. That leaves us in a quandary about what it is that X's causing e might itself event-cause, when X agent-causes e. The view that now emerges seems to be that, if the agent-causing causes anything, it must causally overdetermine the same event as the agent himself agent-causes.[24]

Causings are not attractive. They make the theory of universal causal determination unattractive, and if the latter is unattractive, it surely can't be just for that reason. Suppose you think (1) that every event has a cause (whether an event-cause or an agent-cause or both). Suppose also that you think (2) that all assertions of the form, 'X (agent, event) caused e' require the existence of a causing event, X's causing e. Call X's causing e 'event c'.

---

[23] Overdetermination can be by stochastic or probabilistic causes, as well as by deterministic causes.

[24] For some discussion of this, see Thalberg, *Misconceptions of Mind and Freedom*, 166–7.

But, on the first assumption, c itself has a cause, d, so 'd caused c' is true. On the second assumption, that truth also requires the existence of a causing event, 'd's causing c', which I shall call 'g'. And of course g must have a cause. The result of the combination of these two assumptions will be to create a quite gratuitous infinite regress of events (like the one I attributed to Chisholm above).

I don't say that the regress is vicious; as I said above, it is not. We could accept an infinite number of events or actions. But it is, as I also said, gratuitous and unattractive. To break the regress, one would have to give up either (1) or (2). If we hold on to causings (2), then (1) would have to be rejected. We would reject causal determinism. Since many C-ACT theorists accept that their theories are indeterministic, this is hardly meant as a criticism of C-ACT.[25] But I propose, rather, to jettison (2). And even if we accepted that all or some causings had themselves no causes (so that universal causal determinism were false), the C-ACT view seems quite strange in its views about the effects of causings. But my main reservations about the C-ACT centre on my scepticism about the very existence of causings, not just on their odd causal properties, to which I now turn.

Are there any Causings?

My main complaint against the C-ACT concerns its reification of causings. This may come as something of a surprise to the reader, in light of my metaphysical liberalism. I accept Cambridge events, Cambridge actions, prolific standards for event identity generally, goodness knows what else. Why not causings too? Why doesn't my metaphysical liberalism extend to them as well? Let me explain.

Just what are these causings, postulated by the C-ACT theorist? Chisholm says that they are events, events which are the causings of other events: 'What now of *that* event—the event which is his thus causing e to happen . . . ?'[26] For O'Connor too, causings are events: A's causing of e is 'constituted by the holding of the causal relation between myself and the subevent e'.[27] He says that 'A's causing of e' is uncaused, and it is, of course, events that are caused and uncaused. So both, indeed all, C-ACT theorists accept that there are causings and that these causings are events of some sort.

[25] O'Connor, *Persons and Causes*, 53–5.
[26] Chisholm, 'Reflections on Human Agency', *Idealistic Studies*, 1, 1971: 36–46, 40.
[27] O'Connor, 'Agent Causation', 186.

C-ACT accepts that there is a direct causing, at least whenever an agent acts. But one might suppose that E-ACT, CTA, and indeed anyone who believes that anything ever causes something, must be saddled with causings as well. If, as the E-ACT says, an agent causes an event, then does it not follow, even for E-ACT, that there is an agent-causing of that event, even if that is not what the action is? On the CTA, believing and desiring cause a bodily movement, so does it not follow that there is a causing of the latter by the former? Are we not bound to have causings in our ontology, whether or not they are what actions are?

I wish to argue that there is nothing in what we say generally when we make causal claims (including claims that agents cause events) that forces us to posit causings. So, I want to make a weaker and then a stronger claim. First, the weaker claim: the C-ACT theorist may posit them if he wishes, but the other action theorists are quite free to eschew them. Second, the stronger claim: positing causings is ontologically gratuitous; there are no such things. And any theory that requires them, as does the C-ACT, is in error.

Let's think Davidsonianly for a while. In 'Jack kissed Jill', 'Jill buttered her toast', and 'John ran a mile', we are committed to runnings, butterings, and kissings, to account for all the linguistic facts and to preserve the validity of the inferences that we intuitively take to be valid. If Jack kissed Jill at midnight, then he kissed her; if John ran a mile and Bill ran a mile slowly, then both John and Bill ran a mile. If Jill buttered her toast slowly and with a knife, then she buttered her toast slowly. On Davidson's view, representing these thoughts formally requires quantification over runnings, butterings, and kissings.

Don't we say things that require quantification over causings? Why should the matter be different for causings than it is for butterings? 'Agent X caused event e' follows from 'agent X caused e in the night'; 'c caused e' follows from 'c caused e at night and in Netanya'. So whenever we speak of causation, whichever theory of action we hold, won't we get saddled with causings anyway? If this is right, then E-ACT is going to get agent-causings too, and (as I said above) it is hard to see both how there could be agent-causings and yet these not be what actions are. E-ACT would collapse into C-ACT. And even the CTA is going to get causings too, event-causings, admittedly not of the agent-causing kind.

The Davidsonian argument may work for butterings, kissings, and runnings, but it won't work for causings. Why? Here is an argument against Cartesian dualism that one frequently hears but that I regard as unsound. It is sometimes asked, in criticism of Descartes's view of mind–body interaction: if bodily and mental events causally interact, where do they interact? Descartes's reply that they interact in the pineal gland was an attempt to answer this question, and, so it is said, his failure shows the absurdity of supposing that there is mind–body interaction.

Why is this argument a bad argument, as I think it is? It's the question that is absurd. The question put to Descartes assumes that there are a time and place which modify the causing (as they might modify a buttering, kissing, or a running), that there are a time and place when and where the causing itself took place, but that poor, misguided Descartes got that place wrong. I disagree. In 'c caused e in place p and at time t' (and similarly for other adverbial modifiers), the place and time modifiers are not adverbially modifying the causing but rather are adjectivally modifying the constituent event, c, or e, or both. It is c or e or both that occurred at t in p, and nothing else.

Which event do they modify? c, or e, or c and e? To see which, rewrite 'c caused e in place p at time t' as 'c caused e. It happened in place p at time t'. What happened at t in p? 'It' cannot refer to a causing, because there is no relevant referring term for a causing to which the 'it' can refer back. But what does the 'it' refer to, if not to a causing?

There are three possibilities: to c, to e, to c and e. It is a convention in grammar that 'it' refers back to its closest referring term, which in this case is e. And this sounds right: if I say that the expansion caused the explosion and was asked when or where did *it* occur, I would take it that I am being asked about the explosion. Of course, if Hume's spatial and temporal contiguity requirement is correct, and if c immediately or directly causes e, then c and e will share a spatial and temporal point anyway, so the time and place would be correct, or very nearly so, for the expansion as well as the explosion. But it is the time and location of the explosion and not of the expansion, nor of the expansion and explosion, that is being asked for by the question, 'when did it occur?' in response to my saying that the expansion caused the explosion.[28]

It is e, the effect, which occurs at t and in p. There is no third 'thing', like a 'causing', additional to the cause and the effect, which can be placed and dated. Think of the issue like this: if causation is constant conjunction, or even constant conjunction prefaced by a modal operator ('It is necessary that whenever . . .'), or even if causation can be analysed as a counter-

---

[28] Elliott Sober reminded me of this.

factual about what would have happened if the cause had been absent, it becomes clear why there is no other, third event which could be placed or dated. There are only the two events, the cause and the effect, and the constant conjunction, or the counterfactual truth about the two events. There just ain't anything else that occurs, in virtue of c's and e's occurrence, and *a fortiori* nothing else that has any spatial or temporal location whatever.

Descartes should never have accepted to answer the question of 'where does the interaction take place?'. Interaction isn't a datable and placeable event, any more than causation is. (Interaction just is reciprocal type-level causation.) Rather, causation and interaction are relations that relate datable and placeable events. Descartes can give the place and time of the bodily event, and he can give the time of the mental event (if the latter is non-physical, it has no spatial location), and that must be the end of the placing and dating story that can be told. There is no further appropriate time or place question for Descartes to answer.

So, sentences like 'c caused e in place p and at time t' (or 'agent X agent-caused e in p at t') require a place and a time for c and e, or for the agent, but not for some alleged third thing, the causing itself. We do not need to reify causings simply by holding that some sentences with a causal form are true. If c caused e in p at t, then it was e itself that was in p at t. There are no spatial and temporal modifications that are modifications of causings, which thereby require us to reify those causings.

Return to the examples with which I began the discussion. 'Agent X caused e in the night', and 'c caused e at night and in Netanya', provide nothing analogous to butterings, kissings, and runnings. Butterings, kissings, and runnings can occur at night and in Netanya, but there are no causings that do. In the original examples, it is only event e that occurred at night and in Netanya. All the inferences that need preserving (like that of 'c caused e at night' from 'c caused e at night and in Netanya) will be preserved by having the modifications (like 'at night' and 'in Netanya') modify an event that stands in the causal relation, and without introducing a third event, a causing.

Any more plausible argument for causings as events would have to find cases in which the adverbial modification stuck to the causing and not to the cause or the effect itself. Where this might appear to be the case, I believe one can always offer an alternative way of dealing with these sentences: for example, in 'c caused e quickly', 'quick' is not an adverbial modification of the causing, for causation cannot have happened quickly or slowly, or indeed in any other way at all. Rather, 'quick' is an adjective of pairs of events: c and e are close in time.[29]

How might I deal with 'c's causing e surprised me'? Does this sentence attribute the property of being surprising to the event, c's causing e? I don't have difficulty in general with the idea that events, objects, and so on can have intensional properties amongst their other properties (Recall in Chapter 1 that Napoleon had the property of being eulogized). But if that were the only type of property something could have, I think we should be deeply suspicious. Indeed, I would hold that 'c's causing e was surprising to me' is equivalent to 'I was surprised that c caused e'. The latter requires no quantification over any causings.

Wesley Salmon, and many others, think that there are causal processes: 'One of the fundamental changes that I propose in approaching causality is to take processes rather than events as basic'.[30] Are processes causings, or constructed from causings? If so, are writers like Salmon bound to take causings as entities? As the quotation makes clear, Salmon contrasts events with processes, the latter having greater spatial extent and temporal duration. An example Salmon gives is this. The collision of the baseball with the window is an event; the baseball's travelling from bat to window is a process. Processes, on this view at any rate, are not causings; rather, they are more like stretched events. Processes are to events much as stretch limousines are to cars.

Of course, mightn't my argument thus far just have shown that we do not *have* to reify causings, on the basis of understanding how causal assertions and inferences about causes work? Ordinary event causation is not committed to causings and E-ACT does not collapse into C-ACT after all. But if the C-ACT theorist wishes to introduce causings, for some other reason or for none, is he not free to do so? Can he not simply assert that there are causings?

But I think that my argument shows more than what the above paragraph credits it with. There are two points. First, if there are no properties that we can attribute to causings, since all assertions (save, that causings are causings) apparently about causings are really assertions about an event or events that stand in the causal relation, then causings have no other properties, other than the property of being a causing. An entity with no property

---

[29] Mark Sainsbury led me to see this.
[30] Wesley Salmon, *Scientific Explanation and the Causal Structure of the World*, Princeton: Princeton University Press, 1984: 139 ff.

other than the property of being the type of entity it is seems an absurdity. Such entities, not quite property-less, are still too naked to be taken seriously.

Second, could causings be events, as the C-ACT theorists propose? Even if causings were entities of some sort or other, if they have no spatial or temporal properties (as I argued), it is difficult to see in what sense causings could be events at all, and certainly they could have neither causes nor effects. They would have to be events which had no temporal location, and that seems to be a contradiction. Given that there is no compelling reason to introduce causings, agent-causings or event-causings, we are far better without them in our ontology. We will do better, if we are ACT theorists, to stick to an E-ACT version of the ACT.

The E-ACT

The above discussion leads us to E-ACT as our primary focus. On this version, actions are events that the agent causes, not the causings of those events.

What, if anything, is wrong with the E-ACT? E-ACT says that the event, say my hand's moving, is a basic action when I directly agent-cause the movement. I agent-cause something, but there are no agent-causing events that need to be introduced. The picture that emerges on the E-ACT is this: one might think of causal chains with various nodes on them. Consider only the relation of direct causation, the relation that holds between adjacent nodes. Many of the nodes on the chains will be events. But sometimes, on some causal chains, we find nodes that are occupied by agents themselves, *sans* qualification.

So, on this version, agents can be causes, namely agent-causes. Can agents themselves be effects of other causes? Can there be agent effecthood as well as agent causality? Presumably, they can't be effects in the event causality sense, since event causation requires events as both of its relata. Can they be agent-effects of other agents? There is no provision in the theory for this, nor is it even clear what such a supposition would mean. Agent-effectism seems even less plausible than agent-causalism. So, on the most plausible interpretation of E-ACT, agents can initiate causal chains, but they themselves have no causes in any sense. Hence, the natural affinity of E-ACT for indeterminism.

Do the movements or events agents agent-cause have event-causes as well as agent-causes?[31] I briefly discussed this earlier, and related it to the issue of overdetermination. Taylor says these movements can have causes of both kinds; Chisholm denies that this is possible. Chisholm's view makes us hostages to fortune; neurophysiologists may find the (event) causes of the movements that occur when we intentionally act. On Taylor's view, in cases of unfree action in which both kinds of causation occur, there is a strange kind of overdetermination that is assumed. Taylor's overdeterminism does seem to make agent causation unnecessary and hence otiose, at least in those cases of unfree action in which there are causes of both kinds, since the presence of the event-cause would by itself be sufficient to produce the movement.

A futile attack on the E-ACT is to link the idea of causation with explanation and prediction, and then to argue that since neither of these features attaches to agent causality, agent causality is not any plausible kind of causation. First, to say that an event occurred because an agent X caused it *is* to give some explanation, for it rules out explanations of that event as a mere event over which agent X had no control. So there does seem to be some explanatory force when one says, of an event, that it was agent-caused by X. As far as prediction is concerned, it is the presence of laws rather than causation which allows prediction, and the connection between (event) causation and laws is itself in sufficient dispute to make that a weak place at which to rest one's case against the E-ACT.

So what is wrong with the E-ACT, if indeed anything is? There are two complaints that need distinguishing: the purported analysis of action in terms of agent causation (*a*) is circular and hence non-reductive; (*b*) attempts to explicate the better known by the less well known.

(*a*) Davidson says: 'for then what more have we said when we say the agent caused the action than when we say he was the agent of the action [that he acted]? The concept of cause seems to play no role.'[32] Presumably, *inter alia*, Davidson is claiming here a kind of circularity. He is claiming that the only grasp we have of the idea of an agent causing an event (the purported analysans) is the idea that the agent acted (the purported analysandum), the very idea we were hoping to elucidate. How, it might be asked, could the idea of an agent causing an event elucidate the idea of his acting? The only understanding we have of the idea of an agent's causing something

---

[31] See Thalberg, *Misconceptions of Mind and Freedom*, 167–70, for a discussion of this and for a summary of Taylor's and Chisholm's views on this issue. Also, O'Connor, *Persons and Causes*, 49–66.   [32] Davidson, 'Agency', 52–3.

is garnered from that of action. One intuitively feels that any grasp one has of the idea of an agent causing an event requires a grasp of the idea of action. An agent causing something smuggles in the very idea of action one was hoping to explicate. Certainly, no other account of the idea of agent-causality has been proffered. In so far as we rely on our pre-theoretic understanding of it, the idea of action is already implicit in it.

(*b*) What are the requirements for analysis? Suppose a claim of the form: the Concept of an *F* is just the Concept of a *G*. Certainly, a necessary condition for this is that: (x) $(Fx$ iff $Gx)$. Moreover, the strength of the material biconditional would be insufficient; the biconditional would have to have some modal strength, whether of nomological necessity or metaphysical necessity, so that it could support counterfactuals.

But biconditionals can be read in either direction. Does 'it is necessarily the case that (x) $(Fx$ iff $Gx)$' provide a rational reconstruction of the Concept of *F* in terms of the Concept of *G*, or of the Concept of *G* in terms of the Concept of *F*? The relation of a rational reconstruction is asymmetric; the relation of biconditionality, even when modally qualified, is symmetric.

The idea of rational reconstruction, indeed of analysis generally, is to explicate the less clear by the clearer, to illuminate the problematic in terms of the less problematic. This requirement is pragmatic. There is no objective, non-person-relative, measure of clarity or problematicness. Where there is a genuine disagreement about which of two concepts is better understood than the other, there may be an irresolvable disagreement about the success of a rational reconstruction of one concept in terms of another because of an irresolvable disagreement about the direction in which to read the elucidatory claim of the biconditional. That, alas, is what in the end we may have to conclude about the ACT.[33]

One person's mystery may be another's clarification. In an analysis of an idea, one hopes to use better-understood notions as a basis to make sense of less-well-understood ones. What the C-ACT is claiming is that the idea of an agent causing an event is more intelligible, better understood, than that of an agent's acting, and that, at least relative to the idea of action itself, the idea of such causing is primitive and needs no characterization.

An opponent may well deny this. Indeed, I deny it. But since 'better understood' is person-relative, it is hard to insist that no such rational reconstruction could really afford any measure of enlightenment to anyone.

---

[33] See Rosanna Keefe, 'When does Circularity Matter?', *Proceedings of the Aristotelian Society*, 2002: 275–92.

I do not find that leaning on these pragmatic ideas of relative clarity, being better understood, being less problematic, and so on, is of much help in convincing someone whose intuitions differ from mine on this point. The E-ACT theorist will remind us that, on most views, event causation is pretty mysterious anyway and he will say that it really is not clear that agent causation is in a worse shape than the former.

In summary, what is wrong with E-ACT? Cognizant as I am of not being able to convince the determined opponent, I am on the side of those who do find agent-causality more mysterious than the idea of action. So, it does, by my lights, attempt to explain the less mysterious by the more mysterious. Second, I agree that the idea of agent causation is itself action-laden and hence presupposes a grasp of the idea we are trying to explicate by means of it. I agree with Davidson's judgement quoted above. I can't see that, if we are puzzled about sentences like 'Agent X did so-and-so', where 'doing so-and-so' is one of his basic actions, we are going to be enlightened by saying that that means that X agent-caused the event intrinsic to that basic action. But if my opponent insists that it does enlighten him, and that he is not aiming for a reductive analysis, I do not think that anything I have said thus far will serve as a non-question-begging argument against the E-ACT.

I introduce in the next section what I think of as the real problem with the E-ACT. On the other hand, I regard the C-ACT as generating so many difficulties and problems, especially in its reification of causings, that as a consequence it is unworthy of being taken seriously as a theory of agency.

Taking Stock

Let's pause and take stock. We have found some, even if not always defini-tive, reason to reject both leading theories of action: the causal theory of action and the agent causalist theory. Might it be that, in spite of their dif-ferences, they share a common feature that makes them more similar than one might otherwise have supposed, and which accounts for the defects in both? In my view, such indeed is the case. The CTA, the C-ACT, and the E-ACT all agree that:

(3) Basic or primitive physical actions, like my moving of my hand or my bending of my finger, have events intrinsic to them.

Once (3) is accepted, the question of the relationship between basic phys-ical actions and their intrinsic events arises. It would seem that either they are identical or they are not identical. I reject both options. My rejection of their identity follows from my rejection of the various theories which seek to identify them (the CTA and the E-ACT). Of course, that does not conclusively demonstrate that they are not identical. But for someone who still wishes to plug this option, it will behove him to produce a theory that does attempt to identify them but that escapes my criticisms.

On the other hand, if a basic physical action were not identical to its intrinsic event, if my bending of my finger were not identical to my finger's bending, we would be saddled with an odd dualism, stuck with both my bending of my finger *and* my finger's bending. In Chapter 2, in the case of non-basic actions, we accepted the dualism; there is both my shooting of the gun and the gun's discharge. We needed, though, to disarm the looming overdetermination of the Queen's death that appeared to ensue, and hopefully successfully did so. But the cases before us now are different; they are cases of basic action. In these latter cases, the dualism of basic actions and their intrinsic events just seems foolish.

According to the CTA and the E-ACT, there is no overdetermination (by both basic actions and the events intrinsic to them) of subsequent events, since basic actions are identical to the events intrinsic to them. For those two theories of action, the action just *is* the event (intrinsic to the basic action) caused by my rationalizing mental states, or by me. For the C-ACT, a basic action just *is* the causing of the event intrinsic to it. Notice the assumption shared by all three theories: that there is an event intrinsic to every basic action. Two of the theories identify the event and the action, but all three agree that there is such an event.

(O'Connor's identification of the event intrinsic to a basic action is somewhat more complicated. As he puts it, 'So, in the case of an observable bodily movement such as waving my hand, my action consists of the causal relation I bear to the coming-to-be of the state of determinate intention to wave my hand, plus the sequence of events that flows from that state'.[34] Although this is not quite the sense of 'intrinsic event' that I have been working with hitherto, we might say that, for O'Connor, what is intrinsic to his waving of his hand is the sum of events, {the coming-to-be of his state of determinate intention to wave his hand, the effects of that coming-to-be}. O'Connor does not actually say that the waving of his hand must be one of the events that flows from the coming-to-be of the state of determinate intention to wave his hand, in order for him to wave his hand, although surely he thinks that. A difficulty with his theory relates to its requirement

[34] O'Connor, *Persons and Causes*, 72 n. 11.

of an intention in every case of action, discussed previously in Chapter 3, in addition to the difficulty I introduce below.)

If we do not accept the identity of basic actions and their intrinsic events in the way these theories propose, the alternative seems to be their duality: there are both basic actions and events intrinsic to them. But as I said above, unlike the case of non-basic actions, this duality would stretch one's credulity. Overdetermination looms. Nor is it easy to see how my bending of my finger and my finger's bending could have different causes or effects, which they must have if they are not identical. Finally, in Chapter 2, I argued for the non-identity of action and intrinsic event in the non-basic case, on the grounds that the action and event concerned or involved different things: my killing of the Queen involved her and me, her death involved only her.

But surely that argument cannot be repeated in the case of basic action. What does my bending of my finger involve? Reply: me and my attached finger. What does my finger's bending involve? Reply: perhaps just my attached finger, but not me? But if it involves my attached finger, then it does involve me, since I am not disjoint from my attached finger. (A similar argument was introduced in Chapter 1, to distinguish the analysis of my bending of my finger from the other actions I do by that bending.) In short, to whatever extent these arguments against identity worked in Chapter 2 for non-basic actions and the events intrinsic to them, they do not seem to work even to that extent for basic actions.

If basic actions and their intrinsic events are neither identical nor non-identical, what option might remain open to us for understanding the relationship between basic actions and their intrinsic events? I think a natural suggestion is this: deny (3). We should deny the existence of any such intrinsic events, in cases of basic action.

If (3) is false, then a crucial assumption of the CTA, the E-ACT, and many versions of the C-ACT, is false. When an agent waves his hand, there will be no waving of his hand with which the action could be identified. What of O'Connor's version of the C-ACT? It depends on what events he includes in the sum of events that he claims that the agent agent-causes. If the waving of one's hand is one of the events said 'to flow' from the coming-to-be of the determinate intention to wave, then his theory falls foul of the denial of (3) as well. And yet if the hand waving does not flow from the intention, it is hard to see how, whatever the intention might be an intention to do, the action in question could count as an agent's waving of his hand.

I do not believe that I can 'prove' that my view, the denial of (3), is true, whatever that might mean. What I think I can do is to show that this view

can occupy a perfectly acceptable position in the logical space of alternatives. The argument for it is, in essence, (what I regard as) the greater
unacceptability of the alternatives, identity and duality of basic action and
intrinsic event. Coupled with my disarming of what might be thought to be
its implausible consequences, I regard the case I put forward for the rejection of (3) as a strong one.

It is true that (3) is a standard assumption shared by many action
theorists, as we have seen in Chapter 2. For example, to repeat from that
chapter, David Hamlyn says that '. . . it is undeniable that, when we
make a bodily movement [i.e. when we act], a bodily movement in the
intransitive sense [an event] occurs; when we move an arm, certain arm
movements take place'. Jennifer Hornsby says that 'if John moved$_T$ his
body, then his body moved$_I$'.[35]

What do I mean when I say that when a basic action occurs, no event
intrinsic to that action occurs? My view is that, when X moves his hand,
there is in one sense no such event at all as his hand's moving. All that there
is, is the action. I am not just denying that the basic action and its intrinsic
event are identical. I deny that any such intrinsic event occurs at all, even
one necessary but insufficient for the basic action; *a fortiori*, if there is no
intrinsic event, it can't be identical to anything.[36] No identity of basic action
and intrinsic event, and no duality either, because no intrinsic event.

There is, on this view, a sense of 'event', and of specific event descriptions
(like, 'the moving of his hand'), in which an *exclusive* disjunction is true
in the case of basic actions: either a person moves his hand or his hand
moves.[37] The first is an action; the second is a (mere) event. So if I move my

[35] David Hamlyn, *In and out of the Black Box: On the Philosophy of Cognition*, Oxford:
Blackwell, 1990: 130. Jennifer Hornsby, *Actions*, London: Routledge & Kegan Paul, 1980: 2.
Think of an action as what makes a sentence with the form 'aV_Tb' true (Simon moved his hand'),
and an event as what makes a sentence with the form 'bV_I' true ('Simon's hand moved'). 'a' names
a person, 'b' an object, 'V' stands for a verb, and the subscripts 'I' and 'T' for intransitive and
transitive occurrences of the verb respectively.

[36] Someone might confuse my thesis with the question of inactions, omissions, and forbearances. Most theorists count these as actions. I suppose that, if it is an action, my intentionally
keeping quiet is a basic action, since it is not an action I do by doing something else. Whatever
we might decide about such cases of 'negative' action or inactivity, my claim is about 'positive'
action that evinces activity.

[37] The analogy between my view of action and the Hinton–Snowden–McDowell disjunctive
theory of experience will be apparent. See J. M. Hinton, *Experiences*, Oxford: Oxford University Press, 1973; Paul Snowdon, 'Perception, Vision, and Causation', *Proceedings of the
Aristotelian Society*, 81, 1980–1: 175–92; John McDowell, 'Criteria, Defeasability, and Knowledge', *Proceedings of the British Academy*, 68, 1982: 455–79. The last two are reprinted in J.
Dancy, ed., *Perceptual Knowledge*, Oxford: Oxford University Press, 1988.

hand, it is false (in one sense) that my hand moved or that it changed place, only true that I moved it or that I changed its place.

'His hand moved' and 'his hand changed place' (in one sense) are made true by an event, but by no action; 'he moved his hand' and 'he changed his hand's place' can be made true by a basic action, and when they are, they are made true by no event. When X moves his hand, or when he changes its place, there is no event that occurs intrinsic to *that* basic action. I do not deny (*a*) that many other, perhaps unintentional, non-basic actions of mine occur by my moving of my hand, which will have events intrinsic to them, and (*b*) that many mere or just events occur as a consequence of my moving of my hand.

I am aware that my claim is often met with incredulity. Is it really *false* that when I move my hand, my hand moves? Surely an observer who sees me move my hand, may say: (4) 'I am sure that I saw his hand move. Whether he moved it, or someone or something else did, I don't know.' If this, and many assertions like it, make any sense, how could my claim be true?

I carefully qualified what I said above with the expression, 'in one sense'. For I want to do equal justice to two data, both of which I regard as legitimate:

(5) Metaphysically speaking, when a basic action occurs, it follows that no event intrinsic to that basic action occurs (there is no event intrinsic to the basic action and at least necessary for it);

(6) Assertions like (4) above are sometimes true.

The way in which I reconcile the above metaphysical and linguistic data is by recognizing a systematic ambiguity in the concept of event.

I want to introduce talk of two senses of 'event', or two concepts of event (and of specific event names or descriptions, but I shan't keep repeating this addition). I do not have an account of the concept of event to offer the reader, but I do not need to be in possession of one, in order to make my point. If two concepts, say, concept A and concept B, differ in denotation, they must differ in connotation, whatever that connotation might be. Concept $A \neq$ Concept B. So let me introduce the two concepts of event by giving their differing extensions. My strategy is to characterize the two distinct concepts as best I can, by giving examples of what falls under them.

Thus far in the book, we have used 'event' to refer to both mere events like the eruption of Vesuvius, intrinsic to no action, and events like the Queen's death or the gun's discharge, which are events intrinsic to non-basic actions. Those two kinds of events provide for us one sense of 'event'. Let's call this the passive concept: in its extension are mere events like the eruption of Vesuvius and events intrinsic to actions, if any (like the Queen's death, when I kill her). This sense of 'event' gives us a passive sense, because nothing in its extension *explicitly* demonstrates activity or the hallmark of agency. Do actions, basic or non-basic, fall within the extension[38] of this passive concept? The above qualification 'explicitly' is added for the following reason. Other items may also be in the extension of this concept, but *only* those things which are identical to mere events or events intrinsic to actions, if there are any.

So, in the passive sense of 'event', it does not immediately follow that actions are not events in that sense; that is, it does not immediately follow that they are not in its extension. If they are, one will need to find this out by way of philosophical argument. On this first concept, whether actions, basic or non-basic, count as events is open to philosophical argument. If action have events intrinsic to them and if they are identical to their intrinsic events, actions are also in the extension of this concept of event. If either of these assumptions is false, they are not in that extension.

Using the first concept, one should be pre-philosophically neutral with regard to the question of whether actions are events. To claim that actions are or are not events is a substantial piece of metaphysics, the fruit of honest philosophical labour. The argument of this book has been to show that actions are not events, in the first, passive sense of 'event'. If the arguments of Chapters 1 and 2 are correct, we already know that non-basic actions are not in the extension of this passive concept of event, because we already know that non-basic actions are not identical to the events intrinsic to them. And if the argument of this chapter is correct, we now know that basic actions are not in the extension of this passive concept of event either, since they have no events intrinsic to them at all, to which they might be identical.

(Notice, though, that in the case of *non-basic* actions, no exclusive disjunction is true, even in this passive sense of 'event'. Even though my killing of the Queen is not identical to her death, when I kill her, it *does* follow that the event of her death occurs. The disjunction is only exclusive in the case of basic action.)

The second concept has, in its extension, mere events, events intrinsic to actions, and actions themselves, basic and non-basic, all as items irreducible

---

[38] I speak indifferently both of a concept and an expression having an extension.

to one another. Let's call this the non-passive concept of event. This sense of 'event' is not a passive sense, since some (not all, of course) of the items in its extension explicitly display agency, namely, actions. On this second concept, actions simply are a subclass of events, by stipulation of the concept's extension. In terms of this second concept, actions are events, whatever the metaphysical status of actions might be. There is no philosophical 'finding out' if actions are events in the sense of this second concept. They are, by 'definition'. Since this is only a question of arbitrary classification, and not one of substantive philosophy, nothing of any seriousness hangs on it. No honest philosophical labour is required for this result. Now, one might simply adopt either the passive or the non-passive concept as *the* concept of an event. My method is different. I recognize that there are both of these senses.

Even if actions are *not* events, in the passive sense, we need not deny the similarities, structural or otherwise, between events (narrowly construed to include only mere events and events intrinsic to non-basic actions) and actions. For example, perhaps they are both exemplifyings of properties at a time. But if actions are *not* events in the passive sense of 'event', the significance of the distinction between actions and events lies in the philosophical confirmation of the distinction between activity and passivity. And, *pari passu*, if actions are events in the passive sense, then the significance of that lies in the fact that there is no ultimate philosophical gulf between what we might initially think of as the active and the passive.

So when a person says (4) 'I am sure that I saw his hand move. Whether he moved it, or someone or something else did, I don't know', and if what he says is true, then he is using the non-passive concept of event (or, concept of a moving of a hand) in the first sentence. In (4), 'the moving of his hand' can refer *either* to a passive event of his hand's moving *or* to an action, his moving of his hand. What (4) says, if it is true, is that something occurred that falls within the extension of 'a moving of a hand' in the non-passive sense, but there is uncertainty as to which subset of that extension the item belongs (action or mere event?). But in the passive sense of event, (4) must be false, because when his moving of his hand is a basic action of his, no moving of his hand occurs for anyone to see.

How would I deal with:

(4′) 'I am sure that I saw the gun discharge. Whether he fired the gun, or something else caused it to discharge, I don't know.'

In the case of non-basic actions, (4') can be true in both senses. In the non-passive sense, the account would be the same as the one given above for basic actions.

In the passive sense, the gun's discharge might either be a mere event or an event intrinsic to an action. Although his shooting of the gun ≠ the gun's discharge, and so although the shooting is therefore not in the extension of 'a gun's discharge', in the passive sense, still if the gun's discharge occurs as an event intrinsic to an action and is not a mere event, the shooting must occur as well. So (4') is true, even in the passive sense, for non-basic actions. Since in the case of non-basic action, no exclusive disjunction is true, the occurrence of an intrinsic event does not, obviously, exclude the occurrence of an action as well, namely the one to which it is intrinsic.

Thus, having delineated these two concepts of event, I think I can do justice both to my philosophical claims and to the literal truth of assertions that might appear to contradict them.

Finally, (5) 'Ruben moved his hand' entails (6) 'Ruben's hand was moved by Ruben'. And (6) 'Ruben's hand was moved by Ruben' surely entails (7) 'Ruben's hand moved'.[39] So doesn't the action, my moving of my hand, entail that there was an event, the moving of my hand, after all? The second inference looks as if it is merely a case of simplification.

In fact, there is a missing step. (6) entails (7') 'Ruben's hand was moved', by simplification. I agree that (5) entails (6) and that (6) entails (7'). But does (7') entail (7)?

(6) and (7') both use 'move' in the transitive sense, albeit in the passive voice. (7') is of course elliptical, since anything that was moved was moved by something or someone. But (7) uses 'move' in the intransitive sense. I would say that in the case in which my hand was moved$_t$ by an agent, it does *not* follow that it moved$_i$. If my hand was moved$_t$, say by me, then it did not move$_i$. (7') does not entail (7).

Are All Actions Lacking Intrinsic Events Mental Actions?

Wittgenstein asked: 'What is left over if I subtract the fact that my arm goes up from the fact that I raise my arm?'[40] Wittgenstein's question can arise whenever an action has an event intrinsic to it. If an action (my killing of the

---

[39] Berel Lerner pointed these inferences out to me.

[40] Hugh McCann, 'Volition and Basic Action', *Philosophical Review*, 20, 1974: 451–73, and repr. in his *The Works of Agency*, Ithaca, NY: Cornell University Press, 1998: 75–93. Wittgenstein's question is quoted in McCann, *The Works of Agency*, 75.

Queen) has an event intrinsic to it (namely, the Queen's death), which intrinsic event is itself brought about by a more basic action of the agent (my pulling of the trigger), or by an event intrinsic to that more basic action, we shall finally get to an action (my bending of my finger) which can't be given this sort of analysis, on pain of infinite regress. What analysis are we to give for these basic actions?

Of course, the CTA and the E-ACT had their own ways of solving the regress: the events intrinsic to basic actions are caused either by rationalizing mental states, or by the agent himself, but not by even-more-basic actions or their intrinsic events. But for someone who rejects the CTA and the E-ACT, those options are unavailable.

Hugh McCann says that the way to solve the potential infinite regress problem is to argue that basic actions have no events intrinsic to them at all: 'If there is no result [intrinsic event] to be distinguished from the action, there can be no question as to what makes it a result'.[41] McCann and I would stop the regress in the same way, by denying that basic actions have events intrinsic to them. Call such basic actions 'pure'. My account, unlike McCann's, allows basic physical action. McCann claims to have found actions that have no events intrinsic to them, and hence which stop Wittgenstein's regress, but only in the case of certain mental acts—thinking and willing (to which we might add tryings, on some views). 'That acts of thinking do not have results [events intrinsic to them] means there can be no action–result problem about thinking.'[42] I have reservations, which I have already expressed in Chapter 2, about the purity of acts of thinking. In spite of McCann's arguments to the contrary, I think that there is a strong case for the view that episodes of active thinking do have the occurrence of thoughts as their intrinsic events (there is a lot more to say about this issue, which I do not pursue here).

I could agree with McCann, that some mental actions are or may be pure, that is, have no events intrinsic to them. Acts of will, if and when they occur, may be examples. In cases, if there are any, in which pure mental actions initiate action chains (unlike me, McCann speaks in terms of causal chains rather than action chains), such mental actions might bring the regress suggested in Wittgenstein's question to a halt.

But my main disagreement with McCann is that I do not think that we have to hold that there is such a pure mental action on every action chain, in order to halt the regress. I think that there are physical actions that have

---

[41] McCann, *The Works of Agency*, 87.   [42] ibid. 87.

no events intrinsic to them, and it is they which can halt the regress on those action chains on which they occur. Some physical actions can be pure as well.

Since for McCann these willings and thinkings are the only pure actions there are, he must claim that every action is done by, or is caused by, an act of willing or thinking. On this view, it is from willing or thinking that all other cases of agency stem. It locates basic action 'inside' the agent, in his mind or brain. My view locates much basic action at the physical surface of the agent. We need not, on my theory, be driven inside the agent to find an act of will as a stopping place to account for action.[43]

Presumably, assuming that there are lots of things an agent does, there will have to be, on McCann's theory, an awful lot of willings around as well: '. . . bodily actions typically involve the mental activity of volition or willing and . . . this activity is . . . the basic activity we engage in when . . .' we physically act.[44] Other things being equal, it is unattractive to have to hold that, on every occasion on which I physically act, I am engaging in some mental act, as this view requires. This would lead to the sort of mental overpopulation I have already described. McCann's volitional theory, like the CTA, is an overpopulator.

So what does my theory say about basic actions? In one sense, shockingly little. Actions just are, well, actions. The concept of a basic action is unanalysable, a conceptual primitive. No folk-naturalistic or reconstructive theory that assimilates them to their allegedly intrinsic events, or to anything else, is going to work. Of course, as I have already explained, one might just want to define actions as events: events (in the non-passive sense) include events in the passive sense (intrinsic events, like the gun's discharge, and mere events, like Vesuvius erupting), and actions. But that is only a matter of definitional fiat. It is not a successful reconstructive or naturalistic theory of action.

Basic actions are actions, but not in virtue of some other feature of them. It isn't just that what distinguishes actions from (passive) events is by some feature intrinsic to one but not the other. For that would be compatible with there being some intrinsic feature, F, such that actions but not passive events had F and it was in virtue of having F that some item counted as an action. A view like this is also Carl Ginet's, on mental action. He says that

---

[43] The only discussion I know of this occurs in Stewart Candlish, 'Inner and Outer Basic Actions', *Proceedings of the Aristotelian Society*, n.s., vol. 84, 1984: 83–102.

[44] McCann, *The Works of Agency*, 75.

what makes a mental occurrence a mental action is that the occurrence has this feature: it has 'the actish phenomenal quality'.[45] So for him, the feature that makes something a mental action is intrinsic to the mental action, but it is a feature other than simply being a mental act. It is the feature of having a certain phenomenal quality.

Or, it will be recalled from Chapter 3, that Harry Frankfurt might be best understood as saying that actions and mere movements should be distinguished by their non-historical properties. So, for Frankfurt, there is a non-historical property F, where F is the property of being guided or monitored by the agent, which mere movements lack and movements which are actions possess. Unlike Ginet and Frankfurt, I am not searching for either intrinsic or non-historical properties, by which to distinguish actions from mere movements.

Rather, what I am claiming is that there is no such feature, F, other than the feature itself of being an action (or a feature which presupposes that anything that has it is an action). What makes an action what it is, is nothing other than its being an action. (In case it might mislead, this claim is neutral on the question of whether basic actions have causes.)

Perhaps the great lessons of philosophy are often shockingly small, and my result is merely a part of that tradition. Reductive or what I called in Chapter 3 'reconstructive' philosophies hold out hope for great news: that physical objects are sets of sense data; that societies are sums of their individual members; that numbers are sets of sets; that universals are sets of objects; that causation is constant conjunction; that an action's property of being right is its having the property of maximizing the good; and so on. Add to this: that basic actions are their intrinsic events.

I do not know of one successful reductive or reconstructive theory of this sort. Although, to be sure, one must argue case by case, I believe they all fail. Perhaps it is never such great news to be told that there is no great news to be had at all.

---

[45] Carl Ginet, *On Action*, Cambridge: Cambridge University Press, 1990: 15.

6

A Counterfactual Theory of Causal Explanation

Some Preliminaries

I want to make some preliminary remarks about explanation, without devoting a whole chapter to the topic and without even committing myself to one theory of explanation rather than another. Readers interested in a more extended discussion of explanation, at least along the lines I conceive it, might wish to consult my earlier *Explaining Explanation*.[1]

What gets explained in an explanation is the explanandum; what does the explaining in an explanation is the explanans (plural: explananda and explanantia). In spite of the grammatically singular form of 'explanans', an explanans might contain many 'parts'. On Carl Hempel's D-N model of explanation, the explanans might contain several premisses, each of which is necessary and the conjunction of which is sufficient for deducing the explanandum. On other views of explanation, the explanans might be composed of several sentences, even if they do not figure as premisses in a deductive argument. Hempel also admits a non-deductive type of explanation, the I-S (for 'inductive-statistical') model of explanation. On the I-S model, the explanans inductively supports, to a high degree, the conclusion that it explains.

There is a distinction between explanation (versus no explanation at all) and good explanation (versus a poor one). At least, so I say. Some pragmatic theories of explanation might not have the resources, or desire, to draw the distinction. My own view is that one is able to characterize a quite objective, non-pragmatic account of explanation. But some explanations, objectively and properly so-called, are better than others, also objectively

[1] *Explaining Explanation*, London: Routledge, 1990.

and properly so-called. The goodness of the explanation relates to the interests and concerns of one's audience. So an explanation may be good for some purpose, poor for another. For example, most full explanations (more on full explanations below) might be very poor explanations for almost everyone, since, given that they are so long, they may send all listeners to sleep before being completed.

Why are some explanations better than others? This is a big topic. Here is one example. Suppose ingesting a pound of arsenic, c, causes the Queen's death, e (poor lady, she has been having a rough old time since Chapter 1). The ingestion is a pretty good explanation of the death. But c is only a mediate cause of e. There are connecting events, d, f, g, and so on, such that c immediately causes d which immediately causes f which immediately causes g which finally immediately causes e.

Imagine that g, e's immediate cause, is the physiological state of the Queen just prior to her death. g might be, for most of us, a very much poorer explanation of her death than c, the arsenic ingestion, even if it provides a good explanation for someone with specialized interests in the details of forensic science. Even when an event is the immediate cause for some effect, it does not follow that it is that effect's best explanation for everybody. A mediate cause might provide a better explanation for most of us. So we can speak of the degree to which an explanation explains. Better explanations explain to a higher degree than do poorer ones.

How are causation and explanation related? A principle that I shall use in this chapter is this:

(P) If c causes or is part of the cause of e, where c and e are sufficiently close, then there are some descriptions of c and of e such that c under that description explains e to some degree under that description.

(P) speaks of descriptions. Explanation, unlike causation, creates a non-extensional context, so that descriptions of the cause matter. Causes don't explain effects under every description. Explanation is, as one says, under a description. One might explain the G by the F, and even though the F = the F^*, and the G = the G^*, not be able to explain the G^* by the F^*, or the G^* by the F, or the G by the F^*.

What (P) commits to is the explanatory relevance of every cause, because, if (P) is true, then every cause explains its effect under some appropriate description. I add, but do not explicate, the qualification 'sufficiently close'. I do not know how close, sufficiently close must be. Causes might not explain very distant effects. The Big Bang does not explain the Queen's death, even though it is a remote cause of her death (and indeed of every-thing else, too). So let's just say that the cause and effect must be suffi-ciently close.

When I speak of causes in this chapter, I intend by that to be speaking of event-causes only, not agent-causes (indeed if there are any of the latter). Some of what I say would apply to agent-causes as well, should there be any; with a little adjustment and stretching, I suppose that (P) would be true of them as well.

As I said in the last chapter, causes may be deterministic or non-deterministic (probabilistic), although, as I explain below, I develop a theory of causal explanation only for the case of deterministic causes; its extension to the case of probabilistic causation is far from trivial. The thought that causation at the level of sub-atomic particles is non-deterministic is fairly well entrenched. But I do not assume that all macro-causation (as I shall be calling it) is deterministic causation; even at the level of ordinary physical objects and the events that occur to them, some causation may be non-deterministic. But my aim here is only to give an account of deterministic folk causal explanation. The extension of my account to cover cases of non-deterministic macro-causation will prove extremely difficult, although in my view these difficulties arise in trying to understand the idea of non-deterministic token causation and have nothing especially to do with the concept of explanation. So I ignore them here.[2] So, to repeat, the discussion that ensues is meant only to apply to deterministic event-causes.

In Chapter 4, I argued that intentions are not by themselves rationalizers of action. I have also argued that they are simply not available in numbers sufficient for the requirements of the CTA. But let's assume that we do have a case of action which is preceded and caused by a prior intention to do that action. Even though not all actions are so preceded, some may be.

What is the explanatory power of an intention when it does precede and

---

[2] I follow David Lewis: (roughly) c is a deterministic cause of e iff if c had not occurred, e would not have occurred. (Similarly roughly) c is a non-deterministic cause of e iff if c had not occurred, e would have been less likely to occur.

Probabilistic or non-deterministic accounts of causation work as accounts of causal general-ization, but there is some difficulty in understanding what a non-deterministic account of token causation might be like. This problem of understanding non-deterministic *token* causation would be inherited by any account of explanation that uses non-deterministic causation. For a discussion of this problem about non-deterministic token causation, see James Woodward, 'Supervenience and Singular Causal Statements', in *Explanation and its Limits*, ed. Dudley Knowles, Cambridge: Cambridge University Press, 1990: 211–46.

cause the action intended? In what sense could an intention (say, to do *A*) explain an action token of type *A*? If there is a prior intentional state that causes, or is part of the cause, of the action (and presumably they will certainly be sufficiently close), then the intention to do *A*, under some description, must provide some explanation of the action. And the description of the intention, as 'the intention to do *A*', seems just the right description for the job. So explaining the action by a prior intention, if there is one, explains *something* about the action. For example, it excludes the possibility that the action was an unforeseen consequence of something else that the agent was doing.

But the explanation-by-intention does not possess much explanatory power on its own. Explaining an action by its prior intention, if it has one, is not a good explanation, does not provide much by way of explanation, for most of us most of the time. Intending to *A* leaves it open as to why the agent did it, in the most natural sense of that 'why' question. In a case of action which is preceded by a belief and desire, for example, the belief and desire may only be mediate causes of the action, and the intention may be the immediate, or more immediate, cause of the action, but for most of us the belief, if there is one, and desire will explain more about the action, or explain the action better, than the more immediate cause of the action, the intention.

There is an important distinction to be drawn between partial and full explanation, and in my view many discussions of explanation are vitiated by not addressing this distinction. In truth, each theory of explanation will draw the distinction in its own way, so, since I am not committing myself to any particular theory of explanation, not much can be said about the distinction other than in the most general of terms. But whatever one's theory of full explanation might be, there is always the possibility that, for pragmatic or epistemic or contextual reasons, an explainer will only give part of that full explanation.

Perhaps the explainer is ignorant of all but a part of the explanation; perhaps he gives only part because the rest is so obvious to any reasonable person that it does not bear repetition; perhaps the explainer realizes that in the circumstances he is in, his audience knows part of it and he only has to mention the part that they do not know. The full–partial distinction crosses with the better–worse distinction. Within a single full explanation for something, it might be better to cite, on some occasion, some part rather than another, and, on a different occasion, some other part. If there is more than one full explanation for something (again, more on this below), it might be better to cite one (or part of one) of them, rather than another (or part of another) on one occasion, and on a different occasion conversely.

I do not know if we ever give full explanations; whether we do or not ever advance them will depend on the theory of (full) explanation that we hold. For example, on Hempel's D-N model of explanation, standards for full explanation are set so high that full explanations occur very infrequently, if ever. The higher the standards for full explanation that a theory of explanation sets, the less likely we are to offer them when we actually explain something. But whether or not we ever give full explanations, the idea of a full explanation has conceptual priority relative to the idea of a partial explanation. A partial explanation is just some part of a full explanation.

But isn't it also and equally true that a full explanation is just the sum of all the parts of the explanation, so why do we have here conceptual dependence of partial on full explanation rather than just mutual interdependence between the two ideas? One argument for dependence of partial on full rather than mutual interdependence is this.

Suppose there is some explanandum e. Suppose further that both p and p' are parts of e's explanation. But since e can in principle have more than one explanation, how would we know whether p and p' are parts of the same full explanation of e or each is a part of a different full explanation of e?

We can answer that last question only by first having a grasp of the idea of a full explanation and having some idea of how in principle to individuate full explanations. We must first know how many full explanations are on hand for e and, if more than one, whether the two partial explanations belong as parts to the same or different of e's full explanations. So the idea of full explanation is required in order to understand the idea of a part of an explanation, but not vice versa.

To return to a comment above: one and the same explanandum may have several full explanations. The arsenic-Queen's death provided a case of this. One explanation might be in terms of a more immediate cause of the death, another in terms of a less immediate cause of the same death. This is an example of different full explanations being extracted from different locations on the causal chain leading to the explanandum event. I understand 'full' in such a way that each explanation could be 'full' in its own terms, without the other. Not every theorist of explanation holds this view. David Lewis says, for example, that 'Among the true propositions about the causal history of an event, one is maximal in strength. It is the whole truth on the subject . . . We might call this the whole explanation of the explanandum event, or simply *the* explanation.'[3] This is not my view, since I think that multiple explanations might each offer a whole (full) explanation of the event.

Another case of multiple full explanations for the same event has to do with depth at a single location rather than with different locations on the causal chain leading to the explanandum event. For example, there might be two different full causal explanations of the population reduction in fourteenth-century Europe: one in terms of the occurrence of the Black Death, and the other in terms of the precise aetiological details, relating to the virus, its ability to reproduce in certain conditions, and so on. In short, some explanations are 'deeper' than others are. And it is certainly not true that the deeper, the better. The first explanation, the less deep, might be a better explanation for a group of demographers uninterested in the medical details; the second, the deeper explanation, a better explanation for a group of epidemiologists.

Or, there might be both a causal and a non-causal explanation for the same thing. Again, one explanation may, in the circumstances, be better than the other(s), but it will be true, none the less, that there is more than one full explanation for the action. So, even if every action has a causal explanation, it might be that there is another, non-causal explanation, as well as a second causal explanation, for the same action.

These multiple explanations need not be in competition with one another in any way. As in the examples above, one might be preferable in one set of circumstances; the other in another. Which one of the explanations is appropriate on some specific occasion might depend on the details of that occasion, for example, what is puzzling to the person requiring the explanation and what he already knows. Even on Hempel's D-N model of explanation, one can see how this might arise: more than one premiss set, each conforming to all of Hempel's criteria, might entail the same explanandum. So, in the absence of a further specific argument to the contrary, we should not resist the idea that some one action token can have more than one perfectly legitimate full explanation.

In this chapter, I intend to elucidate a problem about the place of generalizations in the causal explanation of action, when the action has a deter-

---

[3] David Lewis, 'Causal Explanation', in *Philosophical Papers*, ii, Oxford: Oxford University Press, 1986: 218–19.

ministic cause.[4] I do this in the belief that some actions have causal explanations, for otherwise the project would hardly be worthwhile. The causes of action might either be folk-psychological or neurophysiological states of the sort that drive my dancer, ice-skater, hugger, bicycle rider, and so on, of Chapter 4. Even if an action has a folk-psychological cause, I do not assume that it must be a belief-and-desire pair, although it might be. Nor am I assuming, when an action has a folk-psychological cause, that that cause rationalizes the action. As I have argued, a basic desire on its own, or an emotion, or whatever, may cause an action without rationalizing it.

Suppose an action has a cause. How then do matters stand with regard to the action's having an explanation? There must be some causal explanation for the action, since (P) tells us that a cause of the action must explain the action to some degree or other under some description. The causal explanation of an action, if it has one, might not be a good one, but it will still be an explanation, or part of one. I do not assume that every action has a cause, only that some at least do. And those that do, by (P), have some causal explanation. As far as the commitments of this chapter go, some actions might be causeless initiators of action-causal chains. In making this assumption, I part company only from any action theorist, like Timothy O'Connor, who thinks that no action can have a cause.[5]

What options about action explanation would we have if there were actions which were not caused? We could say one of two things: either the occurrences of such actions are inexplicable, or there are non-causal explanations for their occurrence. But I do not investigate that choice here, for actions, if any, which have no cause. I focus only on the causal explanation of actions which do have a cause.

On an action-causal chain like the ones we considered in Chapters 1 and 2, some event c, whatever it might be, may cause and explain a basic action, like my bending of my finger. When we also say that c causes and explains non-basic actions further down the action chain from finger bending, what

---

[4] The topic of explanation and probabilistic causes is far from straightforward, but here is a thought: suppose that some cause c makes action a's occurrence highly probable to 0.8, so we can explain why action a occurred by citing the occurrence of c. But suppose c had occurred but a had not. In that case, could we also have explained a's non-occurrence by citing c? After all, there was a low probability, 0.2, that, given c, a would not occur. c's occurrence is as relevant to a's non-occurrence as it is to a's occurrence. But how can c explain in one situation a, if in another situation it could also have explained a's non-occurrence?

[5] Timothy O'Connor, both in 'Agent Causation', in his *Agents, Causes, and Events*, Oxford and New York: Oxford University Press, 1995, and in *Persons and Causes*, New York: Oxford University Press, 2000.

we must mean is that c causes and explains the events further down the action-causal chain from the basic action that are intrinsic to those non-basic actions. Only on that basis can we say that c causes and explains the non-basic actions.

The Causal Theory of Action Explanation

In Chapters 3, 4, and 5, we examined metaphysical theories about the nature of action: the CTA, the ACT, and my non-reconstructionist alternative. Closely connected, and often confused, with the CTA is a theory of action explanation, the Causal Theory of Action Explanation (hereafter, the CTAE): every action is explained by the rationalizing mental states that non-deviantly cause it. That is, for every action, there is such a causal explanation in terms of rationalizing mental states. It does not need to hold the stronger thesis that *every* explanation of an action is a causal explanation in terms of rationalizing mental states. The CTAE might allow other sorts of action explanations, as long as, for every action, there is also one of the rationalizing-cause kind.

On the CTAE, (1) *every* action has at least one explanation; (2) the explainers in that explanation are its causes; (3) those explainers are appropriate rationalizing folk-psychological states. Davidson's seminal theses are (2) and (3), stated persuasively in his 'Actions, Reasons, and Causes'.[6]

Just what is the relation between the CTA and the CTAE? The CTA and the CTAE certainly seem to be logically distinct theses. One is a metaphysical theory, the other (because about explanation) epistemological. It seems clear that one could reject the CTA, and still believe the CTAE concerning the explanation of action. There might be such causal explanations for actions, even if there were no analysis of actions as events with a specific kind of causal history. So, the CTAE could be true even if the CTA were false.

Could the CTA be true but the CTAE false? If the CTA is true, then every action is an event caused in the right way by certain rationalizing mental states. If the action = the event, and if the event is so caused, then so too is the action. By (P), there must then be a causal explanation for that action by those rationalizing mental states (under some description of them, and no

---

[6] Donald Davidson, 'Action, Reasons, and Causes', repr. in his *Essays on Actions and Events*, Oxford and New York: Clarendon Press, 1980: 3–19. See also the very helpful introduction by Ralf Stoecker, 'Reasons, Actions, and their Relationship', in the collection edited by him, *Reflecting Davidson*, New York: Walter de Gruyter, 1993: 265–90.

doubt under the description of them just as those rationalizing mental states). So the CTAE is bound to be true if the CTA is.

Although the CTA and the CTAE are logically distinct, it is sometimes difficult to keep criticism of them apart, since both require for their truth the existence of certain kinds of causes (rationalizing folk-psychological states), whether these be the causes of the movement which is the action or the explanatory causes of the action unreduced. So my arguments for the unavailability of such causes will equally well tell against the CTAE, if they tell against the CTA. The unavailability argument kills both the CTA and the CTAE stone dead. Still, one might have other reasons for rejecting the CTA, such that those reasons did not equally entail the falsity of the CTAE, and vice versa.

Causation and Generalization

Some philosophers have defended the view that action explanations are never causal explanations. One reason though for thinking that no explanations of actions are causal explanations is the alleged absence of covering laws in the case of action explanations.

Peter Winch, William Dray, A. I. Melden, Charles Taylor, Daniel Taylor, Alan Donagan, and others rejected the view that action explanation was causal explanation. They spoke of rational explanation, teleological explanation, purposive explanation, intentional explanation, and sometimes just of action explanation, contrasting it to causal explanation. But not all of them rejected the idea that actions had causes. That view, that actions have causes but that no action explanations are causal explanations, must accept that some causes do not explain their effects under any description; I find that view difficult to understand.

Only rarely did any of these authors give causelessness of action as the reason why one could not causally explain the action. These authors were writing in the shadow of Carl Hempel's work on explanation. Hempel's explanatory paradigm was unusual in philosophy, in terms of the extensive and dominating hold it had on philosophers, in the area of philosophy with which it dealt.

Although he spoke also of inductive-statistical explanation, Hempel was perhaps at his most influential with his D-N (deductive-nomological) model of explanation, mentioned above. For D-N explanation, Hempel required that the explanandum be deducible from true, empirical premises, at least one of which was a law of nature (or, as he put it, a law-like generalization).

Much of the sort of discussion which today is counted as action theory by philosophers existed in an earlier literature under the head of philosophy of history. Many philosophers of history, and of social science more generally, believed that the D-N model of explanation, with its requirement of law-like generalization, was not appropriate for history and the social sciences. They typically, although not invariably, conceded the D-N paradigm for the natural sciences, but resisted its application to the study of mankind.

Here are examples from Dray, Winch, and Taylor: in historical explanation, '. . . the establishment of a deductive logical connection between explanans and explanandum, based on the inclusion of suitable empirical laws in the former, is neither a necessary nor a sufficient condition of explaining';[7] 'Historical explanation is not the application of generalisations and theories to particular instances: it is the tracing of internal relations';[8] 'If you think of a historical event and try to imagine explaining it in a way which fulfils these criteria [for scientific explanation] you will see the difficulties at once. The problem is to find a universal proposition which both fits the case to be explained and is not falsified by other cases.'[9]

Causal explanations, the D-N model claimed, include or presuppose a law or law-like generalization, and yet there seems to be no such generalization available in the case of actions. To steal a case from Daniel Taylor, Henry VIII seized the monasteries because he wanted their revenue. But not all monarchs, or all English monarchs, who desire revenue (and who believe that seizing the monasteries would be a good, or the best, way to raise revenue) seize the monasteries. Monarchs would only do so if they were in a qualitatively identical situation, in the relevant respects, to the one old Henry was in. But that condition trivializes the search for a law: first, on the grounds of the apparent irremovabilty of the condition, 'relevant respects'; second, on grounds that the generalization is universal in form only by making its application so specific that it will in fact apply to only one case. It is not as if there cannot be laws of nature that apply to only one, or indeed no, case; indeed, there are such laws or law-like generalizations. Ideal gas laws are true of no real gases; frictionless surfaces exist nowhere.

But if we looked for laws in the social sciences and history, these writers

[7] William Dray, 'Historical Explanation of Actions Reconsidered', repr. in Patrick Gardiner, ed., The Philosophy of History, Oxford: Oxford University Press, 1978: 69–70.
[8] Peter Winch, The Idea of a Social Science, London: Routledge & Kegan Paul, 1967: 133.
[9] Daniel Taylor, Explanation and Meaning, Cambridge: Cambridge University Press, 1970: 74.

claimed, we would find that, in the realm of action, *all* of our generalizations would be single-case-specific in their application, and this might be
thought to defeat the whole purpose of insisting on laws in explanation, to
show how the single case fits into a regularity or pattern. Ideal gas laws, in
spite of being strictly true of nothing, still expose a pattern or regularity, but
a single-case-specific 'law' about Henry VIII would not.

There are some well-known gambits in this controversy. First, there is the
Churchland–Ayer response: there are law-like generalizations, with the
explanantia beliefs and desires in the antecedents and the explananda
actions in the consequences.[10] Second, there is Davidson's response, in
terms of the underlying laws covering the case in hand but using terminology different to that of the folk-psychological discourse of the explanans
and explanandum themselves.[11] Third, there is a bite-the-bullet response:
action explanations, unlike causal explanations generally, do not require
laws and hence are not causal explanations at all.

The response I develop in this chapter, which differs from all three of the
above responses, sets out an account of causal explanation generally, which
does not assume or require laws or law-like generalizations at all, not even
in the attenuated way in which Davidson requires them. I aim to show that
some of our action explanations can be causal explanations, in terms of
folk-psychological items, be they belief-and-desire pairs or whatever, even
if there were no relevant covering laws, not even underlying ones couched
in a different, non-folk-psychological vocabulary. And similarly for our
folk-physical explanations, which can be causal yet couched in terms of
ordinary macro-objects, at which level no covering laws can be formulated.
I try to show this by setting out an account of causal explanation that does
not assume the existence of such covering laws at the macro-level. There
are, of course, laws at the micro-level, but my account of causal explanation
at the macro-level does not require that any macro-explanations depend on
there being such.

I assume, following Davidson, that laws are strict, that is, exceptionless.
If it is a deterministic law that Fs are Gs, then every F without exception
must be a G. If it is a stochastic law that $\Pr(G, F) = p$, where $0 < p < 1$, then,
for any finite sample, s, it may well be that the proportion of Fs in s which
are Gs may not be exactly p. However, as one examines Fs indefinitely, the

[10] A. J. Ayer, 'Man as a Subject for Science', in P. Laslett and G. Runciman, eds., *Politics, Philosophy and Society*, Oxford: Basil Blackwell, 1987: 6–24. Paul Churchland, 'The Logical Character of Action-Explanations', *Philosophical Review*, 79, 1970: 214–36.
[11] Donald Davidson, 'Mental Events', reprinted in his *Essays on Actions and Events*.

proportion which are found to be Gs will tend to p, and in the limit, the proportion of Fs which are Gs will be exactly p.[12]

One salient feature of folk-psychological or folk-physical explanations is the apparent absence of such strict deterministic or probabilistic laws expressed in the vocabulary of the same level to back them. (I am assuming that the Churchland–Ayer strategy will not, in the end, be successful.) With these macro-explanations, we are back in the realm of the folk, but without the naturalism. There are no scientific laws that connect beliefs and desires with actions, or the arrival of spring with the melting of the snow. At best, what one finds at this level of folk explanation are (what Davidson called) heteronomic generalizations, or (what Scriven once called) truisms, or (what I prefer to call) conventional wisdom.[13] The snow melts when spring arrives—but not always, not without exceptions, *ceteris paribus*, and so on. But no scientific laws of any kind.

Why do such folk-psychological and folk-physical explanations or macro-explanations (I use the terms interchangeably) work, at least in those cases in which natural science does not overturn them? Some do, of course, get overturned. There is nothing sacrosanct about our conventional, folk wisdom. The folk-physical wisdom on how to cure many minor ailments is surely in error. But it is hard to see how any natural science could overturn the connection between the arrival of spring and the melting of the snow.

There are two answers to the above question that suggest themselves. For the sake of simplicity, I suppose in all of what follows that there are only two levels, a folk-physical or folk-psychological level at which no scientific laws can be formulated and a micro-level at which scientific laws can be formulated, even if the folk-physical explanations do not depend on them.

The first answer, the one I reject, holds that folk or macro-properties, in order to be explanatory, must connect in a specific way (call it 'the *a*-way', whatever it may be) with underlying scientific properties which appear in the strict laws of the micro-science. Let's call this 'the micro-strategy'. Jaegwon Kim, Louise Antony, Philip Petit and Frank Jackson, Jerry Fodor, Gabriel Segal, and Elliott Sober, in different ways and with various qualifi-

---

[12] When Davidson says 'that there are no serious [probabilistic] laws' in some area, he means 'more than [just that there is no] . . . statistical generalization (the statistical laws of physics are serious because they give sharply fixed probabilities, which spring from the nature of the theory) . . .'. Donald Davidson, 'Psychology as Philosophy', in his *Essays on Actions and Events*, 233.

[13] See Donald Davidson's distinction between homonomic and heteronomic generalizations, in 'Mental Events', in Lawrence Foster and J. W. Swanson, eds., *Experience & Theory*, London: Duckworth, 1970: 79–101 and reprinted in Davidson, *Essays on Actions and Events*, 207–27; also Michael Scriven's notion of a truism, in 'Truisms as the Grounds for Historical Explanations', in Patrick Gardiner, ed., *Theories of History*, New York: The Free Press, 1959: 443–75.

cations, are proponents of the micro-strategy.[14] Davidson himself seemed to subscribe to such a micro-strategy: such heteronomic generalizations 'however crude and vague, may provide good reason to believe that underlying the particular case there is a regularity that could be formulated sharply and without caveat'.[15] Various proposals have been advanced for spelling out the specific a-way in which explanatory macro-properties connect with the micro-physical and non-explanatory ones fail to do so.[16]

The second, or macro-strategy, which this chapter seeks to defend, supposes that it is possible to explain why some folk-psychological (and folk-physical) properties like believing and desiring something, are explanatory using only the resources available at the folk level itself. It is consistent with a macro-strategy that one could draw the distinction between explanatory and non-explanatory folk properties, using micro-level information as well, but a macro-strategy need hold only that it is not necessary to do so.[17] Some advocates of the macro-strategy argue more strongly that a micro-strategy will not work, but I do not intend to argue that stronger point here. Peter Menzies, Ernest Sosa, Fred Dretske, and Stephen Schiffer are proponents of the macro-strategy.[18] The macro-strategy attempts to account for folk

---

[14] J. Kim, 'Supervenience and Supervenient Causation', in T. Horgan, ed., *Spindel Conference 1983: Supervenience*, vol. 22, suppl., *The Southern Journal of Philosophy*, 45–56; Louise Antony, 'Anomalous Monism and the Problem of Explanatory Force', *Philosophical Review*, 98, 1989: 153–87, but see esp. 168–74; Jerry Fodor, 'Special Sciences (Or: the Disunity of Science as a Working Hypothesis', *Synthese*, 28, 1974: 97–115, and repr. as ch. 5 in his *Representations: A Philosophical Essays on the Foundations of Cognitive Science*, Brighton: Harvester Press, 1981; Frank Jackson and Philip Pettit, 'Functionalism and Broad Content', *Mind*, 97, 1988: 381–400, also 'Program Explanations: A General Perspective', *Analysis*, 50, 1990: 107–17; Gabriel Segal and Elliott Sober, 'The Causal Efficacy of Content', *Philosophical Studies*, 63, 1991: 1–30.

[15] Davidson, 'Mental Events', 93–4.

[16] Perhaps the most convincing is still Fodor's account, in 'Special Sciences'.

[17] Such a successful macro-strategy would then owe us an account of why we ought to prefer a macro-strategy rather than a micro-strategy if the distinction could otherwise be adequately drawn by both strategies. I attempt to develop an adequate macro-strategy in this chapter, but do not address the question of why it should be preferred to an otherwise adequate micro-strategy.

But here is one thought: why should successful folk explanation be committed to the assumption that there is any level at which strict laws can be formulated? Is it not possible for there to be a world in which folk explanation works, but which is strictly lawless all the way down? At every level, only incompleteable generalizations can be formulated. For some difficulties in formulating a micro-strategic account, see Segal and Sober, 'The Causal Efficacy of Content'.

[18] Peter Menzies argues for what might be called 'the causal autonomy' of supervening or macro-level events. Here is one of his best examples, taken from David Lewis: the high conductivity, the ductility, the opacity, and the distinctive lustre of a metal are all traceable to 'the cloud of free electrons which permeates the metal and which hold the atoms of the metal in a solid state' (pp. 566–7). See his 'Against Causal Reductionism', *Mind*, 97, 1988: 551–74. Also David Owens, 'Levels of Explanation', *Mind*, 98, 1989: 59–79. For Stephen Schiffer, see his 'Ceteris Paribus Laws', *Mind*, 100, 1991: 1–16. For references for Sosa and Dretske, see n. 19.

explanation in terms of the macro-objects, properties, and events at the folk level.

No successful macro-strategy can avoid the use of counterfactuals. The macro-strategy seeks to elucidate the concept of folk-psychological causal explanation by means of counterfactuals about causation, event types, and event tokens. The explanatory macro-strategy *presupposes* the ideas of causation and of a counterfactual; its task is not to elucidate them. Rather, it uses them to get at the idea of causal explanation. Notice in particular that the macro-strategy is not in any way committed to a counterfactual analysis of causation. It is important not to conflate a counterfactual analysis of causal explanation with a counterfactual analysis of causation itself. I am arguing only for the former.

The macro-strategy I shall examine makes liberal use of the idea of macro-causation. It would be desirable, if possible, to develop a macro-strategy for folk or macro-explanation that is as neutral as possible on the question of whether macro-causation disappears in the face of micro-causation (macro-causation is, of course, causation at the folk or macro-level; micro-causation, causation at the micro-level).

If the existence of underlying micro-causation in some sense puts into question the ontological status of folk or macro-causation, then as I understand the alternatives, there are at least three plausible views one might hold about their relationship (the views as I formulate them are undoubtedly vague and need further clarification):

(4) Macro-causal Epiphenomenalism: there is macro-causation, but it is a mere epiphenomenon of micro-causation.

(5) Macro-causal Reductionism: there is macro-causation, but it is not distinct from micro-causation.

(6) Macro-causal Eliminativism: there is no such thing as macro-causation.

The macro-causation required by the macro-strategy which I shall examine is consistent with both (4) and (5); *a fortiori*, it is consistent with a form of dualism about macro-causation and micro-causation that allows an even greater measure of independence and integrity to macro-causation, say a position in the philosophy of mind that speaks of emergent properties. I therefore state the macro-strategy for folk causal explanation making free use of macro-causation, but I intend that everything that I say is consistent with (4) and (5).

Suppose one accepted the eliminativist view (6). Would such a view still allow our folk psychology, and folk physics, the use of counterfactuals? Even if the eliminativist regards as ultimately unacceptable the idea of macro-causal relations, it is more difficult to believe that we must dispense with the use of macro-counterfactuals with explanatory force: if the public had not had such a high demand for petrol, the price would not have risen so dramatically. (I agree that such an eliminativist is not likely to accept a counterfactual analysis of macro-causation, since on his view macro-causation gets eliminated, not analysed.) If we are allowed the use of such macro-counterfactuals by the macro-causal eliminativist, then the explanation macro-strategy could be rewritten, eliminating all references to macro-causation, and replacing them by appropriate macro-counterfactuals. So understood, the explanation macro-strategy is even consistent with (6), as a theory about the sort of folk explanation which replaces causal folk explanation.

Of course, if our imagined eliminativist will not even permit macro-counterfactuals, the explanation macro-strategy fails. But that merely reflects the thought that, on any macro-strategy, the resources of folk psychology or folk physics must at least be rich enough to capture the idea of macro-explanation. Only the most extreme doctrine about the 'unreality' of the macro-level, which robs us even of macro-counterfactuals, deprives folk psychology and folk physics of any explanatory power.

I spoke above about explanation being 'under a description' and creating a non-extensional context. Again,

(7) an event c might explain another event e when c is described as, say, 'the F', but not when described as 'the F^*', even though both descriptions are true of c.

The non-extensionality of explanation cannot be fully captured only by making properties matter, since a property can be explanatory when referred to in one way (e.g. 'red'), and not when referred to in another (e.g. 'the colour of ripe strawberries'). 'Object o is red' may not explain or be explained by what 'object o is the colour of ripe strawberries' explains or is explained by. A property can be named or described in multiple ways, on any theory of property identity. No one, I take it, thinks that 'red' and 'the property I am now thinking about' must refer to different properties. I return to difficulties concerning the extensionality or otherwise of my account at the end of the chapter.

However, in keeping with most of the literature on causal explanation and causal relevance that I shall be discussing, I speak in what follows of an event qua having a certain property, say F, explaining or being explained. It is less cumbersome to express what I wish to say using this locution, but in truth it should always be understood as an event qua a certain name or description, say 'F' or 'the F', being true of it that explains or is explained.

Notice that no description of c like 'the F' is explanatory *per se*. It is explanatory of an event e only relative to some specific description of e like 'the G'; 'the F' may be explanatory relative to e's being described as 'the G' but fail to be explanatory relative to another of e's descriptions, 'the G^*'. I typically omit this qualification in what follows, also for ease of exposition.

The Analysis of Folk Causal Explanation

A specific macro-strategy for accounting for the explanatory force of folk physics and folk psychology (I mean the ensuing discussion to cover both and move freely between examples of the two kinds) is suggested by Ernest Sosa, Fred Dretske, and Stephen Schiffer.[19] Schiffer says that he will ignore a qualification that would be required to deal with relatively rare cases of causal overdetermination, to which I will return later. Schiffer's initial statement of a proposal for such a macro-strategy (one that he will modify below) is this:

(8) the F causally explains the G iff (*a*) the F caused the G, and (*b*) the F would not have caused the G if the F had not been an F.

So, for example, (holding the relevant belief fixed) Henry VIII's desire for revenue causally explains his seizing the monasteries, since that desire (assuming the relevant belief) caused the seizing, and if what occurred had not been a desiring of revenue, it would not have caused the seizing. I presuppose that, in the context in which they are being used, definite descriptions like 'the F' and 'the G' successfully refer to a unique event.

Let 'F' be 'is a cause of G'. (8) would seem to make the cause's property, being a cause of G, an explanatory property of the cause, which intuitively it is not. It is true that the cause of G caused the G, and true that if the cause of G had not been a cause of G, it would not have caused the G, but false that the cause of G causally explains the G. However, when 'F' is 'is a cause of G', (8)(*b*) is a priori true (or analytically true); if the cause of G had not been a cause of G, it would not have caused the G. So, both in (8) and its

---

[19] Stephen Schiffer, 'Ceteris Paribus Laws', 13–14; Ernest Sosa, 'Mind–Body Interaction and Supervenient Causation', *Midwest Studies in Philosophy*, 9, 1984: 277–8; Fred Dretske, in an unpublished manuscript. Dretske and Sosa write about causal relevance, not explanatory relevance, but the lessons are similar.

subsequent improvements, I restrict 'F' and 'G' to cases which do *not* make any of the clauses a priori (or analytic) truths.

As it stands, (8)(b) invites us to consider what would have been the case had some token event not had a property which it in fact did have.[20] Such a formulation might suggest transworld identity, that numerically one and the same token event (or substance, for that matter) can exist both in the actual and in a merely possible world.

Further, even apart from more general worries about transworld identity, some may believe more specifically that at least some properties are essential to the particular events that have those properties. Can we really understand what it would be to consider what would have been the case, had this very token revenue desiring not been a desiring of revenue, or even a desiring of anything at all?

If the reader thinks he can answer these sorts of questions, let him accept (8) as it stands, but for those with doubtful intuitions about these counterfactual questions concerning an actual token event, they should replace the old (8)(b) with its counterpart about a numerically different but qualitatively very similar token (I shall employ this amended formulation in what follows). Let c be the actual token event which is F (hence, c=the F), and c^* be the merely possible token event which fails to be F. c^* resembles c as much as possible (apart, of course, from its failing to be F):

(8)(b*) if there had been another token event c^* in place of the F, which failed to be an F, c^* would not have caused the G.

(8)(b*) will be true only if c^* would not have caused the G, had it occurred instead of c.

(8) has an attractive feature worth remarking. Other things being equal, we ought to prefer a unified account of causal explanation, which applies both to folk and scientific explanation. On any micro-strategy, different accounts will have to be given for causal explanation at a macro-level at which there are no laws and for causal explanation at the micro-level at which are laws. (8), unlike various micro-strategy proposals, yields just such a unified account of causal explanation. (8) can be construed as an analysis of 'the F causally explains the G', *sans qualification* by either 'macro' or 'micro', since it can be used as an analysis of causal explanation at both levels.

---

[20] I cannot here treat general problems about truth-conditions for counterfactuals. I am making well-known assumptions about similarities between possible worlds and the fixity of the laws of nature in the worlds most similar to the actual world.

202202A Counterfactual Theory of Explanation

What can be said against (8)? I consider three objections: (O1) The account is not sufficient for the F to causally explain the G, on the grounds that overgeneral properties do not explain but the account is true of them; (O2) The account is not necessary, on the grounds that overspecific properties explain but the account is not true of them; (O3) The account is not necessary, on the grounds that overdetermining, pre-empting, and other properties explain, but the account is not true of them.[21]

(O1) is raised by Schiffer himself, as an objection to (8). Schiffer thinks that the conjunction of (a) and (b) is a *necessary* but not a *sufficient* condition for the F to causally explain the G. His alleged counter-example to its being sufficient is this: Hugo burped in the presence of Regina, and this caused him to become embarrassed.

A burping by Hugo in the presence of Regina is explanatory of Hugo's becoming embarrassed, because if Hugo's burping in the presence of Regina had not been a burping by Hugo in the presence of Regina, it (we are supposing) would not have caused this instance of embarrassment by him. So far, so good.

But now consider the property, a doing of something by Hugo in the presence of someone, true also of the token burping. If Hugo's burping in the presence of Regina had not been a doing of something by Hugo in the presence of someone, it would not have caused this instance of embarrassment by him. So, (8) makes the property, Hugo's doing something in the presence of someone, explanatory of the embarrassment, when according to Schiffer it in fact is not, and so (8) cannot be providing sufficient conditions for a property's being explanatory. (It would be easy to alter Schiffer's example to provide a folk-psychological example in which the psychological causes rationalize the subsequent action: suppose Henry's desiring revenue and his believing that seizing the monasteries will bring him revenue together causally explain why he seized the monasteries. Then consider just

---

[21] Segal and Sober's 'common cause' objection in Segal and Sober, 'The Causal Efficacy of Content', has no force against the likes of (8), if we are explicating causal explanation (and not causal relevance, if that is a different idea). They claim (pp. 5–6) that an account like (8) fails for the following case: suppose a piece of coal's being hot causes both the coal's being red and a piece of tissue to smoulder. Since, they say, if the piece of coal had not been red, it would not have been hot (they accept a backtracking counterfactual), and so the tissue would not have smouldered, (8) wrongly makes the coal's being red explanatory (causally efficacious?) of the tissue's smouldering.

However, they must be assuming that the coal's being red did cause the tissue to smoulder, since (8) also requires that this be so. But that is a truth only if the coal's being red = the coal's being hot, which is inconsistent with their assumption that the latter causes the former.

his desiring something-or-other, rather than specifically his desiring revenue.)

Schiffer seeks to impose on (8) three further conditions, having to do with manipulability, epistemic accessibility, and being part of a reliable predictive practice, which he says are pragmatic constraints, in order to meet the difficulty generated by these overgeneral properties. Schiffer's pragmatic elaborations are unnecessary. Notice that there is a difference between explanatorily irrelevant properties and explanatorily relevant but overgeneral ones. Suppose that Hugo's burping = the most unusual thing he did that day. From the point of view of explaining Hugo's embarrassment, the event's also being unusual is simply irrelevant. Unusual things don't embarrass Hugo *per se*. (See the next objection, (O2), for more on this case.)

But if that token event is a burping by Hugo in the presence of Regina, it must also be a doing of something by Hugo in the presence of someone. The event qua a doing of something by Hugo in the presence of someone is *not* strictly explanatorily irrelevant to Hugo's embarrassment, in the way in which its being an unusual event was. It is simply not specific enough to capture all of what is explanatorily important, namely, that it was a burping by him in the presence of Regina, even though it will pass the test of (8), since it is entailed by the property that does capture all of what is explanatorily important. In that sense, a doing of something by Hugo in front of someone is 'part' of a burping by Hugo in the presence of Regina, since the latter entails the former.

I disagree with Schiffer about the explanatory force of overgeneral properties. He claims that they do not explain at all; I think that overgeneral properties make for explanations that are both very poor and very partial. This suggests a strategy for dealing with Schiffer's alleged counter-example. I rely on the intuitive idea of the degree of determinateness of a property, without explicating it. For those who think that all properties or universals are fully determinate, one can rephrase the point in terms of more or less determinate specifications of a property.

Suppose one constructs a hierarchy h of logically related properties, running from the more indeterminate (a doing of something by someone in the presence of someone else) to the increasingly more determinate (a burping by Hugo in the presence of Regina). It is *true*, not false as Schiffer asserts, that the doing of something by Hugo in the presence of someone causally explains at least poorly and partially Hugo's embarrassment. There are better and worse explanations, full and partial ones, as we saw earlier, and as we select increasingly determinate properties, they will better and more fully explain his embarrassment.

If we were explicating '. . . at least partially and perhaps rather poorly causally explains . . .', Schiffer's overgeneral properties provide no counter-example at all to (8). Schiffer merely conflates 'no explanation' with 'very little or poor explanation'. Overgeneral properties do provide some degree of explanation, however incomplete and poor. If, on the other hand, we seek an analysis for '. . . fully (or, completely) causally explains . . .' or '. . . explains well . . .', then the property we want is *the most determinate property in h that passes the test required by (8)(a) and (b)*. It does not matter that more indeterminate properties (or, properties as indeterminately described) also pass the relevance test and hence provide incomplete or partial or poor explanations.

Suppose a different case in which Hugo only coughed in front of Regina instead of burping: *voilà*, no embarrassment! Yet, the coughing is also a doing of something by Hugo in front of her, but the doing of something in front of her by him (in this second case) does not explain at all, not even partially and poorly. It can't, because there is no embarrassment to explain. Does this show that the overgeneral property does not explain, even partially and poorly, even in the first case?

It is not easy to see how this could be a difficulty for my view. What this objection shows is that a token of such a very general type, like a doing of something by Hugo in someone's presence, might be explanatory of something in one case (where there is a burping) and a different token of that same type would fail to be explanatory in another, different case (where there is only a coughing). And this must surely be right.

So we need to modify Schiffer's account to deal with the case of explanation by overgeneral properties. Let '*h*' be such a hierarchy of logically related properties, running from the more to the less determinate, at least one of whose members passes the test of (*a*) and (*b*):

(9) the F fully causally explains the G iff (*a*) the F caused the G, and (b) if there had been another token event c^* in place of the F, which failed to be an F, c^* would not have caused the G, and (*c*) in the hierarchy of properties, *h*, to which F belongs, F is the most determinate property in *h* that still meets conditions (*a*) and (*b*).

(O2) is the reverse of the one Schiffer mentions: (9) might be thought to be *sufficient* but not *necessary*. Consider the overspecific property, being a burping by Hugo when he is wearing a blue shirt in the presence of Regina.

On the supposition with which we are working, that he was wearing a blue shirt was irrelevant to the explanation of why Hugo felt embarrassed. If he had not been wearing a blue shirt while burping, the burp would have caused the very same embarrassment. For example, a burp while wearing a white shirt would still have caused this same embarrassment.

Hugo's burping in the presence of Regina while wearing a blue shirt fails the test required by (9)(b), but *if* it is a property explanatory of his embarrassment all the same, in spite of the inclusion of the explanatorily irrelevant information about his shirt colour, it follows that (9) cannot provide a necessary condition for a folk property's being so explanatory.

Is there a rationalizing folk-psychological example that makes the same point? I believe there is. Suppose I walk to a store to purchase some milk. Why did I walk there? I desired some milk, and I believe that the store stocks milk in bottles with a blue top. My belief is too specific, since all I wanted was milk in some type of container or other, which type making no difference to me. I would have walked to the store, had I believed that there was milk there in red-topped bottles instead. Of course, one might well argue that if someone believes that there is milk in blue-topped bottles there, then it follows that he believes that there is milk there too. And so it may be. The question, though, is whether his believing that there is milk at the store in blue-topped bottles, in conjunction with his desire for milk, is explanatory of his walking to the store and, if so, to what extent.

To deal with this problem, we shall have to distinguish two different positions on what the addition of overspecific irrelevant information does to an otherwise acceptable explanation. Some, like Wesley Salmon, think that an overspecific property provides no explanation at all of an explanandum. Recall Salmon's sugar that dissolves in holy water and John Jones, his male friend, who also takes birth control pills and never becomes pregnant; Salmon distinguishes explanations from arguments by claiming that additional irrelevant premises do not alter the validity of an argument, but are 'fatal' for explanations.[22] Others will merely hold that overspecific properties provide worse explanations, since they are irrelevantly specific, but explanations of some sort none the less.

Call the first view 'the destruction by irrelevance view' (the d-i view). Call the second 'the worsening by irrelevance view' (the w-i view). On the d-i view, no difficulty for (9) arises. If being a burping by Hugo in the presence

[22] See Wesley Salmon, 'The Third Dogma of Empiricism', in Robert Butts and Jaako Hintikka, eds., *Basic Problems in Methodology and Linguistics*, Dordrecht: Reidel, 1977: 149–66.

of Regina is the most determinate property such that (*a*) and (*b*) are true, then even more determinate properties like the property of being a burping by Hugo while wearing a blue shirt in the presence of Regina are such that (9)(*b*) is false of them and hence they are simply not explanatory, fully or otherwise. There is an event that is *not* a burping by Hugo in front of Regina while wearing a blue shirt that will still cause Hugo's embarrassment, namely when he burps in front of Regina in a white shirt, etc. On the d-i view, these cases provide no counter-example to (9) after all. For an overspecific property that fails to explain at all, both the left-hand side and the right-hand side of the analysis will be false.

The difficulty for (9) arises only on the w-i view. On this view, some properties, like the property of being a burping by Hugo while wearing a blue shirt in the presence of Regina, are such that (*b*) is false of them but they are, on this view, to some degree at least, still explanatory. Isn't the left-hand side of the analysis true but the right-hand side false, on the w-i view?

I shall not explicitly rewrite (9), but the way in which this difficulty can be surmounted is this. Say that a property F provides a succinct explanation for the G (whether full or partial) if F is the most determinate property for which (*b*) is true. Then consider any property H that is more determinate than F, but for which (*b*) is false. Say that H provides an excessive explanation for the G (whether full or partial) just when there is some property F ($F \neq H$) which provides a succinct explanation for the G and to which H is related in the way I have described. Thus, (9) can be maintained whether the d-i or w-i view is correct.[23]

Would Hugo have been embarrassed if he had burped in some other female's presence? Was his embarrassment Regina-specific? (9) helps us sort out these questions. If he would not have been embarrassed except in the presence of Regina, then the explanatory property or anyway explanatorily succinct property (depending on whether one takes the d-i or the w-i view) of the burp is that it was a burp in the presence of Regina. If he would have been embarrassed in the presence of any other female, then the explanatory

---

[23] Suppose that this lump of stuff would have dissolved, whether it had been salt or sugar. Now, to say of this lump that its being salt explains its dissolving is overspecific, since it would have dissolved had it been sugar or salt.

However, its being salt is surely, one might think, not an overspecific explanation of its dissolution; it is more succinct than the disjunction, not less so. I think that this stuff's being salt *is* overspecific compared to the disjunction, perhaps despite initial reactions, but it is a long story. See John Meixner, 'Homogeneity and Explanatory Depth', *Philosophy of Science*, 46, 1979: 366–81.

property or explanatorily succinct property of the burp would be that it was a burp in the presence of a female, and that it was a burp in the presence of Regina would be an overspecific property for the purposes of explanation, even when the burp was in fact a burp in the presence of Regina, and hence either non-explanatory (on the d-i view) or anyway excessive (on the w-i view).

(O3) Ernest LePore and Barry Loewer, in their discussion of the causal relevance of psychological properties (and this would apply to folk-physical properties as well), raise another objection to the macro-strategy (although they do not employ this terminology).[24] Their objection is a version of (O3). They claim that an account similar to (8) is a sufficient but not a necessary condition for the F to causally explain the G. Their claim is that (8), and its likes, are too strong, since they would make the underlying micro-property taken from the strict law, if there is one, irrelevant to the causal explanation of the outcome.

Let F be some macro-property, and let V be the disjunction of micro-properties M, P, and Q, with which F is connected.[25] Suppose that this F, this token desiring of revenue, (a) was in fact an M, (b) could have been P or Q but wasn't, and (c) that there is a strict law connecting being V and desiring revenue. (8), and its subsequent improvements, make the desiring of revenue being an M explanatorily irrelevant to the seizing of the monasteries.

Given a plausible view about the truth conditions for counterfactuals, it is false that if the desiring of the revenue had not been M, the desiring (with the belief fixed) would not have caused the seizing. In a closest possible world in which the desiring of revenue isn't an M, since the desiring won't be altogether microproperty-less in that world, it has some other micro-property that is an element of V: it is a P or a Q, and in that close world the monasteries get seized after all. So the relevant counterfactual is false, with the result that (8), and of course (9), would make the token desiring of revenue's actual micro-property, taken from a strict law which links that micro-property to the seizing, explanatorily irrelevant to the seizing.[26] Let's

[24] Ernest LePore and Barry Loewer, 'Mind Matters', *Journal of Philosophy*, 84, 1987: 630–42. See 638–40.

[25] I use the deliberately vague 'connected', in order to avoid any discussion about the nature of the macro–micro relation. Some will think that F supervenes on each element of V; others, that $F = V$; still others that the connection is merely nomic in some sense. Readers may plug in their favourite views here about this issue, since nothing I say depends on how this connection is to be understood.

[26] One might swallow the view that the micro-properties connected to a desiring of revenue *are* explanatorily irrelevant to the seizing of the monasteries. The micro-properties connected to

call M, the micro-property that such a thing actually does have, its L-L property, and P or Q, the other elements in V, the micro-properties it would have if it were not M, its L-L alternative properties.

Such a possibility may have occurred to the reader while discussing poor Hugo's embarrassment. Suppose his burp had instead been a hiccup (or, he had hiccupped instead of burped). Surely he would have suffered the very same bout of embarrassment. Although this possibility does not concern a macro-property and a disjunction of micro-properties, the fact that there would be, in such a case, a disjunction of properties, each disjunct of which, if instantiated, would explain the explanandum, raises issues similar to LePore and Loewer's example.

I hereafter call the sort of case LePore and Loewer describe an 'L-L' case. We also have cases that Schiffer referred to as 'rare' or 'special' cases of overdetermination. We need, then, to deal with two sorts of problems: L-L cases, and 'rare' cases of overdetermination.

In what way are the cases of overdetermination that I shall consider 'special' or 'rare'? Special overdetermination does not focus on two events, but on two properties of one event. Suppose c is both F and F^*. c causes e. Had c remained F but not been F^*, c would still have caused e; had c remained F^* but not been F, c would still have caused e. If c had been neither F nor F^*, c would not have caused e. For example, suppose a switch does not light a light just by being turned on. Rather, if I turn on the switch quickly, the light lights, and if I turn on the switch with my left hand, the light also lights. Now imagine I turn on the switch quickly, and with my left hand. The light's lighting is overdetermined, in the special or rare sense.

So, the two cases can be summarized in this way. In a case of property overdetermination, c is both F and F^*, and c causes e, c would not cause e if it had been neither F nor F^*, and had c not been F, it would still have been F^* and have caused e, and had c not been F^*, it would still have been F and have caused e. In an L-L case, c is F, is *not* F^*, and c causes e, but had c not been F, c would then have been F^* and caused e. (One can of course re-express this using the idea of a possible event c^* that lacked some of the properties that the actual event c had, or which had some that c lacked, as in $(8)(b^*)$.) L-L cases differ from cases of causal pre-emption, which I do not

---

a revenue desiring are uncontroversially explanatorily relevant to the micro-properties connected to a monastery seizing, but it does not follow that they are explanatorily relevant as well to the monastery seizing. I shall discuss their objection as it stands, as if the micro-properties *are* explanatorily relevant to the monastery seizing, but it would be possible to adopt this alternative strategy in dealing with LePore and Lower's objection.

discuss, for a reason I mentioned in the Introduction. In a case of causal pre-emption, c would be both F and F*; in an L-L case, c is F but is not F*.

A counter-example to (8) or (9) will arise whenever: (*a*) there is some disjunction of properties, say $F \vee F^*$, such that a token event c would cause an effect e when it has any one of the properties of the disjunction, (*b*) c has at least one of those properties, (*c*) and the most similar world in which c does not have that property is a world in which it has (still or instead) another of those properties. In such a case, although the F does causally explain the G, it is false that if that event had not been an F, it would not have caused the G. These conditions for a counter-example to (8) or (9) will be met in both cases: L-L cases, and cases of property overdetermination.

How shall we deal with these counter-examples? The basic idea is that the explanatory relevance of a property like F, when there is another property like F* as in the cases above, cannot be explicated at the level of F itself, but only at the level of the non-redundant disjunction of F and F*. In the sense in which I will require the term, a disjunction is *redundant* relative to some test t if it passes t, but if a disjunction with at least one fewer disjunct (or a single disjunct of that disjunction) passes t just as well. So, in the case at hand, we are imagining the *least* differences there would have to be between c^* and c, in order for it to be true that c does, but c^* would not, cause the G.

(*b*) must be rewritten as follows:

(10) the F fully causally explains the G iff (*a*) the F caused the G, and (*b*) either (i) if there had been another token event c^* in place of the F, which failed to be an F, c^* would not have caused the G, *or* (ii) there is a non-redundant disjunction of properties V, of which F is an element, such that if c^* had not had any of the properties which are elements of V, c^* would not have caused the G, and (*c*) in the hierarchy (or hierarchies, in the disjunctive case) of properties, h, to which F (or the elements of V) belongs, F (or each element of V) is the most determinate property in h that still meets conditions (*a*) and (*b*).

Although (10) correctly makes overdetermining and L-L properties explanatory, a worry might arise that (10) will now wrongly make intuitively non-explanatory properties, for example, L-L alternative properties, or irrelevant properties, or perhaps both of two overdetermining properties, explanatory as well.

The easiest case to deal with is property overdetermination. In a case of property overdetermination, the right-hand side of (10) is true for both overdetermining properties, F and F*, since both are members of the non-redundant disjunction, $F \vee F^*$, but this is acceptable, or anyway arguably so. Each of c's being F and c's being F^* does fully explain the G since c causes the G when it has both or either. On the other hand, for those who doubt whether overdeterminers are causes and hence causally explanatory of what they overdetermine, it would be a straightforward matter to add a further clause that denied that there was any explanation by either of the two overdetermining properties in the case in which more than a single property met the other conditions on the right-hand side of (10). And for those who are prepared to concede that each overdeterminer causes and hence explains, but that each does so on its own only partly, a clause can be added which weakens the explanation to mere partial explanation for such cases.

(10) correctly allows L-L properties as explanatory. Such properties are elements of the sort of non-redundant disjunction mentioned in (b)(ii). But does (10) wrongly make either (i) L-L *alternative* properties, or (ii) intuitively *irrelevant* properties, all of which we wish *not* to count as explanatory in the circumstances, explanatory? Let me take each in turn.

(i) It is crucial first to see why (10) does not make L-L alternative properties explanatory, as indeed it should not. Hugo burps, and (10) makes burping (F) explanatory. Hugo does not hiccup. But if he had hiccupped instead, he would also have been embarrassed, so the relevant disjunction in (10) must include both hiccupping (F^*) and burping (F), since there is a connection between hiccupping or burping and becoming embarrassed. Doesn't (10) now wrongly make hiccupping (F^*) as well as burping (F) explanatory of Hugo's actual embarrassment? But that could not be correct; Hugo's actual embarrassment could not be explained by something he did *not* do but only could have done! But his hiccupping as well as his burping is a member of the relevant non-redundant disjunction.

On the occasions on which c is F and *not* actually F^* (as in any L-L example), it is of course false that c's being F^* explains the G. But (10) gets this right, since (10)(a) is not true: 'the F^*' does not refer at all, or anyway does not refer to c, since the property F^* is a property that c does *not* actually have. (Hugo *didn't* hiccup.) So the F^* did not cause e, since the F did.

There is no need to go further and examine the truth of the counterfactuals mentioned in either (b)(i) or (b)(ii). *Even though these counterfactuals are true both for the L-L alternative properties and for the L-L properties*, since (10)(a) is not true for any L-L alternative property, no L-L alternative property F^*, which is a property a cause like c would have had under certain counterfactual conditions, is explanatory of an actual effect. Of course, an L-L alternative property could be explanatory in different circumstances, but we are explicating 'the F *does* fully causally explain the G', not 'the F *could* have fully causally explained the G'.

(ii) Consider now some intuitively non-explanatory, irrelevant property D and some intuitively explanatory property F, both of which are properties that the explanans event c actually does possess. Moreover, consider the disjunction, $F \vee D$. Does (10) make D explanatory, on the grounds that it is a disjunct of a disjunction that passes (10)? No, it does not, since the qualification that requires the disjunction to be *non-redundant* ensures that a property like $F \vee D$ fails to pass (10), since F alone passes the test imposed by (10).

(10) as emended does adequately explicate our intuitive idea of explanatory relevance, without recourse to the *explicit* assumption of there being laws in which the explanatory properties appear (whether this is really so will depend on one's account of the truth conditions for counterfactuals), and indeed without recourse to any micro-level information whatsoever.

Extensionality Problems

Epistemology and metaphysics come together, to give us our conception of explanation. That explanation has an epistemic face to it is evidenced by its non-extensionality. Even if the causal relation is extensional, the relation of causal explanation is not.

Extensionality is a single idea, but the question of extensionality arises for different types of expressions of a language. As Susan Haack puts it,

A context is *extensional* if co-referential expressions—singular terms with the same denotation, predicates with the same extension, or sentences with the same truth-value—are substitutable within it without changing the truth-value of the whole, '*salva veritate*', i.e., if *Leibniz' law* holds for it; otherwise, it is *intensional*.[27]

In what follows, I use 'intensional' and 'non-extensional' synonymously.

Let's call the first sort of truth-preserving substitutability of singular terms with the same denotation 'transparency'; the second sort, substitutability of predicates with the same extension, 'predicate extensionality'; the third sort, substitutability of sentences with the same truth-value, 'sentence extensionality' (or, 'truth-functionality').

In which of these ways is explanation intensional? John listens to his favourite nature programme, and on it there is a dog, Fido, which, as John

27 Susan Haack, *Philosophy of Logics*, Cambridge: Cambridge University Press, 1978: 246.

is told, has a heart. John does not know that that animal is the Queen's oldest corgi, and, being both a biological ignoramus and a non-reader of Quine, does not know that all and only animals with hearts have kidneys. Unbeknownst to poor John, Fido's other name is 'Rover'.

Suppose Fido's having a heart explains why Fido's blood circulates. Explanation is neither predicate extensional nor truth-functional, since it is neither the case that Fido's having a kidney explains why Fido's blood circulates, nor that John's being ignorant of biology (since 'John is ignorant of biology' has the same truth-value as 'Fido has a heart') explains why Fido's blood circulates.

Is explanation transparent for co-designating terms, definite descriptions, and names? Explanation is not transparent, because substitution of 'the Queen's oldest corgi' for 'Fido', produces a falsehood. The Queen's oldest corgi's having a heart does not explain why Fido's blood circulates. Similarly, Rover's having a heart does not explain why Fido's blood circulates. 'Explanations' such as these, far from providing enlightenment, would merely produce puzzlement and incomprehension. What on earth does Rover's having a heart have to do with Fido's blood circulating? Are Fido and Rover joined by some machine, so that Rover's heart pumps blood around Fido's body? How unusual!

But, all this having been said, is it really *false* that the Queen's oldest corgi's (or Rover's) having a heart explains why Fido's blood circulates? If someone, unlike John, did believe that Fido was the Queen's oldest corgi, or that Fido=Rover, then for that person it would be an explanation of sorts. Armed with that knowledge, he would not be misled into the joined-by-some-machine hypothesis.

Let's call such an explanation 'derivatively explanatory'. An explanation may be derivatively explanatory for a person only if it is explanatory in virtue of that person's belief that some a posteriori identity claim is true. Fido's having a heart explains Fido's blood circulation *sans* qualification; if Fido = the G, then the G's having a heart may derivatively explain why Fido's blood circulates only for the person who believes the a posteriori identity.

To understand non-derivative explanation, we imagine someone who does not believe any a posteriori identities about Fido, for example: that Fido = Rover, that Fido is the Queen's oldest corgi, and so on. The person does not fail to believe that Fido = Fido, and similar a priori identities. There are explanatory failures of the sort I indicated above, arising from the lack of substitutability of the various kinds, if explanation is taken to be non-derivative explanation, which is the sense which I shall want hereafter.

There is a fourth sort of extensionality that we shall need. Consider two predicates, 'F' and 'G', which stand for or name the same property, whatever the criterion of property identity the reader prefers, but surely stronger than just coextensionality. Indeed, if coextensionality were enough, this type of extensionality would merely collapse into predicate extensionality. Call any pair of such predicates 'co-typical predicates'. A context is co-typical predicate extensional if there is substitutability *salva veritate* of predicates that are co-typical.

The property of being red = the property of being the colour of ripe strawberries. Consider the sentence 'John believes that roses are red'. The context following 'John believes that . . .' is not co-typical predicate extensional since it does not follow that John believes that roses are the colour of ripe strawberries.

Co-typical predicate extensionality is similar to transparency, as far as explanation is concerned. Suppose that the flame's turning red explains the reading on the meter. It does not follow that the flame's turning the colour of ripe strawberries explains the meter reading, except derivatively for the person who happens to know that red is the colour of ripe strawberries. In the non-derivative sense, explanation is not co-typical property extensional. It is not only properties (or objects) that matter to explanation, but also how we refer to or designate them. Using one name or definite description of a thing or property may be explanatory, whereas using a different name or description of the thing or property may not be, except derivatively to the person who knows the relevant a posteriori identity.

Problems for my Analysis

My analysis, put simply and without introducing the various necessary complications, of 'the F causally explains the G' (in the non-derivative sense) was: (*a*) the F caused the G, and (*b*) if there had been another token event c^* in place of the F, which failed to be an F, c^* would not have caused the G. (And (*c*) was the condition about the hierarchy of properties.) But how could my analysis be adequate? If explanation has an epistemic aspect, it is implausible that the analysis as it stands, in terms of causation and a counterfactual about causation, gets at that epistemic aspect. If the epistemic aspect of explanation appears in its non-extensionality, then the failure of the analysis to get at that epistemic aspect should be evidenced by the fact that the right-hand side (RHS) and the left-hand side (LHS) of the analysis do not match in respect of extensionality/non-extensionality.

Such indeed appears to be the case.[28] The LHS of the analysis (of non-derivative causal explanation) is non-extensional, in all of the senses described. It does not admit of substitution *salva veritate* of sentences with the same truth-value, co-designating names or definite descriptions, co-extensive properties, or even co-typical properties, as we have just observed. If the RHS is a correct analysis of the LHS, the RHS must be non-extensional in just the same ways; if it is not, we can find a case in which the LHS is false but the RHS, true.

The counterfactual in clause (*b*) on the RHS certainly makes properties matter; its sensitivity to properties disallows the substitutability of co-extensive properties. 'If *x* had not had a heart, its blood would not have circulated' is true, but, happily for my analysis, it does not follow that if *x* had not had a kidney, its blood would not have circulated, since the possible world in which it has no kidney but retains a heart and its blood keeps circulating is closer to the actual world than is the possible world in which it has no kidney but retains a heart and its blood does not circulate. So in the possible world in which it loses its kidneys, its blood keeps circulating. Thus far, the LHS and RHS display the same measure of non-extensionality. Replacing 'has a heart' by 'has a kidney' produces falsehoods on both sides of the biconditional. My analysis can explain why Fido's having a kidney does not explain the circulation of his blood.

The central problem for my analysis is with transparency and co-typical predicate extensionality. Let me restrict the discussion to the latter, although the same issues arise for the former (with, I hope, the same resolution). The flame's turning red causally explains the meter reading iff the flame's turning red caused the meter reading and if the flame had not turned red (suppose for instance that it had turned blue), its turning colour would not have caused the meter reading. Both the LHS and the RHS are true. So far, so good.

Red is the colour of ripe strawberries. Now consider: (CP) the flame's turning the colour of ripe strawberries causally explains the meter reading iff the flame's turning the colour of ripe strawberries caused the meter reading and if the flame had not turned the colour of ripe strawberries, the flame's turning colour would not have caused the meter reading. It is false

---

[28] I think Paul Noordhof first led me to see this.

that the flame's turning the colour of ripe strawberries causally explains the meter reading. So the LHS is false.

What about the RHS of the analysis? In the actual world, the colour of ripe strawberries is red and the flame does turn red. The counterfactual asks us to consider a possible world in which the flame does not turn the colour of ripe strawberries. What is that world like? It seems plain that the counterfactual is holding fixed the actual colour of ripe strawberries, and asks us to consider the possible world in which the flame does not turn *that* colour, that is, does not turn red.

If so, then the RHS of the analysis is true: the flame's turning the colour of ripe strawberries did cause the meter reading, and if the flame had not turned that colour (i.e. red), it would not have caused the meter reading. The possible world in which the colour of ripe strawberries is red and the flame does not turn the colour of ripe strawberries (i.e. does not turn red and hence does not cause the meter reading) is closer to the actual world than the world in which the colour of ripe strawberries is blue and the flame does not turn the colour of ripe strawberries (does not turn blue, so does turn red and hence does cause the meter reading). For simplicity, I am assuming that the flame can only turn red or blue, and that no other colour is available for the flame to turn. Nothing in my argument depends on the simplification.

The first possible world differs from the actual world in point of two local alterations (the colour the flame turns and the non-occurrence of the meter reading); the second in terms of very many local alterations (the colour of loads of strawberries), even though the meter reading does occur in that second possible world, just as it does in the actual world. The LHS is false, but the RHS is true, so the analysis cannot be right.

How might we deal with this apparent counter-example to my analysis? My analysis thus far of the concept of causal *explanation* in terms of causation and counterfactuals about causation omits from the analysans anything obviously epistemological. Perhaps the two problems, the counter-example to the analysis and the omission from the analysis of an epistemological component, are related. The above remark about derivative and non-derivative explanation gives us, I think, the clue we need. Recall that some explanations, the derivative ones, only work because of beliefs about a posteriori identities. The flame's turning the colour of ripe strawberries could indeed *derivatively* explain the meter reading, but *only* when it was believed that red is the colour of ripe strawberries. If we were offering an analysis of derivative explanation, the LHS would be true, as is the RHS, not false as we assumed. So there is no counter-example after all to my analysis, if it is construed as an analysis of derivative explanation.

In the analysis of non-derivative explanation, what is needed on the RHS of the analysis is a fourth clause, (d), that adds the missing epistemological aspect to the analysans. The clause needs to make the RHS as a whole true for the flame's turning red (since the LHS is true: the flame's turning red does causally explain the meter reading) but make the RHS as a whole false for the flame's turning the colour of ripe strawberries (since the LHS is false: the flame's turning the colour of ripe strawberries does not non-derivatively explain the meter reading):

(d) If a person did not believe any a posteriori identities about the F, he would (still) believe (a) and (b).

(d) is true for 'the flame's turning red'. If a person believes no a posteriori identities about the flame's turning red, he will still believe that the flame's turning red caused the meter reading, and that if the flame had not turned red, it would not have caused the reading. On the other hand, (d), and hence the RHS, is false for 'the flame's turning the colour of ripe strawberries'. If a person does not believe any a posteriori identities about the flame's turning the colour of ripe strawberries (and in particular does not believe that it is identical to the flame's turning red), he will not believe (a) and (b), for he won't, in that circumstance, believe that the flame's turning the colour of ripe strawberries caused the meter reading or that if the flame had not turned the colour of ripe strawberries, it would not have caused the reading.

This solution, as far as I can see, works for all a posteriori identities, whether necessary (being water = being composed of H_2O molecules) or contingent (red = the colour of ripe strawberries), *except* for the one that links the explanans property explicitly with the effect specified in (a) and (b) (red = the colour such that something's turning it causes the meter reading), which identity we will have to specifically exclude. (d) also explicates the epistemological content in our concept of causal explanation.

Conclusion

What have we learned about action explanation, or anyway about those that are causal explanations? We have learned something about their analysis, in particular that they do not require, at least in any explicit way, a statement of a covering law or law-like generalization. As is well known, this has often been taken as a disproof of the thesis that some action explanations are causal: covering laws were simply too hard to come by. Unlike Davidson's well-known resolution of this problem, mine does not even require the backing of laws at some lower, or more fundamental level, although it certainly permits there being such.

Appendix on the Epistemology of Action: Certainty and Basic Physical Action

Philosophers of knowledge not so very long ago were much exercised with the topic of infallible, indubitable, or certain contingent knowledge. Could claims about the contents of one's present experience be certain, as many empiricists supposed? Could claims about one's own existence be indubitable, as Descartes argued? Some philosophers were prepared to extend the list of what can be known with certainty to include beliefs about one's own basic actions, or anyway about some of them, for it seemed that the knowledge a person can have about his basic actions has a peculiar and rather special kind of authority.

An example of this is Stuart Hampshire and H. L. A. Hart's 'Decision, Intention, and Certainty'.[1] The main thrust of the article was to argue that a person's beliefs about his own actions, wants, and the like are not based on any sort of observational evidence, and this is, of course, not the same thing as these beliefs being known with certainty.[2] Moreover, beliefs about actions were of interest to Hampshire and Hart mainly in so far as they were beliefs about one's future actions, based on the intentions persons have regarding their future performances.

However, Hampshire and Hart did claim in addition that '. . . in this article we are concerned with only one case of the kind of *certainty* . . . that cannot be associated with any appeal to evidence: namely . . . a man's

---

[1] Stuart Hampshire and H. L. A. Hart, 'Decision, Intention and Certainty', *Mind*, 67, 1958: 1–12.

[2] The contemporary *locus classicus* for discussion of knowledge of one's own actions not resting on observational evidence is Professor Anscombe's *Intention*, Oxford: Blackwell, 1963: 49 ff.

knowledge of his own *present* and future voluntary actions' (emphasis added).[3] They had in mind what I have been calling 'physical actions', and it is the certainty or otherwise of that class of actions that shall occupy me in this appendix. If one focuses on mental actions, the topic may not remain distinct from the question of the certainty of the mental in general. I have said something in Chapter 2 about Descartes's claim of certainty for his knowledge that he is thinking, a mental activity. In any event, I have nothing further to say about the certainty of one's mental actions, say acts of will or tryings, if there are such and if some of them are also basic if or when they occur.

Although Hampshire and Hart admit that 'there is a sense in which our own declarations about our current actions may be mistaken' (p. 9), this qualification has to do with the unintended consequences of what a person does intentionally, so that a person might misidentify or fail to identify his unintended, non-basic actions. Concerning such *basic* physical actions as there are (although they do not put the point in this way), perhaps the moving of parts of one's own body, their view seems to have been that a person can know for certain at *t* what they are doing at *t*.

Can we have Certain Knowledge of our Basic Physical Actions?

I use but do not explicate the idea of certainty or certain knowledge, beyond the limited assumption needed for this appendix: the idea of certainty involves the thought that belief entails the truth of what is believed.[4]

There is a weaker and a stronger claim of Cartesian certainty concerning one's token basic physical actions. The weak claim, (1), is that an agent can have certain knowledge that he is acting when he basically physically acts; that is, that he can know for certain that he is doing something or other, whether or not he can know for sure what it is that he is doing. A stronger claim, (2), is that, for at least some token basic physical action, *a*, if the agent is *a*-ing, then he can have certain knowledge that he is *a*-ing. The agent couldn't be wrong as to whether or not he is *a*-ing. Stronger still is the last claim, but altered to apply either (3) to all rather than some of an agent's basic physical actions, or (4) at least to all of the agent's basic physical actions of the same action type as *a*.

A distinction is sometimes drawn in the literature, between certainty and self-warrant. Roughly, certainty that *p* is defined as: 'X believes that *p*'

---

[3] ibid. 1.

[4] For a good discussion and pertinent distinctions, see Roderick Firth, 'The Anatomy of Certainty', *Philosophical Review*, 1967: 3–27.

entails 'p'; its being self-warranting that p is defined as: 'p' entails 'X believes that p'. I don't think that even basic physical action is, in any sense, self-warranting. An agent can basically physically act without believing that he is acting, either in that way or in any way at all. In the sense discussed in Chapter 4, I would claim that when a person basically physically acts, he may be disposed to believe that he is acting and indeed disposed to believe that he is acting in that specific way. But dispositions to believe are not beliefs, not even dispositional beliefs.

The certainty claims about basic physical action are these:

(5) There is no possible world in which a person believes that he is doing something, and it is false that there is something that he is doing.

(6) For at least some token basic physical action description, 'a-ing', there is no possible world in which a person believes that he is a-ing and he is not a-ing.

The quotation from Hampshire and Hart seems to commit them to (6). In any event, I am interested in the truth or otherwise of (5) and (6), not in the accuracy of the attribution.

The distinction between (5) and (6) is controversial, since some philosophers have said that for a person to believe that he is acting is always for him to have in mind some specific act type, say, 'A', such that he believes that he is a-ing and that his a-ing is a token of the type A. Even if that view were correct, one might still maintain that one of the two beliefs was certain and the other not, but the distinction would become much more problematic.

Some Counter-Examples

Here are two examples that question the possibility of certainty even about one's own basic physical action. William James cites both.[5] (*a*) Professor Strümpell describes his 'wonderful anaesthetic boy': 'Passively holding still his fingers did not affect him. He thought constantly that he opened and shut his hand, whereas it was really fixed.' (*b*) Dr Landry describes a blindfolded patient thus: 'If, having the intention of executing a certain movement, *I prevent him*, he does not perceive it, and supposes the limb to have taken the position he intended to give it'.

If opening and closing one's hand or 'executing a certain movement with a limb', at least on the occasions being considered, are basic physical actions, both Strümpell's and Landry's cases show that both (5) and (6) cannot be sustained. In both cases, the person has done nothing, or anyway

---

[5] William James, *The Principles of Psychology*, ii, London: Macmillan, n.d.: 489–92.

executed no physical action, but falsely believes that he has done something, and indeed falsely believes that he has *a*-ed, where '*a*-ing' is a basic
physical action description. That is, the agent believes that '*a*-ing' refers to
his token basic physical action when it in fact refers to nothing.

The wonderful anaesthetic boy falsely believed that he opened his hand;
Landry's patient falsely believed that he had executed a certain movement
with a limb. In both cases, no physical action occurred, basic or otherwise.
Of course, one cannot 'disprove' (6), which is an existential generalization,
by way of disconfirming examples. But I think that the two examples cited
by William James do undermine any plausibility that (6) might initially be
thought to have.

Another counter-example to the two certainty claims might be this.
Phantom limb cases concern sensations in non-existent limbs, but I can see
no reason for thinking that there could not be cases of phantom limb
actions (indeed, perhaps there are). If, unbeknownst to a person, his hand
were amputated, he, if blindfolded, might still falsely believe that he moved
the fingers of that hand in various ways.

The examples would make the same point if, for example, the wonderful
anaesthetic boy's hand had been opened and shut after all, but not by him,
but rather by some force made invisible to him. The boy might then have
falsely believed concerning some mere physical occurrence involving his
body, the opening and closing of his hand, that it was a basic action of his,
when in fact it was not. James's counter-examples do not have to concern
beliefs about action rendered false by total lack of movement; the counter-
examples could also concern beliefs about action rendered false by the
occurrence of mere bodily movements that are not actions. So not only can
a person falsely believe that he is basically physically acting when nothing
relevant whatever occurs. Concerning some mere event or happening, perhaps the opening of his hand, a person could falsely believe that that mere
event is his basic physical action (his opening of his hand) when it is not an
action at all.

Perhaps we are looking at the wrong sort of beliefs about basic physical
action in order to find certainty. The belief a person has that he is basically
physically acting, and the belief that he has that he is *a*-ing, are positive
action beliefs. The examples James cites show that, if movings of one's body
are basic physical actions, then a person's positive basic action beliefs cannot be certain. On the other hand, the belief of a person that he is *not* engaging in any physical action whatever, and the belief that he is *not a*-ing, not
doing any action of type *A*, are negative action beliefs. Perhaps a person can

be certain about his negative basic physical action beliefs. Such claims would go like this:

(7) There is no possible world in which a person believes that he is doing nothing at all, and there is something that he is doing.

(8) For at least some token basic physical action description, '*a*-ing', there is no possible world in which a person believes that he is not *a*-ing and he is *a*-ing (namely, there is no possible world in which a person believes that he is not doing any basic action of type *A* but in fact he is doing a basic action of type *A*).

Notice that any philosophical doubts, mentioned above, concerning the distinction between the two positive action beliefs, (*a*) the belief that one is doing something or other and (*b*) the belief that one is *a*-ing, will not apply in the case of negative action beliefs. A person can surely (*c*) believe that he is not acting at all, without (*d*) there being any specific token basic physical action description '*a*-ing' whatever such that he believes that he is not *a*-ing.

What connection if any, is there between positive and negative action beliefs? Belief is not closed under logical implication, and arguably not even under known logical implication. Of course, the person who believes that he is bending his left index finger, and who believes that bending and straightening the same index finger at the same time is conceptually impossible, may indeed also believe that he is not straightening his left index finger. But even if he does not actually believe that he is not straightening his left index finger, surely he at least must be disposed to believe that he is not straightening that index finger.

On the other hand, one can't infer any positive action belief, or even just a disposition to hold any positive action belief, from a negative action belief, even if the assumption of belief in the conceptual impossibility is added. Suppose a person simply believes that he is not straightening his index finger. There is no positive action belief, or disposition thereto, that he thereby must have, on the basis of that fact alone (plus his belief in the conceptual impossibility of both bending and straightening the same finger at the same time).

Notice that (7) and (8) concern beliefs about what is not the case, which is of course not the same thing as having no beliefs at all. The impossibility in question, claimed by (7) and (8), does *not* consist in a person's acting when he fails to believe anything whatever regarding his actions, but only when he has a negative action belief, when he *actually believes* that he is not doing something or anything.[6]

Suppose that 'the opening of my hand' and 'the closing of my hand' are, on the occasions under investigation at any rate, token basic physical action descriptions, uttered by Professor Strümpell's wonderful anaesthetic boy. That is, if they refer to anything at all, they refer to one of his basic physical actions. The boy is *not* asked whether he has opened and shut his hand, to which he gave the wrong answer, but rather he is asked whether he has *not* opened and shut his hand.

As we have seen, Professor Strümpell's wonderful anaesthetic boy can believe that he has opened and closed his hand when he has not, but how could he believe that he has not opened and closed his hand when he has? Perhaps, if he were to believe that he has *not* opened and shut his hand, he could not fail to be correct. In general, if a person believes that he has not *a*-ed, where '*a*' is a token basic physical action description in the sense I explained, then isn't it true that he has not *a*-ed (as (8) asserts)?

Are (7) and (8) true? Let me defend the thesis from an unsuccessful line of attack, before I consider an objection which will force us to reconsider and reword the thesis. The following case, quoted by Hugh McCann, when duly altered, might make one wrongly doubt (8) (not that McCann himself uses it for any such purpose):

'Watch what I'm doing: I'm touching each of my fingertips against my thumb . . . Let me see how well you can do that with your left hand.'

I could scarcely do it at all. When I ordered the index finger down, the middle finger, perhaps, wavered towards my thumb. Successive attempts made it apparent that my left-hand fingers and my wishes for them were at odds.[7]

Let me slightly amend the example, to produce examples of negative, rather than positive, action belief. It seems plain that McCann's case could

---

[6] There is a long tradition of taking certain sorts of non-changes as a kind of change, so that in an extended sense refraining from acting counts as a kind of acting. See Myles Brand, 'The Language of Not Doing', *The American Philosophical Quarterly*, 8, 1971: 45–53. A person lying in bed, with no thought about rising, may well be doing nothing with respect to his rising. A person lying in bed, who knows that his non-arising will annoy someone whom he wishes to annoy, may well be refraining from arising. (Most parents of teenagers know of this case all too well.) A person who does nothing at all with respect to rising must both (*a*) not rise and (*b*) not be refraining from rising.

[7] E. Hodgins, *Episode: Report on the Accident inside my Skull*, New York: Atheneum Press, 1964: 27, quoted by Hugh McCann, in 'Trying, Paralysis, and Volition', *Review of Metaphysics*, 28, 1974: 423–42.

be amended so that the person was blindfolded and anaesthetized in such a way that he could not observe or feel what had happened. He might then falsely believe that he had bent his index finger, when in fact his middle finger had wavered ('the middle finger . . . wavered').

Suppose the person believes, consciously and explicitly, that bending one finger while waving another on the same hand at the same time is physically impossible for him. Believing the impossibility, he might then have or acquire the desire and intention not to wave his middle finger, since he wants to bend his index finger.

If bending an index finger and waving a middle finger are or could be basic actions for him on this occasion, then, so it might be held, the person in McCann's case might believe that he had *not* waved his middle finger (because he believed that all that he had done was to bend his index finger and believed that that is incompatible with him waving his middle finger), when in fact he had waved his middle finger. So (8), it will be claimed, is false. Again, he believes that he has *not* waved his middle finger, because he believes that he has bent his index finger, and believes the incompatibility of index finger bending and middle finger waving, but because of the wish–finger mismatch, he does wave his middle finger after all. Doesn't this show that (8) is false? He holds, does he not, a negative basic physical action belief ('I have not waved my middle finger') that is false?

In fact, the amended case does not constitute a counter-example to (8), and the language with which McCann describes the case explains why. We can bring this out by asking this question: did the person really wave his middle finger or not? True, the person believes that he is *not* waving his middle finger. The case is a counter-example, though, only if it is true that he did wave his middle finger when he believed that he was not waving it. There is a strong argument for it being the case that he does not wave his middle finger at all.

What then happens, if he does not wave his middle finger? I think that what happens in this example is that a mere event occurs, a wavering of his middle finger, which is intrinsic to no action of his at all, but is only a bodily occurrence involving his finger. As McCann says, 'the middle finger . . . wavered', not that he waved it. If, when I am thinking about something unpleasant, I shudder or twitch, the shuddering or twitching is a mere event, nothing I do in the actional sense (even though it is true that I shudder or that I twitch, these doings are not actions of mine). They are not even unintended actions of mine; they are no actions of mine at all. They are involuntary reactions of my body. So it seems one might think of the finger

wavering in this way. It is simply an involuntary bodily response to whatever is going on inside the person. As the shuddering or twitching is to the
unpleasant thought, so is the middle finger wavering to the wish to bend the
index finger.

A steadfast opponent, wishing to treat this case as a counter-example to
(8), might argue that this is a case of the agent's middle finger waving *action*,
in spite of what I have just said. True, the person intends and wishes not to
wave his middle finger, but why can't his action then simply be an *unintentional* waving of his middle finger? When we thought in terms of the accordion effect, in Chapter 2, the picture that emerged was that a basic physical
action, itself intended or at least not unintended in the sense I explained,
might have unintended, often increasingly remote, events as effects. Subject
to certain not very clearly defined limitations, such events were intrinsic to
the agent's non-basic actions, and were such that he could be said to do
these other actions by doing the basic one. Some of these actions could
count as the agent's unintended actions. If we apply the accordion effect to
this case, why can't the middle finger wavering be an event intrinsic to such
an unintended action, so that he does wave his middle finger after all? How
can I just assume that the middle finger wavering is a mere event, like shuddering or twitching, rather than an event intrinsic to an unintended action,
which in this case would be the unintended action of his waving of his
middle finger?

The distinction between basic and non-basic action is exhaustive. So,
if there were, in this case, such an unintended action as his waving of his
middle finger, it would have to be either a basic or a non-basic action. Recall
that we have attributed to the agent the desire and intention *not* to wave his
middle finger, since what he wanted to do is to bend the index finger and
thought that the two actions, bending and waving, would be incompatible
for him. His waving of his middle finger, if there were such an action, would
have to be unintended by him in the case as I have described it, and unintended in the strong sense that it is something he intended not to do (and not
just in the weaker sense that he might do it without intending to have done
it).

Could his middle finger waving be a non-basic action? Non-basic actions
can certainly be unintentional in that strong sense; a person might do something unintentionally that he actually intended not to do. But the topic
under discussion is certainty about one's *basic* physical actions. If the
waving were a non-basic action, we would not be addressing the topic we
have set ourselves, in so far as we focus on the waving.

(But, in any event, the middle finger waving, had there been such an action, could not be an example of a non-basic physical action, since, in the example as McCann described it, there is no other physical action that the person did such that he might have waved his middle finger by doing it. Might the basic action in this case be a mental action, such as his trying or attempting to bend his index finger? Perhaps he unintentionally waved his middle finger *by* trying to bend his index finger? I won't, in this appendix, rehearse my arguments about the ubiquity of tryings or willings as mental acts. But more to the point, the purpose of this appendix is to explore the question of the certainty of basic *physical* action. (8) makes a claim about basic physical actions, not about basic non-physical ones. Invoking tryings as basic actions at this point, which are mental actions if they are anything at all, would defeat that purpose.)

For the purposes of the discussion in this appendix, the possibility of the middle finger waving being a basic physical action is more plausible. Could the finger waving be a basic physical action? If the argument of Chapter 2 is correct, no basic physical action can be unintentional in this strong sense. A person can't basically physically act in a way in which he desires and intends not to act. If he desires and intends not to do something, say wave his middle finger, and yet his middle finger waves, the case is compelling for the waving, or wavering, to be a mere event. So there is no such action at all, basic or non-basic, in the case described, as his waving of his middle finger. There is only the mere event, the wavering of his finger. The finger just wavers, without that wavering being in any sense under the agent's control.

What happens when the person begins to understand the systematic mismatch between his wishes or intentions and fingers, as may happen with permanent cross wiring? Indeed, suppose he is fitted with Ginet's mismatch machine.[8] Ginet's cases are expressed as a mismatch between action and volition. When he has a volition to bend his index finger, the person knows that he will wave his middle finger. What he really wants or intends to do is to wave his middle finger. So he volitions to bend his index finger, knowing that he will wave his middle finger as a result. I am not sure that I really understand this supposition. I shan't pursue some of the difficulties I have in understanding the mismatch: in what sense can the person really have a bona-fide volition to do *a*, when what he wants to do, intends to do, wishes to do, is rather to do something else, *b*? Is he just pretending to have a

---

[8] Carl Ginet, *On Action*, Cambridge: Cambridge University Press, 1990: 42–4.

certain volition, in order to get the result he needs from the systematic mismatch machine? But a sham volition is no volition at all.

But let's accept the Ginet mismatch as a possibility. I agree in that case that the story now has been altered so that the person is now genuinely acting, he waves his middle finger, and that this waving would be a basic physical action (again, discounting volitions as basic actions). A crucial difference in the amended case is that the waving of the middle finger is now intended, deliberate, done on purpose, and so can count as a basic physical action of the agent. Certainly, the waving of his middle finger is no longer something that he intends *not* to do.

But (8) is still untouched, for, knowing of the systematic mismatch, he will now believe that he has *not* bent his index finger (not: that he has not waved his middle finger). Given his understanding of the systematic mismatch, what he has done, and what he will believe that he has done, is to wave his middle finger. What he has not done, and what he will believe that he has not done, is to bend his index finger. Not doing something and belief about not doing it stay together. In Ginet's systematic case, the systematic mismatch is allegedly between volitions and actions; the match remains between beliefs, negative and positive, and actions. Thus far, the certainty of negative basic physical action belief, (8), is untouched.

In *The Man who Mistook his Wife for a Hat*,[9] Oliver Sacks describes a number of cases of patients with neurophysiological injuries resulting in loss of proprioception, 'that continuous but unconscious sensory flow from the movable parts of our body (muscles, tendons, joints) by which their position and tone and motion is continually monitored and adjusted, but in a way which is hidden from us because it is automatic and unconscious' (p. 42). Patients who have lost this 'sense' are unable to see their own body as 'their own'. In one case, a man in a hospital bed finds a leg in bed with him. Assuming that it has been put there as a practical joke, he flings it in disgust from the bed, only to find that somehow he follows the leg out of bed, and ends up sitting on the floor, with this alien leg now inexplicably attached to him. In another case, Christina suddenly begins to feel 'disembodied', having lost throughout her entire body, from head to toes, the proprioception lost only in the leg by the man in hospital. Christina felt that no part of her body was hers.

As with many of the 'pathological cases' of action, it is not clear how we

---

[9] Oliver Sacks, *The Man who Mistook his Wife for a Hat*, London: Pan Books, 1986. Page references in the text are to this volume.

are best to describe them, since we are using the vocabulary and structure derived from non-pathological cases. There is no suggestion that Christina or the man in hospital cannot act, and if they act at all, they must basically act in some way or other. So Christina might in fact move her body, say bend a finger. What does she believe? Sacks's brief account does not tell us. It only tells us that she regards her body as 'alien'.

It is crucial that it is their bodies that they consider to be alien, and not their actions themselves. That is: they do not consider the actions as not theirs. What might 'considering one's actions as alien' mean, and why would it matter? One thing it might mean is this: then when Christina, for example, in fact acts in some way, she would not believe that it is *she* who is acting in that way. But that would only be to say that action is not self-warranting, not that it is not certain.

But if she considers her actions as alien, as not her own, might that not mean something else? When she believe that she is not acting in some way, might she be acting in that way all the same? That would count decisively against (8), but nothing in the story suggests, let alone requires, that description. She appears to know when she acts and when she does not, it is just that the acting 'feels' strange. The man in hospital believes that he has thrown a leg out of bed and indeed that is precisely what he has done. He simply does not know that it is *his* leg.

If the body is what is thought of as alien, as the two stories suggest, then what he or she must believe is that that they are acting but that the control they have is exercised over objects that are not any part of their bodies. Christina might feel as we would feel, in the speculation in Chapter 2, if we could directly control physical objects that were no part of our body. If Uri Geller bends a spoon as one of his basic actions, it does not follow that the spoon is connected to him by the sense of proprioception. This reading of the story also presents no challenge to (8). For Sacks's stories to challenge (8), it is the actions themselves which would have to be considered alien, understood as I have indicated, and not just the objects on which the actions are directed. But nothing in the story as presented requires or even encourages us to take the story in this way.

All the same, in my view, even (7) and (8) cannot be true. Consider finally this case. We convince Professor Strümpell's wonderful anaesthetic boy that the nerves responsible for opening his hand have been irreparably severed. In fact, this is not true; they are entirely intact. We also tell him that the friendly neighbourhood neurophysiologist will cause the movement that is an opening of his hand, but of course a movement for which he will be in no way responsible (no such neurophysiologist is in fact on the scene).

For whatever reason you would like to imagine, we ask him to try and open his hand none the less, perhaps telling him that the attempt is for him to see just how ineffectual he is. He accepts, and sees his hand opening, but falsely believes that he has not opened his hand, and that the hand's opening is only a result of the neurophysiologist's activity. Hasn't he in fact opened his hand, falsely believing that he has not opened his hand? Isn't (8) false? Doesn't he believe, even *while* he is opening his hand, that he is not opening his hand, because he believes that the neurophysiologist is opening his hand instead of him?

One possible line of response is to argue that, if he believes that it is not possible for him to open his hand, then he cannot try or intend to open his hand either, on the grounds that a person cannot try or intend to do what he believes it impossible for him to do.[10] This response is controversial, but suppose it were so. And if so, he won't open his hand after all. But then, his belief will not be false.

We can slightly amend the case to bypass this objection. In order for the amended wonderful anaesthetic boy case to work, what must be true is that the boy believes that he has not opened his hand when he has done so. He need not believe that it is impossible for him to open his hand. He might believe that his nerves are such that they work rather erratically—on any particular occasion, there is only a 1 per cent chance that they will work properly. So he tries to open his hand. Lo and behold, this occasion was the 1 in a 100. He does open his hand.

He does, of course, now see that his hand is open. But, given such a low probability, it is reasonable for him to believe, on the basis of the evidence that he has, that he has not opened his hand and that on this occasion the hand opening is a consequence of the neurophysiologist's intervention. (Pick any percentage you wish, such that it allows him enough scope to try and open his hand yet is small enough to justify his believing that he did not succeed in opening it on this occasion.) So he will be wrong: he is opening his hand, in spite of his belief that he is not. There is a convincing counter-example to (8).

---

[10] See the extensive literature on this question, e.g. Michael Bratman, *Intention, Plans, and Practical Reason*, Cambridge, Mass.: Harvard University Press, 1987: 37–41; Myles Brand, *Intending and Acting*, Cambridge, Mass.: MIT Press, 1984: 148–52; Alfred Mele, *Springs of Action*, New York: Oxford University Press, 1992, ch. 8.

BIBLIOGRAPHY

Books

Anscombe, G. E. M., *Intention*, Oxford: Basil Blackwell, 1963.

Audi, Robert, *Action, Intention, and Reason*, Ithaca, NY: Cornell University Press, 1993.

Baker, Lynne Rudder, *Saving Belief*, Princeton: Princeton University Press, 1987.

Bennett, Jonathan, *Events and their Names*, Oxford: Oxford University Press, 1988.

Bishop, John, *Natural Agency*, Cambridge: Cambridge University Press, 1989.

Bogdan, Radu, ed., *Belief: Form, Content, and Function*, Oxford: Oxford University Press, 1986.

Brand, Myles, *Intending and Acting*, Cambridge, Mass.: MIT Press, 1984.

—— and Walton D., eds., *Action Theory*, Dordrecht: Reidel, 1976.

Bratman, Michael, *Intention, Plans, and Practical Reason*, Cambridge, Mass.: Harvard University Press, 1987.

Butts, Robert, and Hintikka, Jaakko, eds., *Basic Problems in Methodology and Linguistics*, Dordrecht: Reidel, 1977.

Chisholm, Roderick, *Person and Object*, London: Allen & Unwin, 1976.

Clark, Romane, and Welsh, Paul, *Introduction to Logic*, Princeton: van Nostrand, 1962.

Crane, Tim, *Elements of Mind*, Oxford: Oxford University Press, 2001.

Dancy, Jonathan, ed., *Perceptual Knowledge*, Oxford: Oxford University Press, 1988.

Davidson, Donald, *Essays on Actions and Events*, Oxford and New York: Clarendon Press, 1980.

Davis, Lawrence, *Theory of Action*, Englewood Cliffs, NJ: Prentice-Hall, 1979.

Dennett, Daniel, *Content and Consciousness*, London: Routledge, 1993.

Donagan, Alan, *Choice: The Essential Element in Human Action*, London: Routledge & Kegan Paul, 1987.

Dummett, Michael, *Frege: Philosophy of Language*, London: Duckworth, 1973.

Elster, Jon, *Sour Grapes*, Cambridge: Cambridge University Press, 1985.

—— *Nuts and Bolts*, Cambridge: Cambridge University Press, 1989.

Fodor, Jerry, *Representations: A Philosophical Essay on the Foundations of Cognitive Science*, Brighton: Harvester Press, 1981.

Foster, Lawrence, and Swanson, J. W., eds., *Experience & Theory*, London: Duckworth, 1970.

Frankfurt, Harry, *The Importance of What we Care about*, Cambridge: Cambridge University Press, 1988.

Gardiner, Patrick, ed., *Theories of History*, New York: The Free Press, 1959.

——ed., *The Philosophy of History*, Oxford: Oxford University Press, 1978.

Geach, Peter, *Mental Acts*, London: Routledge & Kegan Paul, 1964.

—— *God and the Soul*, London: Routledge & Kegan Paul, 1969.

—— *Logic Matters*, Oxford: Blackwell, 1981.

Ginet, Carl, *On Action*, Cambridge: Cambridge University Press, 1990.

Goldman, Alvin, *A Theory of Human Action*, Princeton: Princeton University Press, 1970.

Goodman, Nelson, *The Structure of Appearance*, Indianapolis: Bobbs-Merrill, 1977.

Haack, Susan, *Philosophy of Logics*, Cambridge: Cambridge University Press, 1978.

Hamlyn, David, *In and out of the Black Box: On the Philosophy of Cognition*, Oxford: Blackwell, 1990.

Hinton, J. M., *Experiences*, Oxford: Oxford University Press, 1973.

Hodgins, E., *Episode: Report on the Accident inside my Skull*, New York: Atheneum Press, 1964.

Holmström-Hintikka, Ghita, and Tuomela, Raimo, eds., *Contemporary Action Theory*, Dordrecht: Kluwer Academic Publishers, 1997.

Horgan, T., ed., *Spindel Conference 1983: Supervenience*, *The Southern Journal of Philosophy*, 22, Supplement, 1984.

Hornsby, Jennifer, *Actions*, London: Routledge & Kegan Paul, 1980.

—— *Simple Mindedness*, Cambridge, Mass.: Harvard University Press, 1997.

James, William, *The Principles of Psychology*, ii, London: Macmillan, n.d.

Kane, Robert, ed., *Free Will*, Oxford: Blackwell, 2002.

Kant, I., *Moral Law*, ed. H. J. Paton, London: Hutchinson, 1969.

Knowles, Dudley, ed., *Explanation and its Limits*, Cambridge: Cambridge University Press, 1990.

Laslett, P., and Runciman, G., eds., *Politics, Philosophy and Society*, Oxford: Blackwell, 1987.

Lehrer, Keith, ed., *Freedom and Determinism*, New York: Random House, 1966.

Lepore, Ernest, and van Gulick, Robert, eds., *John Searle and his Critics*, Oxford: Blackwell, 1992.

Lewis, David, *Philosophical Papers*, ii, Oxford: Oxford University Press, 1986.

Lombard, Lawrence, *Events: A Metaphysical Study*, London: Routledge & Kegan Paul, 1986.

McCann, Hugh, *The Works of Agency*, Ithaca, NY: Cornell University Press, 1988.

McDowell, John, 1998, *Meaning, Knowledge, and Reality*, Cambridge, Mass.: Harvard University Press, 1998.

McGinn, Colin, *Logical Properties*, Oxford: Oxford University Press, 2000.

Mackie, J. L., *The Cement of the Universe*, Oxford: Clarendon Press, 1974.

Marks, Joel, ed., *The Ways of Desire*, Chicago: Precedent Publishing Company, 1986.

Melden, A. I., *Free Action*, London: Routledge & Kegan Paul, 1961.

Mele, Alfred, *Springs of Action*, New York: Oxford University Press, 1992.

Mellor, Hugh, *Real Time*, Cambridge: Cambridge University Press, 1981.

Mill, J. S., *A System of Logic*, London: Longman, 1970.

O'Connor, Timothy, *Agents, Causes, Events*, Oxford and New York: Oxford University Press, 1995.

—— *Persons and Causes*, Oxford and New York: Oxford University Press, 2000.

O'Shaughnessy, Brian, *The Will: A Dual Aspect Theory*, i and ii, Cambridge: Cambridge University Press, 1980.

Peacocke, Christopher, *A Study of Concepts*, Cambridge, Mass: MIT Press, 1992.

Phillips Griffiths, A., ed., *Knowledge and Belief*, Oxford: Oxford University Press, 1968.

Pick, Rabbi Eli, *Guide to Sabbath Observance*, Southfield, Mich.: Targum Press Ltd., 1998.

Popper, Karl, *The Logic of Scientific Discovery*, 6th edn., London: Hutchinson & Co., 1972.

Raz, Joseph, ed., *Practical Reasoning*, Oxford: Oxford University Press, 1978.

Reid, Thomas, *Essays on the Active Powers of the Human Mind*, repr. by Cambridge, Mass.: MIT Press, 1969.

Ruben, David-Hillel, *The Metaphysics of the Social World*, London: Routledge & Kegan Paul, 1985.

—— *Explaining Explanation*, London: Routledge, 1990.

Ryle, Gilbert, *The Concept of Mind*, Harmondsworth: Penguin Books, 1963.

Sacks, Oliver, *The Man who Mistook his Wife for a Hat*, London: Pan Books, 1986.

Sainsbury, R. M., *Paradoxes*, Cambridge: Cambridge University Press, 1988.

Salmon, Wesley, *Scientific Explanation and the Causal Structure of the World*, Princeton: Princeton University Press, 1984.

Searle, John, *Intentionality*, Cambridge and New York: Cambridge University Press, 1984.

Sosa, Ernest, and Tooley, Michael, eds., *Causation*, Oxford: Oxford University Press, 1993.

Sternberg, Robert, Forsythe, George, Hedlund, Jennifer, Horvath, Joseph, Wagner, Richard, Williams, Wendy, Snook, Scott, and Grigorenko, Elena, *Practical Intelligence in Everyday Life*, Cambridge: Cambridge University Press, 2000.

Steward, Helen, *The Ontology of the Mind*, Oxford: Clarendon Press, 1997.

Stoecker, Ralf, *Reflecting Davidson*, New York: Walter de Gruyter, 1993.

Swinburne, Richard, *Is there a God?* Oxford: Oxford University Press, 1999.

Taylor, Charles, *The Explanation of Behaviour*, London: Routledge & Kegan Paul, 1964.

Taylor, Daniel, *Explanation and Meaning*, Cambridge: Cambridge University Press, 1970.

Taylor, Richard, *Action and Purpose*, Englewood Cliffs, NJ: Prentice-Hall, 1966.

—— *Metaphysics*, Englewood Cliffs, NJ: Prentice-Hall, 1992.

Teichmann, Roger, ed., *Logic, Cause, and Action: Essays in Honour of Elizabeth Anscombe*, Royal Institute of Philosophy Supplements, vol. 46, Cambridge: Cambridge University Press, 2000.

Thalberg, Irving, *Misconceptions of Mind and Freedom*, Lanham, Md.: University Press of America, 1983.

Thomson, Judith Jarvis, *Acts and Other Events*, Ithaca, NY and London: Cornell University Press, 1977.

Velleman, J. David, *Practical Reflection*, Princeton: Princeton University Press, 1989.

von Wright, G. H., *Norm and Action*, London: Routledge & Kegan Paul, 1963.

Wagner, Steven, and Warner, Richard, eds., *Naturalism: A Critical Appraisal*, Notre Dame, Ind.: University of Notre Dame Press, 1993.

Watkins, John, *Science and Scepticism*, Princeton: Princeton University Press, 1984.

Watson, Gary, ed., *Free Will*, Oxford Readings in Philosophy, Oxford: Oxford University Press, 1982.

White, A., ed., *The Philosophy of Action*, Oxford: Oxford University Press, 1968.

Wiggins, David, *Sameness and Substance*, Oxford: Blackwell, 1980.

Wilkes, Kathleen, *Real People*, Oxford: Clarendon Press, 1999.

Winch, Peter, *The Idea of a Social Science*, London: Routledge & Kegan Paul, 1967.

Articles

Adams, Frederick, and Mele, Alfred, 'The Role of Intention in Intentional Action', *Canadian Journal of Philosophy*, 19, 1989: 511–32.

Antony, Louise, 'Anomalous Monism and the Problem of Explanatory Force', *Philosophical Review*, 98, 1989: 153–87.

Audi, Robert, 'Believing and Affirming', *Mind*, 91, 1982: 115–20.

—— 'Dispositional Beliefs and Dispositions to Believe', *Nous*, 28, 1994: 419–34.

Ayer, A. J., 'Man as a Subject for Science', in P. Laslett and G. Runciman, eds., *Politics, Philosophy and Society*, Oxford: Blackwell, 1987: 6–24.

Bach, Kent, 'A Representational Theory of Action', *Philosophical Studies*, 34, 1978: 361–79.

—— 'Actions are not Events', *Mind*, 89, 1980: 114–20.

Bennett, Jonathan 'Shooting, Killing and Dying', *Canadian Journal of Philosophy*, 2, Mar. 1973: 315–23.

Bishop, John, 'Agent-Causation', *Mind*, 92, 1983: 61–79.

—— 'Naturalising Mental Action', in Ghita Holmström-Hintikka and Raimo Tuomela, eds., *Contemporary Action Theory*, i, Dordrecht: Kluwer Academic Press, 1997: 251–66.

Braithwaite, R. B., 'The Nature of Believing', repr. in A. Phillips Griffiths, ed., *Knowledge and Belief*, Oxford: Oxford University Press, 1968: 28–40.

Brand, Myles, 'The Language of Not Doing', *The American Philosophical Quarterly*, 8, 1971: 45–53.

Bratman, Michael, 'Two Problems about Human Agency', *Proceedings of the Aristotelian Society 2000–1*, n.s., vol. 101, London, 2001: 309–26.

Butterfield, Jeremy, 'Prior's Conception of Time', *Proceedings of the Aristotelian Society*, 84, 1983–4: 193–209.

Candlish, Stewart, 'Inner and Outer Basic Actions', *Proceedings of the Aristotelian Society*, n.s., vol. 84, 1984: 83–102.

Chisholm, Roderick, 'Freedom and Action', in Keith Lehrer, ed., *Freedom and Determinism*, Random House: New York, 1966: 11–44.

—— 'Reflections on Human Agency', *Idealistic Studies*, 1, 1971: 36–46.

—— 'Agency', in *Person and Object*, London: Allen & Unwin, 1976: 53–88.

Churchland, Paul, 'The Logical Character of Action-Explanations', *Philosophical Review*, 79, 1970: 214–36.

Clarke, Randolph, 'Toward a Credible Agent-Causal Account of Free Will', in Timothy O'Connor, *Agents, Causes, Events*, Oxford and New York: Oxford University Press, 201–15.

Costa, Michael, 'Causal Theories of Action', *Canadian Journal of Philosophy*, 17, 1987: 831–52.

Crimmins, Mark, 'Tacitness and Virtual Beliefs', *Mind & Language*, 7, 1992: 240–63.

Danto, Arthur, 'Basic Actions', repr. in Alan White, ed., *The Philosophy of Action*, Oxford: Oxford University Press, 1968: 43–58.

Davidson, Donald, 'Mental Events', in Lawrence Foster and J. W. Swanson, eds., *Experience & Theory*, London: Duckworth, 1970: 79–101, and repr. in his *Essays on Actions and Events*, Oxford and New York: Clarendon Press, 1980: 207–27.

—— 'Psychology as Philosophy', in his *Essays on Actions and Events*, Oxford and New York: Clarendon Press, 1980: 229–44.

—— 'The Logical Form of Action Sentences', in his *Essays on Actions and Events*, Oxford and New York: Clarendon Press, 1980: 105–48.

—— 'Actions, Reasons, and Causes', repr. in his *Essays on Actions and Events*, Oxford and New York: Clarendon Press, 1980: 3–19.

—— 'Agency', in his *Essays on Actions and Events*, Oxford and New York: Clarendon Press, 1980.

—— 'Causal Relations', *Journal of Philosophy*, 64, 1967: 691–703.

Davis, Wayne, 'The Two Senses of Desire', in Joel Marks, ed., *The Ways of Desire*, Chicago: Precedent Publishing Company, 1986.

Dray, William, 'Historical Explanation of Actions Reconsidered', repr. in Patrick Gardiner, ed., *The Philosophy of History*, Oxford: Oxford University Press, 1978: 69–70.

Ducasse, C. J., 'On the Logic and Epistemology of the Causal Relation', repr. in Ernest Sosa and Michael Tooley, eds., *Causation*, Oxford: Oxford University Press, 1993: 125–36.

Feinberg, Joel, 'Action and Responsibility', repr. in A. White, ed., *The Philosophy of Action*, Oxford: Oxford University Press, 1968: 95–119.

Firth, Roderick, 'The Anatomy of Certainty', *Philosophical Review*, 1967: 3–27.

Fodor, Jerry, 'Special Sciences (Or: the Disunity of Science as a Working Hypothesis', *Synthese*, 28, 1974: 97–115, and repr. as ch. 5 in his *Representations: A Philosophical Essay on the Foundations of Cognitive Science*, Brighton: Harvester Press, 1981.

Foot, Philippa, 'Moral Beliefs', *Proceedings of the Aristotelian Society*, 59, 1958–9: 83–104.

Frankfurt, Harry, 'The Problem of Action', repr. in *The Importance of What we Care about*, Cambridge: Cambridge University Press, 1988: 69–79.

—— 'Freedom of the Will and the Concept of a Person', *Journal of Philosophy*, 68, 1971: 5–20, repr. in Gary Watson, ed., *Free Will*, Oxford Readings in Philosophy, Oxford: Oxford University Press, 1982: 81–95, and in Frankfurt, *The Importance of What we Care about*, Cambridge: Cambridge University Press, 1988: 11–25.

Geach, Peter, 'Some Problems about Time', *Proceedings of the British Academy*, 1965.

Hampshire, Stuart, and Hart, H. L. A., 'Decision, Intention and Certainty', *Mind*, 67, 1958: 1–12.

Helm, Paul, 'Detecting Change', *Ratio*, 19, 1977: 34–8.

Humberstone, I. L., 'Wanting as Believing', *Canadian Journal of Philosophy*, 17, 1987: 49–62.

Hurley, Susan, 'Animal Action in the Space of Reasons', *Mind and Language*, forthcoming.

Hursthouse, Rosalind, 'Arational Action', *The Journal of Philosophy*, 88, 1991: 57–68.

—— 'Intention', in Roger Teichmann, ed., *Logic, Cause, and Action: Essays in Honour of Elizabeth Anscombe*, Royal Institue of Philosphy Supplements, vol. 46, Cambridge: Cambridge University Press, 2000.

Jackson, Frank, and Pettit, Philip, 'Functionalism and Broad Content', *Mind*, 97, 1988: 381–400.

——— 'Program Explanations: A General Perspective', *Analysis*, 50, 1990: 107–17.

Jeffrey, Richard, 'Preference among Preferences', *Journal of Philosophy*, 71, 1974: 377–91.

Johnston, Mark, 'Is there a Problem about Persistence', *Mind*, suppl. vol. 61, 1987: 107–35.

—— 'Constitution is not Identity', *Mind*, 101, 1992: 89–105.

Kane, Robert, 'Free Will: New Directions for an Ancient Problem', in his, ed., *Free Will*, Oxford: Blackwell, 2002: 222–48.

Keefe, Rosanna, 'When does Circularity Matter?' *Proceedings of the Aristotelian Society*, 2002: 275–92.

Kim, J., 'Noncausal Connections', *Nous*, 8, 1974: 41–52.

—— 'Supervenience and Supervenient Causation', in T. Horgan, ed., *Spindel Conference 1983: Supervenience*, vol. 22, suppl., *The Southern Journal of Philosophy*, 1984: 45–56.

Lacey, H. M., 'Quine on the Logic and Ontology of Time', *Australasian Journal of Philosophy*, 49, 1971: 47–67.

LePore, Ernest, and Loewer, Barry, 'Mind Matters', *Journal of Philosophy*, 84, 1987: 630–42.

Lewis, David, 'Extrinsic Properties', *Philosophical Studies*, 44, 1983: 197–200.

—— 'Causal Explanation', in *Philosophical Papers*, ii, Oxford: Oxford University Press, 1986: 214–40.

Lombard, Lawrence, 'Actions, Results, and the Time of Killing', *Philosophia*, 8, 1978–9: 341–54.

—— 'The Cambridge Solution to the Time of a Killing', *Philosophia*, 30, forthcoming, 1–14.

Lycan, William, 'Tacit Belief', in Radu Bogdan, ed., *Belief: Form, Content, and Function*, Oxford: Oxford University Press, 1986: 61–82.

—— and Pappas, George, 'What is Eliminative Materialism?' *Australasian Journal of Philosophy*, 50, 1972: 149–59.

McCann, Hugh, 'Trying, Paralysis, and Volition', *Review of Metaphysics*, 28, 1974: 423–42.

—— 'Volition and Basic Action', *Philosophical Review*, 20, 1974: 451–73, and repr. in his *The Works of Agency*, Ithaca, NY: Cornell University Press, 1998: 75–93.

McDowell, John, 'Criteria, Defeasability, and Knowledge', *Proceedings of the British Academy*, 68, 1982: 455–79.

Mackie, J. L., 'Causes and Conditions', *American Philosophical Quarterly*, 2, 1965: 245–64.

Meixner, John, 'Homogeneity and Explanatory Depth', *Philosophy of Science*, 46, 1979: 366–81.

Mele, Alfred, 'Acting for Reasons and Acting Intentionally', *Pacific Philosophical Quarterly*, 73, 1992: 355–74.

Menzies, Peter, 'Against Causal Reductionism', *Mind*, 97, 1988: 551–74.

O'Connor, Timothy, 'Agent Causation', in his *Agents, Causes, Events*, Oxford and New York: Oxford University Press, 1995: 173–200.

Owens, David, 'Levels of Explanation', *Mind*, 98, 1989: 59–79.

Peacocke, Christopher, 'Demonstrative Thought and Psychological Explanation', *Synthese*, 49, 1981: 187–217.

Pietroski, Paul, 'Actions, Adjuncts, and Agency', *Mind*, 107, 1998: 73–111.

Price, Huw, 'Defending Desire-as-Belief', *Mind*, 98, 1989: 119–27.

Rescher, Nicholas, 'Axioms for the Part Relation', *Philosophical Studies*, 6, 1955: 8–11.

Ruben, David-Hillel, 'A Puzzle about Posthumous Predication', *Philosophical Review*, 97, 1988: 211–36.

—— 'Review of *Natural Agency*', *Mind*, 100, 1991: 287–90.

—— 'Mental Overpopulation and the Problem of Action', *Journal of Philosophical Research*, 20, 1995: 511–24.

Salmon, Wesley, 'The Third Dogma of Empiricism', in Robert Butts and Jaakko Hintikka, eds., *Basic Problems in Methodology and Linguistics*, Dordrecht: Reidel, 1977: 149–66.

Schiffer, Stephen, 'Ceteris Paribus Laws', *Mind*, 100, 1991: 1–16.

Scriven, Michael, 'Truisms as the Grounds for Historical Explanations', in Patrick Gardiner, ed., *Theories of History*, New York: The Free Press, 1959: 443–75.

Searle, John, 'Consciousness, Unconsciousness, and Intentionality', *Philosophical Topics*, 17, 1989: 193–209.

Segal, Gabriel, and Sober, Elliott, 'The Causal Efficacy of Content', *Philosophical Studies*, 63, 1991: 1–30.

Shorter, Michael, 'Subjective and Objective Time', in *Proceedings of the Aristotelian Society*, suppl. vol. 60, 1986: 223–34.

Silverstein, Harry, S., 'The Evil of Death', *The Journal of Philosophy*, 77, 1980: 401–24.

Smith, Terence Paul, 'On the Applicability of a Criterion of Change', *Ratio*, 25, 1973: 325–33.

Snowdon, Paul, 'Perception, Vision, and Causation', *Proceedings of the Aristotelian Society*, 81, 1980–1: 175–92.

Sosa, Ernest, 'Mind–Body Interaction and Supervenient Causation', *Midwest Studies in Philosophy*, 9, 1984: 277–8.

Stanley, Jason, and Williamson, Timothy, 'Knowing How', *Journal of Philosophy*, 98, 2001.

Stich, Stephen, 'Beliefs and Subdoxastic States', *Philosophy of Science*, 45, 1978: 499–518.

Stoecker, Ralf, 'Reasons, Actions, and their Relationship', in Stoecker, ed., *Reflecting Davidson*, New York: Walter de Gruyter, 1993: 265–90.

Thalberg, Irving, 'How does Agent Causality Work?' in M. Brand and D. Walton, eds., *Action Theory*, Dordrecht: Reidel, 1980: 213–38.

Velleman, J. David, 'What Happens when Someone Acts?' *Mind*, 101, 1992: 461–81.

Vermazen, Bruce, 'Occurrent and Standing Wants', in *Bowling Green Studies in Applied Philosophy: Action & Responsibility*, Bowling Green, Oh.: Bowling Green State University, 1980: 48–54.

von Wright, G. H., 'On so-called Practical Inference', in Joseph Raz, ed., *Practical Reasoning*, Oxford: Oxford University Press, 1978: 46–62.

Wakefield, Jerome, and Dreyfus, Hubert, 'Intentionality and the Phenomenology of Action', in E. Lepore and Robert van Gulick, eds., *John Searle and his Critics*, Oxford: Blackwell, 1992: 263–66.

Winch, Peter, 'Understanding a Primitive Society', *The American Philosophical Quarterly*, 1, 1964: 307–24.

Woodward, James, 'Supervenience and Singular Causal Statements', in Dudley Knowles, ed., *Explanation and its Limits*, Cambridge: Cambridge University Press, 1990: 211–46.

Index